Theories of Visual Perception

Theories of Visual Perception

SECOND EDITION

Ian E. Gordon
University of Exeter

JOHN WILEY & SONS
Chichester · New York · Weinheim · Brisbane · Toronto · Singapore

Copyright © 1997 by John Wiley & Sons Ltd,
Baffins Lane, Chichester,
West Sussex PO19 1UD, England

National   01243 779777
International (+44) 1243 779777
e-mail (for orders and customer service enquiries): cs-books@wiley.co.uk
Visit our Home Page on http://www.wiley.co.uk
or http://www.wiley.com

Reprinted August 1998

Other Wiley Editorial Offices

John Wiley & Sons, Inc., 605 Third Avenue,
New York, NY 10158-0012, USA

VCH Verlagsgesellschaft mbH
Pappelallee 3, 0-69469 Weinheim, Germany

Jacaranda Wiley Ltd, 33 Park Road, Milton,
Queensland 4064, Australia

John Wiley & Sons (Canada) Ltd, 22 Worcester Road,
Rexdale, Ontario M9W 1L1, Canada

John Wiley & Sons (Asia) Pte Ltd, 2 Clementi Loop #02-01,
Jin Xing Distripark, Singapore 129809

Library of Congress Cataloging-in-Publication Data

Gordon, Ian E.
    Theories of visual perception / Ian E. Gordon. — 2nd ed.
        p.   cm.
    Includes bibliographical references and index.
    ISBN 0-471-96933-8 (cloth). — ISBN 0-471-96825-0 (pbk.)
    1. Visual perception.   I. Title.
    BF241.G67   1996
    152.14—dc20   96–30819
                                                   CIP

British Library Cataloguing in Publication Data

A catalogue record for this book is available from the British Library

ISBN 0-471-96933-8 (cased)
ISBN 0-471-96825-0 (paper)

Typeset in 10/12pt Times by Dorwyn Ltd, Rowlands Castle, Hants
Printed and bound in Great Britain by Bookcraft (Bath) Ltd
This book is printed on acid-free paper responsibly manufactured from sustainable forestation,
for which at least two trees are planted for each one used for paper production.

In memory of Charles Gordon
1899–1994

Contents

Preface to the second edition

This second edition has been extensively rewritten. Chapter 2 places Fechner's work into a wider historical context and certain important errors have been corrected. Chapter 3 on Gestalt psychology has been expanded to show how the theory was part of a long tradition of work by physicists and mathematicians on the Minimum Principle. The section on more recent work relating to Gestalt ideas has also been expanded. Chapter 4 on probabilistic functionalism has been changed in order to show how Brunswik's thinking was an early recognition of the importance of the 'inference revolution' in psychology. Chapter 5 on the neurophysiological approach to theorizing now contains an introductory account of connectionist networks, replacing that previously included in Chapter 8 on the computational approach. In Chapter 5, it is hoped that a new section on modularity in perceptual input systems will lead to a more balanced appraisal of empiricism. J.J. Gibson's discussion of art has been removed from Chapter 7, leaving room for a fuller description of more recent work on invariants and affordances. Chapter 8 on the computational approach is largely unaltered, apart from transferring the section on connectionist networks to an earlier chapter. The author is aware of more recent developments in this area; however, feedback from undergraduates suggests that, as an introduction to the topic, the chapter is already sufficiently demanding. Chapter 9 now includes an account of Ramachandran's utilitarian theory of vision.

Bettina Newman of the Graphics Department, Exeter University, redrew many of the original figures and has prepared new ones for this edition.

ACKNOWLEDGEMENTS

The reception of the first edition of this book was heartening. With very few exceptions, reviewers were generous towards the book and appreciated its aim: to make some of the major approaches to theorizing about visual perception accessible to a readership of undergraduates and interested lay people.

Some reviewers went beyond the call of duty and sent the author detailed comments about the contents of the book. These have been invaluable during the preparation of this new edition and have made it possible to correct errors of fact and interpretation. Two reviewers must be acknowledged publicly.

Dr Robert O'Shea of the University of Otago pointed to a number of inaccuracies in the book and listed some clumsy or infelicitous passages. He also offered many helpful suggestions for improving the book's structure, which we have tried to do in this second edition. It is a pleasure to acknowledge this generous help.

The author expresses his grateful thanks to Professor Lester Krueger of Ohio State University. As a distinguished theorist with a special interest in psychophysical laws, Professor Krueger was able to point out serious errors of fact and interpretation in Chapter 2. Every effort has been made to correct these in this edition. Professor Krueger also offered invaluable advice on many other issues, particularly the history and significance of the inference revolution: Chapters 2 and 4 have been rewritten to give due importance to this intellectual landmark. As one who has translated classic works in psychology from the German, Professor Krueger was also very helpful in correcting the author's use of certain important terms in Gestalt theory and also directed him to a number of important publications of which he was unaware. Many of what we hope are improvements in the second edition would not have been possible without this very generous advice.

Exeter psychology students are nothing if not frank. Five generations have now worked through *Theories of Visual Perception* and have not hesitated to tell the author which parts they disliked (at grave risk to their careers). Such direct criticisms from a target readership have been invaluable.

Finally, the author reiterates his gratitude to his friend and colleague, Dave Earle. He was always there when needed, and usually knew the answer.

Ian Gordon
Exeter, April 1996

1

An introduction to theories of visual perception

There are many theories of visual perception. Few psychologists know them all; no teaching department includes more than a small subset in its perception courses; and the theories are often very different from each other—a fact which can prove perplexing to students. In this short introductory chapter an attempt will be made to explain why theories concerned with a single sense— vision—should differ so markedly in their style and content. The bias towards vision in general theories of perception is also explained. The chapter is intended to provide a general orientation, particularly for those who are new to the study of visual perception and whose knowledge is grounded in areas other than psychology, such as philosophy, physiology, or the visual arts. More advanced students will know when to skip certain sections.

We shall begin with a few general remarks about theories, particularly as they have developed in psychology and related disciplines. Note that the remarks represent an oversimplification of the continuing debate about the nature of scientific theories. Further, some of the work to be described later in the book does not strictly qualify for the label 'theory': we shall include some very general approaches to perception, such as psychophysics and artificial intelligence, which are of great intellectual and technical importance, but which could be adopted by workers approaching the problems of visual perception from very different theoretical starting points. Nevertheless, these approaches have been adopted in order to explain the phenomena of vision; for this reason they are appropriate subjects for inclusion in this book.

SCIENTIFIC THEORIES AND THE STUDY OF PERCEPTION

This section aims merely to form an appropriate framework for subsequent evaluations of perceptual theories. Readers who wish to learn more about current thinking in the philosophy of science should consult the references given at the end of the chapter.

The majority of those who have worked on perceptual problems have adopted the standards and assumptions of experimental science. That is to say, when theorizing about phenomena they have attempted to meet certain accepted scientific criteria (see, for example, Popper, 1960). These may be briefly summarized.

1. Theories should offer economical accounts of a range of facts. A theory is not much use if a description of it is as long as that required to describe the relevant phenomena.
2. Theories should attempt to explain phenomena, or at least suggest causal links between them.
3. Theories should be testable. They should be stated in such a manner that deductions can be made which are empirically testable.

These points may be illustrated by reference to a theory which arose following detailed scientific studies of human colour matching and discrimination, the Young–Helmholtz theory of colour vision (Helmholtz, 1909/1924).

Humans can see several million different colours. And our colour vision is *trichromatic* in that much of our colour experience can be matched by suitable mixtures of three primary lights. One of the first scientific theories of colour vision, the Young–Helmholtz theory, used the remarkable fact of trichromacy as its starting point. The theory (which will be described more fully later in this book) clearly satisfies the first of the above criteria. Colour vision is described in terms of three mathematical curves, each representing the absorption properties of a hypothetical receptor in the eye. The curves are, in effect, an elegant way of summarizing human colour sensitivity.

But the Young–Helmholtz theory also attempts to *explain* colour vision. It holds that there are three types of receptor in the eye, each sensitive to a portion of the spectrum, and that it is the combined activity of these receptors which underlies colour sensitivity and explains why it is trichromatic. The theory meets the second of the listed criteria.

The Young–Helmholtz theory is no longer accepted as a completely adequate theory of colour vision. It cannot account for changes in the appearance of coloured lights when their intensity changes; it does not explain why yellow appears always as a unitary, primary, colour; it has difficulty in accounting for certain forms of human colour deficiency. However, the fact that these weaknesses can be demonstrated means that the theory is clearly testable.

Most theories of perception have this in common: like the Young–Helmholtz theory they attempt to satisfy the basic criteria listed above. For this reason they merit the label 'scientific'. But it is important to stress that despite having this common property, theories can differ greatly. This is certainly the case with theories of visual perception, as we shall see.

THE VARIETY OF THEORIES OF VISUAL PERCEPTION

The reasons why the theories of perception to be described in this book are so different from one another are themselves many and varied.

Different theoretical orientations

During the course of this book, the reader will see something of the great variety of approaches to the study of perception. Some of these arise because workers adopt very different starting points. Consider, for example, the differences between structuralists and functionalists. In the last century a structuralist approach involved breaking down experience into constituent sensations using a method of anaylsis known as introspection. As a method, this proved to be unprofitable, even invalid. However, there are still those who believe that, for example, when responses to simple mixtures of light can be explained, an understanding of colour perception under complex real-life conditions will gradually emerge.

By contrast, a functionalist account of any perceptual mechanism or system will tend to begin with the question: What is it *for*? How might such a mechanism have evolved? What evolutionary advantage might it confer? This attitude will tend to encourage certain types of research. For example, one outcome will be that the study of visual systems other than human ones will seem relevant: how does each relate to the environment in which it evolved? We shall show that one of the strengths of the computational approach outlined in Chapter 8 is that it searches for basic mechanisms of vision while at the same time recognizing the importance of constraints set by the environment within which the mechanisms evolved. (And it is of interest that one computational theorist has examined the landing behaviour of . . . the house fly.)

Another major theoretical approach arises from the philosophical movement, phenomenology. In our daily lives, each of us experiences a stable and coherent world, a world of surfaces and things. We make no conscious effort here: the world is as we see it. Yet, as we shall see, some theorists claim that seeing this stable world may require us to go beyond the evidence of our senses. When rectangular objects are tilted, the images on our retinae become trapezoidal, but the objects retain their rectangular appearance. A coloured surface seen under different illuminants will reflect different patterns of light to the eye, and yet its colour may remain unchanged. We may be fully aware of an entire object, even though part of it is obscured. Phenomena such as these are familiar to artists, particularly those seeking to produce realistic representations of the world. It is also easy to convince observers that there are problems here, using controlled laboratory demonstrations.

The question is, to which of these two different aspects of seeing should research be directed: the trained and analytic, or the everyday world of experience? Phenomenologists believe that it is the experiences of everyday life which need to be explained, and we shall see something of this approach in a description of Gestalt theory (Chapter 3). However, we shall also see that many other approaches to the study of visual perception are far removed from phenomenology.[1]

There is an important but less formal aspect to the relationship between perceptual theory and philosophical orientation. Scholars in psychology rarely work in complete isolation. What is going on around them exerts an influence. Brunswik, for example, started his career in proximity to the Vienna school of logical positivists. As a result, the early focus of his work was upon that which is physically measurable (see Gigerenzer and Murray, 1987). When he arrived in the USA in 1937, American psychology was under the sway of Behaviourism: many experimenters spent their time running rats down mazes. Two years after his arrival in the USA, Brunswik published an experiment involving . . . rats running down a maze.

In Chapter 3 we shall describe how a central tenet of Gestalt theory—Prägnanz—has a strong aesthetic component. In the liberal years of the Weimar republic at that time there existed a remarkable organization: the Bauhaus. This very influential institution, directed initially by the architect Walter Gropius, ran courses that were taught by artists such as Kandinsky, Klee and Albers. By 1937, the graphic design taught in the Bauhaus drew on the principles of Gestalt psychology. With this sort of influence around them, it is small wonder that the Gestalt theorists were in turn interested in art and aesthetics and gave an aesthetic principle such importance in their theory.

Levels of explanation

An important issue concerns the level at which perception should be described and explained. Many have preferred to look for possible physiological mechanisms which could mediate certain aspects of seeing. Others, by contrast, have insisted that the proper language with which to describe human perception is the language of psychology.

These differences also determine the relative importance attached to bottom-up versus top-down factors in perceiving, terms which will be explained later in the book. One who works in the belief that seeing begins with the responses of peripheral 'modular' mechanisms (which are assumed to be automatic or reflexive in their action and unaffected by higher-level processes such as knowledge, reasoning, habits and so on) is unlikely to spend much time worrying about the perception of, say, caricatures. Those who do think about such things may accept that perceptual input systems do certain jobs,

---

[1] That said, from now on we shall not hesitate to appeal to the reader's direct experience of things in order to strengthen an argument.

but that the interesting questions arise when we ask how perceptual inputs are used to construct our experience of the world (including caricatures).

In more recent times, a different approach to perception has emerged: simulation of perceptual mechanisms. One of the goals of those who work in the discipline of artificial intelligence is to build machines that can see. The importance of this in the development of intelligent machines is obvious. Now the proof about a machine (usually a computer program) designed to solve some visual problem lies in the fact that either it works or it doesn't. This is a new means of testing theories, and it is a very stringent one. The question is, of course: Is a simulation an explanation?

Errors as evidence

This is a minor point, but worth noting. There are basic disagreements between theorists concerning how much can be learned from errors in perceiving. Two attitudes exist. The first holds that forcing a system into error is a long-established scientific method: that when and how a system breaks down gives us a privileged glimpse into the normal workings of that system. A lot of experimental psychology has followed this maxim. Among the phenomena which psychologists have studied are lapses of attention, errors in logical reasoning, slips of the tongue, effects of long-term blindness, and language breakdown following brain damage. In studying visual perception, many have looked to illusions as clues to normal functioning: and illusions will feature large in this book.

On the other hand, there are those who argue, first, that illusions are rare in daily experience—it takes special stimulus configurations, often highly artificial ones, to induce them—and that once perception under more natural conditions is understood, explanations of illusions will follow naturally. For example, stereophonic sound, now available in most high-fi systems, is an illusion. But the illusion of something moving through the space between two loudspeakers is no longer mysterious: we know the basis of normal sound localization; that the cues of intensity and phase can be used to generate an illusion is not at all mysterious.

The availability of models

Much scientific thought has been shaped, directly or indirectly, by the models or metaphors currently available to theorists. This is an important point and is worth expanding upon.

In the seventeenth century Descartes was developing what were to become very influential views on the mind–body problem. The essence of Cartesian dualism is that the human body is a physical machine controlled by the mind. Descartes believed that this control is exercised *via* 'animal spirits' flowing through channels in the body, with the pineal gland in the brain forming the point where the body interacts with the mind (or soul).

It is interesting to ask what physical models would have been known to Descartes at the time he was writing his *Discourse on Method*, which was published in 1637. The answer is that in the royal parks of France there were a number of remarkable automata. These were mechanical human-like figures driven by water pressure and connected to hidden pipes in such a manner that the weight of people crossing adjacent flagstones caused them to move. Familiarity with these ingenious machines (which are mentioned in his writings) must have shaped Descartes' thoughts on dualism.

The nineteenth century was a period of great social change. The full impact of new technology had created the large industrial cities of the Western world. Pockets of discontent throughout Europe convinced many that social revolution was imminent. Indeed, a new stereotype emerged: the bomb-throwing anarchist. During this same period the most widely admired and influential model of brain function—that proposed by the neurologist Hughlings Jackson (1835–1911)—stated that the function of the most recently evolved, 'higher' centres of the brain was to exert control over the older and more primitive functions of the rest.

> When the highest centres were damaged there was a release of the lower functions. In normal functioning the highest centres were 'protected' and partially insulated from the lower; in cases of brain damage they were the first to suffer dissolution.
>
> (Hearnshaw, 1964)

Substituting 'revolution' for 'damage' and 'social classes' for 'centres', allows us to speculate that this model of the brain might be more than just a neutral account of clinical and anatomical data. It could be revealing some of the hidden anxieties of an upper-class British scholar.

For the past 30 years or so, psychological theorists in a variety of areas have based their models upon the modern digital computer. The result is that contemporary descriptions within psychology have been peppered with terms such as *stages, retrieval, control, content-addressable memory, buffer memory, information*, and so on. For some, the computer has become an intriguing and indispensible model of the human brain.

As we shall show in Chapter 5, a new model is now available to psychologists and neurophysiologists: the connectionist network. This is already beginning to exert its effects on visual research and theory, and it seems likely that the effects will spread. An example of a connectionist model used to test a theory will be given in Chapter 8.

The relevance of all this to the question concerning the variety of theories of visual perception is simply that the model which a particular theorist adopts, or is influenced by, will in turn influence the type of theory which he or she eventually develops.

New techniques

This source of ideas (which commonly grow into theories) is one which is stressed infrequently in formal treatments of the philosophy of science or the history of psychology. However, new techniques and methods of analysis have had a significant influence on the study of perception. Techniques do not of themselves exert a direct influence upon theorizing, rather they open up new possibilities for exploring and modelling phenomena.

In the early 1950s the first twin-track tape recorders became available. In retrospect, this seems a fairly minor technical advance. But it was a machine of this type that allowed Cherry (1953) to conduct his famous experiments on dichotic listening in which he showed, for example, that a person who is shadowing a message in one ear may learn very little about a message delivered simultaneously to the other. Although the sex of the speaker can be identified, the content of what the person is saying cannot, nor can the language in which it is being said. This single demonstration stimulated a host of similar studies, and these led eventually to Broadbent's widely influential book, *Perception and Communication* (Broadbent, 1958).

The threshold performance of the eye used to be described under two headings: sensitivity and acuity. The first was concerned with the smallest amounts of light energy that the eye could detect; the second referred to the resolving power of the eye—the smallest changes in stimulation that could be detected.

It had been found by researchers in optics that the performance of a lens could be described in terms of its ability to transmit the imaging of a *grating*. Advances in this area led to the use of sinusoidally modulated gratings and new terminology appeared: 'modular transfer function', 'spatial frequency analysis', and so on.

When such techniques were applied to the vertebrate eye, success was rapid. A new way of describing the performance of the eye, which combined measures of sensitivity *and* acuity, became available: *the contrast sensitivity function*. Equally exciting was the idea that the eye may have channels tuned to different spatial frequencies. The impact of this technique and this idea will be described more fully in Chapter 5.

THE FOCUS OF RESEARCH AND THEORY: REGIONS OF CONCERN

Readers who are new to the study of psychology will realize, as they work through this book, that vision is a bewilderingly complicated sense. There are so many aspects of seeing that no theorist can hope to embrace them all. There has to be some selection. We shall now delineate what we shall call *regions* of potential interest to theorists, and then try to show how the choice of regions leads to differences between theories.

A starting point for perception is commonly a change or event in the world.[2] However, perceivers can become aware of only a small subset of such events: humans, for example, are not perpetually aware of ultraviolet radiation, although we can deduce that it must have been present once the pain of sunburn begins. It follows that part of the understanding of perception must be based on knowledge of things and events in the world: their physics, their regularities, the dimensions along which they vary. The study of such things is, of course, the study of the perceiver's *ecology*. To date, the study of ecologies has been the province of geologists, geographers and biologists, but this is an area of increasing relevance to the psychologist, as will become apparent in subsequent chapters. We can therefore say that the first of our regions of interest is simply the environment or ecology in which an organism perceives.

A second region of concern is that comprising stimuli. Potentially detectable objects and events generate stimuli. At source, these are known as *distal stimuli*. The form they take on arriving at sense organs determines their role as *proximal stimuli*. Knowledge of the important properties of distal and proximal stimuli has come mainly from physics (light, sound, heat, pressure) and chemistry (volatile substances). We shall show later in this book that the degree to which proximal stimuli can specify distal stimuli has been the subject of vigorous debate (Chapters 6 and 7).

A third region of concern is that defined by the perceiver's sensory surfaces and associated peripheral neurons. Stimuli cannot be perceived until their energy has been transduced into neural codes. It is important to know the nature of this transduction: how light is absorbed by the eye, how changes in frequency affect the ear, how substances are absorbed by the nasal membranes. Important questions concern the pathways taken by neural messages, the codes which are used to represent differences in quality, intensity and duration, and the interactions which take place between neurons. Anatomists and physiologists have sought answers to these questions for more than a century, and are still doing so. Some theories of visual perception give great prominence to events in this region (Chapter 8).

In some organisms the connection between the reception of an incoming sensory signal and the initiation of a response may be a simple one. However, in many others, perceptual inputs are processed by brains. This brings us to a fourth region of enquiry.

The problems associated with the study of the brain are almost too obvious to list. Most behaviour of complex animals depends upon brain processes, but

---

[2] We can, of course, become aware of some of the events which occur within our bodies.

these are commonly not available to direct study and must be explored indirectly—by making inferences from behaviour. Indeed, the whole of the activity labelled 'psychology' can be viewed as an attempt to gain insights into how brains perform their functions. Very often, and for good reasons, the term 'mind' has been preferred to 'brain'. We shall not become enmeshed in the notorious mind/brain problem[3]; rather we shall bypass it in subsequent expositions, noting simply that mind and its relation to brain has been the subject of lengthy debate by psychologists and philosophers, while the direct study of the brain has been the province of neurophysiologists and neuroanatomists, some of whose work will be described later in this book.

A fifth region of interest is that of effector or motor systems. Stimuli trigger numerous kinds of events in the body. For example, the pupil constricts in response to light (careful study of this response has enabled researchers to detect which wavelengths of light animals are or are not sensitive to). However, the most easily observed responses to stimulation are motor responses. Perceivers are not passive, they move around in the world and in this way partially determine the stimulation they receive.

It is interesting to note here that there is a strong evolutionary link between movement and vision. Coren (1986) has pointed out that when various members within a particular phylum are compared, the more mobile the species, the better developed is its visual apparatus. Within the phylum *Mollusca*, for example, bivalves such as the clam move very little and have only primitive light receptors; in more mobile species, such as the scallop, light receptors are grouped into eye spots; and the most active members of the phylum, the octopus and the squid, have eyes which rival those of vertebrates in their state of development.

At a more general level, the study of motor activity is simply the study of behaviour: what organisms actually do. And this is, of course, the major concern of experimental psychology.

Finally, we come back to the environment. The behaviour of organisms does not take place in a vacuum, but in the world. And so this classification ends where it began: with the physical world in which living things dwell and upon which they act in so many different ways.

The foregoing is merely a sketch, an oversimplification, and as such it must not be taken too seriously. Indeed, as schemes such as the one just outlined cannot be arrived at in a theoretically neutral manner, they are risky. For example, it will be stated in later chapters that there are those who hold that movement of the observer is a vital component of perceiving. Such theorists would argue strongly that to delineate the motor aspect of perception as a separate 'region', as was done above, does violence to the truth. Nevertheless, although our classificatory scheme skates over some major theoretical

---

[3] Useful references are included in the notes at the end of this chapter.

difficulties, we shall use it as a way of highlighting important characteristics of particular theories. One thing the scheme does is to help explain the variety to be found among those theories of perception which have emerged during the first hundred years of experimental psychology.

All general theories of perception refer directly or indirectly to the brain. They must, for the brain is the seat of all psychological functions. Leaving this to one side, we can note something else about such theories. The point will be defended in subsequent chapters; for now we shall simply assert that, commonly, the greater the number of what we have called regions that are included in a theory, the more that theory tends to be general in form. This is almost a tautology. More importantly, as will be shown, *the particular subset of possible regions among which underlying relationships are sought differs from theory to theory*. It is this fact which makes general perceptual theories so confusingly varied, as a few examples will show.

Consider first theories which are somewhat restricted in focus. Three-factor theories of colour vision (one of which will be described more fully in a later chapter) state that there are three pigments in the cone cells of the eye, each maximally sensitive to a particular region of the visible spectrum. These theories clearly attempt to link two of the regions we have delineated: proximal stimuli and the sensory surface of the eye. The brain is also involved, of course, because the theories attempt to explain part of our general response to light. But three-factor theories are not general theories, even of colour vision. They explain the appearance only of what are described as 'film colours', the colours we see when looking at surfaces through narrow apertures. Three-factor theories cannot predict the appearance of coloured textured surfaces, nor can they fully explain how we see objects as having stable colours under different illuminants. The theories cannot do these things because, in their present form, they do not embrace enough regions to enable them to do so.

Now consider another group of phenomena and the different ways in which they can be approached theoretically. As an object recedes from the eye, the angle it subtends there diminishes in a lawful manner. This simple fact is known from the application of geometry to aspects of the physical world, which tells us about the relationship between distal and proximal stimuli. The same geometry (using the theorem of similar triangles) permits the calculation of corresponding changes in the size of retinal images (our third region). Although these calculations can be performed in three distinct regions, in this case the manner in which the effects of distance on stimulation are described is not really important. Descriptions of things and events in the three regions can be rendered essentially equivalent.

We can now ask about the size of the smallest stimulus that an observer can detect: how far can the object recede (or shrink) before it becomes invisible? This obviously involves the sizes of visual angles and their corresponding retinal images. Either description will do for most purposes, unless we wish to relate detection to the number of cells per unit area of the retina, in which case image size may be the more convenient. (Note that we cannot use object size alone as an adequate description: a standard playing card held fifty centimetres in front of the eye subtends a greater angle than the average car fifty metres away.) And while the brain exerts an important influence on threshold performance, the performance as such is commonly described only in terms of visual angles or retinal image sizes.

However, when someone is asked to estimate or match the apparent size of a receding object, it is usually found that, within wide limits, perceived size is not affected by distance. This phenomenon is known as 'size constancy' and will be cited frequently in later chapters for it raises interesting theoretical issues. But note that any perceptual theory which attempts to explain size constancy (and other phenomena of perceptual stability) cannot do so if analysis is limited solely to one or two of our regions. This is because at least four regions are involved: the world, in which objects approach and recede from the eye and which forms the context in which they are seen; accompanying changes in stimulation; and central factors which must be cited to explain (a) how perceivers manage to compensate for the shrinking visual image and (b) how artists who wish to depict the three-dimensional world are able to overcome constancy and respond to the true visual angles of things. And as size constancy is stronger when the observer is free to move his or her head and eyes, a complete account of the phenomenon will also have to include the contribution made by the motor system.

Although general theories of perception never attempt to incorporate *all* the regions we have described, most are concerned with more than two. Which regions are focused upon depends upon the attitude and assumptions of the theorist. It is this possibility of choice that is largely responsible for the great variety among perceptual theories generally and theories of vision in particular.

THEORIES OF VISUAL PERCEPTION

The title of this book requires a little explanation. A more appropriate title might be *Some Theories . . .*, for it has been possible to describe only a selection of theoretical approaches. And of these only one is exclusively visual in its domain: the computational approach to vision. The remainder all include some discussion of perception in other modalities. But the title *Theories of Visual Perception* was chosen deliberately. All the general theoretical approaches to be described focus much more closely on vision than on any other sense. In fact, removal of the visual content from any of the theories would reduce each to a very short statement. Why should this be so?

One answer is that we are a species in whom the visual sense is very highly developed, and we are interested in ourselves. Touch is important, particularly in establishing our earliest emotional ties, and few would wish to live without hearing—not to be able to converse or listen to music would be a tragic loss for all of us. But our waking experience is largely visual. In fact, 'waking up' is mainly opening our eyes and noticing things. To lose consciousness is essentially to stop seeing (we stop hearing also, but this is not what we spontaneously remember about it). All this is mirrored in our language: for example, the ensemble of adjectives available to describe the visual appearance of things far exceeds that available for describing their sounds or smells. The bias among theories of perception is merely a natural reflection of the importance of vision to those perceivers about whom we are most curious: ourselves.

There is a second, rather more trivial, reason why visual phenomena dominate work in perception: the stimuli are easier to produce. In later chapters numerous examples will be given of important discoveries which have been made using remarkably simple visual stimuli. These are often no more complicated than carefully drawn lines, narrow beams of pure light, or simple clusters of dots. Provided these can be displayed under carefully controlled conditions, major explorations of visual function become possible. In fact, in the remainder of this book probably the most complicated single stimulus to be referred to is a picture of a human face.

The situation in other modalities is not so simple. Substances for quantitative research into the sense of smell must be blasted up into the nasal passages. Controlled pain induction requires quite elaborate procedures. Production of sound stimuli with precisely controlled duration, frequency, intensity and phase requires expensive equipment. Suppose, for example, one wished to deliver two words to a subject, one to each ear, and that it was important that the words arrived exactly simultaneously, it could take several days (and some fancy electronics) to set up the experiment. Contrast this with the ease with which pairs of words can be displayed visually.

Finally, it should be acknowledged that because vision is the sense which has received the most research attention in the past hundred years, an extraordinary number of visual phenomena have been discovered. The problem lies in accommodating them within satisfactory general theories.

THE ORGANIZATION OF THE REMAINING CHAPTERS

Chapter 2: Psychophysics and the concept of the threshold

This chapter will show how measurement was first introduced into the study of perception and how this led to claims that it was possible to measure sensations. It will then outline some of the basic methods designed to measure sensory and perceptual thresholds. It will be shown how—even at this basic level of exploring the area between being able and being unable to perceive an event—a theory is required. Thus at the start of perceptual processing there is a mystery: What *is* a threshold? Different interpretations are reviewed.

Chapter 3: The Gestalt theory

This theory emerged, in part, as a reaction against the view that perceptions are bundles of sensations. Gestalt psychologists were able to show that when two or more stimuli are present simultaneously, their interactions may lead to a percept which is very different from those arising from the stimuli in isolation. The theory stresses the dynamic aspects of perceiving and claims that there are major organizing principles at work in the central nervous system which cause perception to be as stable, coherent and simple as conditions allow. The Gestalt explanations of these organizing tendencies are rooted in a long tradition in physics and related disciplines which maintains that physical systems tend to follow a Minimum Principle. This will be explained in some detail. Finally, some of the more recent work which is beginning to support and quantify Gestalt principles will be described.

Chapter 4: Brunswik's probabilistic functionalism

Brunswik's functional approach stresses that perception must have evolved to take advantage of the ways in which the environment offers potential information about itself. It is the nature of this potential information that it is essentially *statistical*: the cues which an organism receives are seldom perfectly reliable or valid. As a result, perceiving has to be flexible as stimulation may come in different forms and *via* different modalities. In order to survive, perceivers must make a series of successful bets concerning the quality of sensory evidence they receive. Brunswik held that these ideas demanded a different research programme than that represented by classical psychophysics, one in which the complexities of the environment are adequately sampled and represented. Brunswik's pioneering role in what has been described as 'the inference revolution' will be described.

Chapter 5: The neurophysiological approach to visual perception

Replacing hypothetical constructs by possible neural mechanisms has always appealed to some theorists. And there has long been a two-way traffic between psychology and neurophysiology, in that discoveries about the nervous system cannot fail to exert some influence upon psychologists; at the same time, the work of neurophysiologists commonly represents an attempt to explain phenomena discovered in psychological research.

Chapter 5 describes some areas in which reliable data from psychological experiments have led to psychological theories, which have then been enriched by neurological discoveries and the importation into the theories of neurological mechanisms and concepts. A new model, the connectionist network, will be introduced. Finally, the limits on attempts to explain psychological phenomena using the language of neurophysiology will be discussed.

Chapter 6: Empiricism: perception as a constructive process

There have long been those who believe that perception of the world cannot be based solely on the evidence provided by the senses. Sensory data, it is argued, are often erratic, impoverished and distorted. In short, they alone cannot furnish what is needed to build the stable, coherent world of everyday experience.

The empiricist or constructivist paradigm is built on the assumption that perception results from a combination of sensory data and inferential cognitive processes. Perceivers act as intuitive scientists, forming and testing hypotheses about the world. In this manner they are able to go beyond the imperfect evidence of their senses. It will be shown that this view—that perception is essentially an indirect process—can be combined with the assertion that perceptual input systems are modular in their design.

Chapter 7: Direct perception and ecological optics

In contrast with empiricists/constructivists, J.J. Gibson and his followers have asserted that perception of the natural environment can indeed be based on the evidence of the senses. The claim is that stimulation arising from the world (in contrast with that which is commonly presented in laboratory experiments) may be extraordinarily rich in information—a richness that is augmented by active exploration by perceivers. The problem is to discover regularities in the complex, ever-changing inputs provided by the senses.

Adherents of this theory maintain that a perceiver and its environmental niche should be treated as aspects of the same reality: the one cannot be understood without reference to the other. More recent research on the concept of the 'fit' between organisms and environments will be reviewed. A brief description of advanced studies of optic flow will be included.

Chapter 8: Marr's computational approach to visual perception

This is an account of the computational approach to vision, as exemplified by the work of David Marr. Marr's theory of vision derives from work in artificial intelligence and is considered by many contemporary workers to be the most important theoretical development of recent years. Marr develops a framework for the analysis of any information-processing system, including vision. The essence of this is the formal distinction between different levels of understanding: the goal of a particular process (the computational theory), the rules or procedures by which this goal might be attained (the algorithm) and possible mechanisms with which to instantiate the rules (the hardware implementation). The approach will be described in general, together with detailed accounts of some successful applications.

Chapter 9: Overview and conclusions

This chapter comprises an overview and some general comments on theorizing in visual perception. An attempt is made to show how knowledge of the successes and failures of the various general theories of visual perception might be used to guide subsequent theorizing. The question of what a theory of visual perception should attempt to achieve is discussed, and certain fundamental difficulties are highlighted.

THE STYLE OF THIS BOOK

The responses of students and others to whom the author has taught perception have shaped an approach to theoretical matters which will be followed in this book. It has always seemed helpful to describe a theory as sympathetically as possible, before offering criticisms of it. In this way, more clarity is achievable than would be possible if the criticisms were interwoven into the initial description.

This separation of presentation and criticism has another justification: those who have developed general theories of perception in the past were not fools; we should assume that they did the best they could with the knowledge available to them at the time, and for this they deserve respect. It is hoped that by introducing their work sympathetically, this respect will have been accorded.

A note on history

An attempt will be made in each of the following chapters to tell a story, to say how a state of affairs has evolved. This is the way in which the author has always tried to make sense of things, and the way in which he has taught his subject. Every effort has been made in this book to describe the history accurately. However, the reader should beware of one thing: the author is not an historian.

In a lecture describing the historical background to his work on the theory of quantum electrodynamics, for which he was awarded the 1965 Nobel Prize, the physicist Richard Feynman said:

> By the way, what I have just outlined is what I call a 'physicist's history of physics', which is never correct. What I am telling you is a sort of conventionalized myth-story that the physicists tell to their students, and those students tell to their students, and is not necessarily related to the actual historical development, which I do not really know!
>
> (Feynman, 1985)

In like manner, when, for example, we describe in Chapter 3 how Max Wertheimer broke a journey in 1910 in order to buy the toy which eventually led to the development of Gestalt theory, he might have had more important things on his mind: we do not really know. But that is the story.

Finally, the theoretical aspects of any subject are always the most abstract. In reading about a number of theories of visual perception, there is a danger that something will be lost: the powerful fascination of visual phenomena. The reason why so many people are drawn to the study of vision is in part aesthetic: the eye does wonderful things. To finish this chapter, we include an illusion which has been published since the first edition of this book (Figure 1.1). This single figure encapsulates what, for many, is the thrill of visual research.

NOTES ON CHAPTER 1

The following references may be helpful introductions to theory in science generally and psychology in particular.

Chalmers (1982). This is a very good introduction to scientific explanation generally, with some reference to problems within psychology.

Churchland (1984). This is a short but useful paperback outlining modern thinking on the philosophy of mind.

Quine and Ullian (1970). This describes the ways in which science is based upon belief.

Dennet (1991) is a remarkable attempt to develop a new theory of consciousness. The book contains many examples of fascinating perceptual phenomena and some remarkably provocative thought experiments, for example, on the problems of knowing what it is like to be another creature, what would happen if all the reds a person saw were experimentally changed to greens, whether we would be able to describe the experience of adapting to an inversion of our visual input. This book is highly recommended.

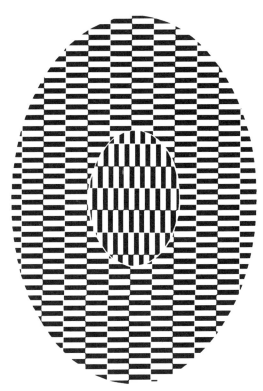

Figure 1.1   A new illusion, discovered by Hine, Cook and Rogers (1995). Move this page from side to side and notice how the central region of the figure moves relative to its background. (Reprinted from Hine, Cook, and Rogers (1995), with kind permission from Elsevier Science Ltd)

2

Psychophysics and the concept of the threshold

Most readers will have had an experience similar to the following when entering a dark room. At first, nothing can be discerned. After a few minutes in the dark, it becomes obvious that (to be melodramatic) you are not alone. What is happening in this situation—between the moment of invisibility and that of visibility? What is the nature of the border between these two states? This chapter will be about *thresholds*, their measurement and the debate about what they are. To provide orientation in terms of the classificatory scheme outlined in Chapter 1: an interest in thresholds leads to consideration of the relationship between properties of a proximal stimulus and the sensation (or response) elicited by that stimulus.

Two types of threshold are traditionally distinguished in sensory research. *Absolute thresholds* are measures of the least amounts of stimulus energy that can be detected. *Difference* (or *relative*) *thresholds* represent the minimum changes in stimuli that can be detected and are often used as measures of the acuity or resolving power of a sense. It is also possible to measure perceptual thresholds—for example, what is the minimum time it takes to recognize a face, to read a word, or to distinguish between a square and a triangle. These will not be discussed in this chapter, although they will feature elsewhere in this book.

Psychophysics is a set of techniques designed to explore thresholds. Much of what is known about the workings of perceptual systems has been discovered by applying these techniques. Indeed, most of the data to be described in the remainder of this book have come from experiments using techniques drawn from the psychophysical repertoire. This has been a very impressive achievement; to have made important discoveries about the workings of visual systems without being able to enter or tamper with them has been one of the most notable contributions of experimental psychology. It is more than a century since the results of the first psychophysical experiment were published, and yet this method of investigation is still in use in laboratories throughout the world.

Psychophysics has done more than simply provide techniques for the exploration of the senses: it has given rise to *theories* of the threshold. Examining theoretical successes and failures where the phenomena are relatively straightforward and generally not in dispute will be a useful preliminary to later discussions of theories in more complex areas of perception. That said, the reader may be surprised to learn of the amount of disagreement there is in this field. Even here, among what might appear to be the basic processes of vision—detection and discrimination—there is active debate among theorists, as will be shown.

In terms of our classification of regions which theorists attempt to link, we shall see that the central concern of this chapter is how the brain makes decisions concerning information from the sense organs, and the relationship between these decisions and properties of the proximal stimuli which have activated processes in the sense organs.

One reason for beginning with a treatment of psychophysics and thresholds arose from thinking about the various kinds of person who might read this book. Some readers will never have had an opportunity to carry out perceptual experiments. And yet any text on visual perception will refer to many such experiments; it must, for they are the main source of our knowledge concerning vision. A familiarity with the basic psychophysical techniques is an essential prerequisite for understanding perceptual research. Not all researches involve purely psychophysical techniques and only a minority are concerned with perception of weak stimuli or minimum differences between stimuli. Nevertheless, the methodological rigour established within psychophysics has proved invaluable in the experimental exploration of perception.

By the end of this chapter, any reader should be able to attempt a perceptual experiment. For example, many parents must have wondered what it is about their face that induces smiling in their newborn infants. Similarly, many dog owners must have asked themselves how well their pets can see distant objects. To answer such questions is not as straightforward as it may seem, but it can be done, and through entirely harmless procedures. It is hoped that this chapter will at least show how to think of ways of tackling such problems.

Our main aim, however, is to examine the concept of a sensory threshold. It is demonstrably true that there are sounds we cannot hear, contours we cannot see and odours we cannot smell. We can tell when these stimuli are present, for we have instruments to tell us so. And when the strengths of the stimuli are increased we may then be able to detect them. (We also know that other species can often detect stimuli which we cannot: the visual acuity of some hawks has been estimated as being so high that they could detect the movement of the hour hand of a clock.) Now the question is: What happens as the intensity of a stimulus is raised from a value at which we cannot detect it to one at which we can? Is there a value such that the stimulus makes an impact which is simply insufficient to send a message to the brain, and another, just greater, when the message *is* transmitted? Is there, in other words, a sensory *threshold*? This is the theoretical problem to be dealt with in this chapter. We shall review the historical development of the concept of the threshold and then try to show why this once dominant idea in perception has been challenged in the past few years.

The remaining contents of this chapter are organized around the following related topics:

- Number and measurement
- Classical psychophysics
- The classical theory of the threshold
- The neural quantum theory
- The theory of signal detection
- Direct scaling techniques
- General remarks on psychophysics

NUMBER AND MEASUREMENT

Number and measurement play so large a part in twentieth-century life that we tend to take them for granted. Following a little education we are expected to know the distance to the sun, the atomic weight of hydrogen, the value of the gravitational constant. Children are now routinely taught to count to base 2 as well as to base 10. Many families in the richer countries use electronic calculators; a high proportion own computers. No one expresses surprise or admiration when a space vehicle arrives back on earth within minutes of its estimated time of arrival. Our society depends upon a great deal of measurement and calculation and we accept this as quite normal.

Imagine, however, the excitement which the discovery of number and measurements must have caused. The ancient Greeks, who had a deep interest in aesthetics, found that if a vibrating string is divided into two equal lengths, each will sound the octave of the original. Dividing the string 3 : 2 produces the interval of a perfect fifth: 3 : 4 yields a perfect fourth. How uncanny: simple ratios between integers producing perfect harmonic intervals. What a strange relationship between mathematics and music.

When Greek mathematicians divided the circumference of a circle by the diameter they found the answer to be an irrational number: pi = 3.141592654. . . . They then discovered that if a line is divided into two portions, *a* and *b*, such that the ratio of *a* to *b* equals that of *b* to the whole (that is, *a* : *b* = *b* : *a* + *b*), then this proportion or Golden Section has remarkable properties. A rectangle constructed from such a golden section seems balanced and pleasing; it also has the property that it can be subdivided into other rect-angles, the sides of which are also golden sections (see Figure 2.1). And the formula for the golden section can be converted into a simple expression: $(-1 + \sqrt{5})/2$. The solution of this expression to nine decimal places is 0.618033989, the Golden Ratio. Note, however, that this too is an irrational number (be-cause $\sqrt{5}$ has no simple integer solution), and now imagine the initial impact of these discoveries: at the heart of a strange and seemingly powerful aesthetic rule—used in the construction of the Parthenon (and the basis of Le Cor-busier's architectural concept of the *modular* 2000 years later)—is another number which is not an integer. Small wonder that the properties of $\sqrt{5}$ became a guarded secret known only to small religious sects.

Interest in measurement and the fascination with numbers persisted over the centuries. From the eighteenth century onwards successful measurement was increasingly the mark of a mature science. Many gains in understanding stemmed from the ability to measure things. Engineers learned how to quantify important properties of materials in terms of the concepts of stress, strain and elasticity. Chemists produced estimates of the atomic weights of elements. Many of the main physical constants, such as gravity, received numerical values. And much important scientific work during the eighteenth and nineteenth centuries made use of a marvellous mathematical tool: the calculus.

So far, however, we have made no reference to the measurement of any *human* attribute. True, certain pioneers had collected data on skull shape and

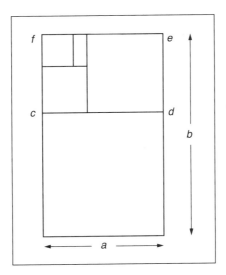

Figure 2.1   The Golden Rectangle, $a : b = 0.618$. If the shorter side, a, is projected onto the longer, b, a new Golden Rectangle is formed (*cdef*). This process may be repeated indefinitely

size and attempted to relate these to the cultural and evolutionary development of different peoples (providing a pseudoscientific basis for future racism; see Gould, 1981), but there had been little or no measurement of what people could do. Then, in 1846, a German physiologist published the results of a simple experiment which was to become a catalyst for the new science of experimental psychology. The experiment had succeeded in measuring a human sensory threshold.

CLASSICAL PSYCHOPHYSICS

Weber's and Fechner's Laws

E.H. Weber was professor of physiology at Leipzig when he published an account of some experiments on the sense of touch: *Der Tatsinn und das Gemeingefühl* (1846). During these experiments Weber had observers make judgements between pairs of lifted weights. His concern was with the smallest difference that could be detected and how this varied with absolute weight.

German physiology at that time used some strange units of weight. We shall therefore illustrate Weber's findings using fictitious data. Basically, what Weber discovered was that if he started with a standard weight of, say, 10 grams, then a second weight could just be felt as heavier if it was raised to 12 grams; this stimulus value was defined as the *Just Noticeable Difference* (JND). But if the standard weight was 100 grams, then a second weight would seem just noticeably heavier when it was raised, not by 2 grams, but by 20. In other words, the JND was not a fixed amount; it was a *ratio* of the standard. These researches were then repeated in the visual and auditory modalities, with similar results.

Weber's finding was later elevated to the status of a law, having this form:

$$\Delta I/I = k \tag{1}$$

In (1) ΔI is the JND change in the intensity of the stimulus, I is the original intensity (the standard stimulus) and k is a constant for a particular sensory modality. Other *Weber fractions*, as they became known, have now been established in every sensory modality.

The significance of Weber's research is fourfold. First, he discovered a law which is still valid (although, as we shall see, there are those who consider that it needs to be modified). Second, Weber fractions have continuing practical usefulness. For example, should a lighting engineer wish to increase the perceived brightness of illumination in part of a room, the relevant Weber fraction is a good guide to what change will be noticeable. Third, Weber had shown how a fundamental property of a sense modality could be discovered by the systematic use of a non-destructive, simple procedure. Finally, the extension of Weber's work by Fechner created a new subject, psychophysics, which was to be of great importance in launching the new science of experimental psychology.

The true nature of the relationship between Weber's data and Fechner's subsequent use of them has been disputed (see Boring, 1950, for a detailed account of the history of psychophysics), but this need not concern us here. What is important is the way in which Weber's main finding was interpreted by Gustav Fechner.

Fechner (1801–1887), a successful professor of physics by the age of 33, had an abiding interest in philosophy. It is known (Boring, 1950) that he suffered a breakdown in midlife and resigned his chair. Fechner later described how, following his illness, he had an insight which was to change the direction of his career. We shall describe this insight as clearly as possible, again using fictitious data to simplify the account. It is important to remember (a) that actual threshold data are never as clear-cut as the hypothetical ones below, and (b) a constant Weber fraction for weight is assumed: in fact the fraction changes somewhat with absolute stimulus magnitude. These facts will not invalidate the demonstration.

Imagine a set of determinations of JNDs carried out in the following, rather unusual, manner. Starting with a weight of 100 g, we shall assume that over the range of stimuli in which we are interested the Weber fraction is 20 per cent. It follows that the first JND we should record will be 20 g. In other words, a weight of 100 g + 20 g = 120 g should feel just noticeably heavier than a weight of 100 g (more formally, we can say that it will be reliably detected as being the heavier of the two weights presented).

Next, substitute 120 g as a new standard and measure another JND. With the Weber fraction constant at 20 per cent, this should occur with a weight of 120 g + 24 g (20 per cent of 120), or 144 g. Proceed in this manner for a number of successive determinations of sequential JNDs. Weber's Law implies that if such an exercise was carried out, the following results would be recorded (all units are in grams and have been rounded up for clarity):

Standard stimulus:	100	120	144	173	208	250	300
JND at:		120	144	173	208	250	300	360

These results can be displayed in an alternative form:

Change required to produce JND:	20	24	29	35	42	50	60
JND step:		1	2	3	4	5	6	7

The key to Fechner's insight is contained in the last two lines. It can be seen that as the change in the standard necessary to produce each JND is growing rapidly, the JNDs are simply incrementing. As we have said, real experiments never turn out as cleanly as this hypothetical one, but the implications of Weber's Law are unambiguous.

Fechner's insight was that *JNDs might parallel sensations*. At one moment the standard and comparison stimuli cannot be differentiated; they feel the same. However, with a slight increase in the comparison stimulus the difference becomes just perceptible—but is not this felt difference a *sensation* of heaviness?

It takes but a little imagination to understand Fechner's excitement so many years ago. Was this the beginning of an answer to one of the age-old problems of philosophy, namely the relation between mind and body, the mental and physical? To produce incremental, *arithmetic* steps in sensation, the physical stimulus must grow *geometrically*. (A geometric progression is one in which the ratio of a number to its predecessor is always the same.) Measurement had revealed a link between the laws of physics and the laws of the mind; the external and internal worlds could be linked *via* a simple mathematical equation.

Fechner was the first to write Weber's Law in the form given above. However, he had long believed in the importance of the *logarithmic principle* (see Krueger, 1989, note 1),[1] and geometric progressions are equivalently described as logarithmic. With the logarithmic principle in mind, Fechner proceeded to formulate his own psychophysical law as follows.

Let S = the strength of a sensation

Let ΔS = a subjective JND, in other words the sensation induced by a just noticeable change in stimulus intensity, ΔI

Assume that all subjective JNDs are equal and that at absolute threshold the strength of sensation is zero. Weber's Law (equation (1)) is

$$\Delta I/I = k \tag{1}$$

which is the same as

$$\Delta I = kI \tag{2}$$

Assuming that JNDs are sensations, we can write

$$\Delta S = c \tag{3}$$

where ΔS is the subjective just noticeable change and c is a scaling factor which adjusts for the particular units of measurement adopted.

Now, instead of considering discrete differences, such as particular difference thresholds, assume that there is an underlying *continuous* function

---

[1] Bernoulli (1954/1738) had earlier claimed that human happiness is related logarithmically to wealth; for example, however rich someone is, a 10-fold increase in wealth will produce the same increment of happiness.

relating sensation and stimulation. Let ΔS and ΔI become very small, so that they can be reperesented in terms of the integral calculus as dS and dI, respectively. Assume, further, that every ΔS has the same subjective magnitude—no matter what intensity level is adopted as the standard stimulus, a just noticeable change to it will feel the same (equation (3)).

At this point Fechner combined equations (2) and (3) and used the mathematical technique of integration to generate the following expression:

$$S = (c/k) \log_e I \tag{4}$$

In (4), k is the Weber fraction from equation (1), c is the scaling constant from equation (3) and $\log_e$ is the natural logarithm, with e the irrational constant 2.7182 . . . (Fechner used logs to base e because of certain important proofs associated with the integral calculus.)

Some readers may be confused by these mathematical manoeuvres. However, the essence of Fechner's Law can be described very simply. What the law states is that sensation is a logarithmic function of stimulus intensity, the steepness of the function being determined by the constant k. As k is the Weber fraction, the steepness of the logarithmic function will be inversely related to acuity: the smaller the value of k, the better the observer's acuity.

In many textbooks, Fechner's Law is written in a simplified form as:

$$Sensation = k \log (Stimulus\ intensity) \tag{5}$$

where k represents a weighting constant for each modality (and includes the relevant Weber fraction) and the logarithmic multiplier represents the exponential or geometric growth in stimulus intensity required to yield successive JNDs. Stated in another way, the law implies that to predict the growth of sensation produced by an increase in stimulation, mutliply the logarithm of the stimulus value by a constant typical of the modality being explored.

One way of thinking about this is that the laws of both Weber and Fechner *compress* the stimulus intensity dimension. If we make the plausible assumption that it is advantageous for organisms to be able to detect weak stimuli (predators in dim light, faint noises, smells of distant prey) then there will be evolutionary pressure to develop high sensory sensitivity. However, the natural variation in, for example, light intensities is vast: the brightest midday sun is 1000 million times as intense as dim moonlight. An organism which is sensitive enough to be capable of functioning in dim light may still need to operate in the massively greater intensities at the other end of the range. Here, too, it may be important to be able to detect change, but more crudely. It might therefore be an economical use of neural resources to have sensory systems working in the way described by the laws of Weber and Fechner; that is, by effectively compressing the intensity scale.

Fechner's contribution in this area was two-fold. First, he reinforced the idea that scales relating sensory sensitivity and stimulus intensity sensitivity are compressed; magnitude of sensation does not grow linearly with stimulation. Second, he initiated the development of psychophysical methods for the exploration of sensation and perception, which was the start of experimental psychology.

During the remainder of his career Fechner did further theoretical work and developed other techniques for the exploration of sensation and perception. Below is a brief description of some of these techniques—the main classical psychophysical methods—the development of which Fechner inspired and which have proved so valuable in the exploration of the human senses.

The psychophysical methods

The essence of all methods is that stimuli are presented in a systematic manner and that the observer's task is simplified by requiring him or her to make one of a restricted set of responses (see Woodworth and Schlosberg, 1955). We shall illustrate the three main classical methods with reference to the measurement of a difference threshold, an index of the acuity or resolving power within a sense. It will be easy to see how the techniques could be applied to the measurement of absolute thresholds.

The methods of limits or minimal changes

A standard stimulus is selected and the difference threshold assessed by systematically changing the value of a comparison stimulus. For example, suppose we wish to measure the difference threshold for brightness. One way to do this is to select a particular intensity of light for the standard and display this as a lit rectangle. A second rectangle is presented which is noticeably more intense than the first; the observer will be able to say, effortlessly, that this comparison stimulus is brighter. Then the intensity of the comparison stimulus is reduced by a fixed amount and both stimuli are presented again. As this procedure is repeated, the observer will at some point say that the two stimuli appear to be the same or equal. Further changes are made to the comparison stimulus until eventually the observer responds by saying that it now looks darker. At this point the trial is stopped and a note made of the points at which the response 'brighter' changed to 'equal', and this to 'darker'. The threshold on this trial is estimated from these changeover values. On the next trial the variable comparison stimulus is set to a markedly lower value and moved upwards in intensity. These upward and downward trials alternate, with the starting points randomized to prevent anticipation or counting on the part of the observer. A typical threshold determination will require about 20 trials, which should yield a good estimate of the observer's brightness discrimination in this region of the intensity range.

This procedure is pleasant to use and observers find it simple and sensible. Provided that care is taken to control variables such as stimulus duration (observers tend to take much longer over decisions made close to threshold), the method usually yields clean data. Incidentally, a similar procedure, involving only upward trials, was once used to test the threshold of detonation of explosives. The variable stimulus in this case being the height from which a detonating weight was dropped (presumably by testers nicknamed Lefty).

The method of constant stimuli

The essence of this method is that a set of comparison stimuli are selected to present against one standard stimulus. The standard is presented, together with one particular comparison stimulus, for several trials. On each trial the observer must say which of the two stimuli is greater (or smaller, louder, etc.). The proportion of correct guesses is recorded and another comparison stimulus is then chosen, repeating the procedure. The spatial or temporal positions of the standard and comparison stimuli are randomized on each presentation. The threshold is calculated from a plot of the magnitude of the comparison stimulus against the proportion of correct guesses on each set of trials (sometimes using transformed or 'normalized' data for statistical reasons). As a detail, it should be added that in certain applications of this psychophysical method (for example, when measuring some absolute sensory thresholds) a number of 'catch' trials may be presented in which no stimuli are actually delivered: these enable the experimenter to make estimates of the observer's guessing behaviour.

The adjustment method

This is the most straightforward of all methods. It is very close to the common-sense view of what a threshold should be and is something many of us do in our daily lives when tuning radio or television receivers.

The adjustment method involves fixing the value of the standard while setting the comparison stimulus to a value that is obviously different. The observer is then instructed to alter the setting of the comparison stimulus until the two stimuli appear equal, and the setting is recorded. (Alternatively, the two stimuli may be identical at the start, the observer's task being to adjust the variable comparison stimulus until it appears to be just different.) The observer is not required to make any verbal response; he or she simply keeps altering one of the two stimuli. Several trials are run and average settings used to calculate the difference threshold. Observers find the adjustment method pleasant and easy to use.

Other psychophysical techniques

The classical psychophysical techniques have been refined and added to over the years. *Tracking procedures* vary stimulus values continuously while the observer attempts to maintain them just around threshold. *Staircase procedures* are based on the method of limits, but include decision rules for the selection of stimuli which are based on the observer's immediately preceding performance. Under these conditions performance slowly converges upon the threshold value of the stimulus.

Experimental precautions

The reader who has persisted through all this detail is now almost ready to measure a sensory threshold. Almost, but not quite. In all sensory research it is necessary to take certain precautions. For example, in most visual studies it is necessary to control and measure the room illumination as that will affect the visual threshold. And one needs to keep the observer under that illumination for a period before the threshold determination in order to adjust his or her state of light adaptation. Changing the intensity of a visual stimulus is not always completely straightforward: for example, one cannot just use resistors to dim lights without making sure that the change in temperature of the light source has not produced a corresponding change in colour—tungsten lights get redder as they get dimmer. Finally, the whole question of motivating an observer to endure prolonged testing is not without its problems. Nevertheless, the methods described do work and any intelligent person can be taught to use them to produce good scientific data.

Many of the extraordinary things which we know about perception generally and the senses in particular have stemmed from the application of these basic psychophysical methods. For example, a dark-adapted observer's absolute threshold for light is equivalent to detecting a candle flame at a distance of 30 miles. This means that some rod cells of the retina must fire when they have absorbed only one or two quanta of light. As one cannot have less light than one quantum, the rod cells of the retina have clearly reached an evolutionary limit: they will never improve. Psychophysics has also proved that the sensitive hair cells of the inner ear, which are responsible for transducing sound-induced movement into neural impulses, must respond when they move through a distance less than the diameter of a hydrogen atom. If the ear was any more sensitive we would hear the random movements of molecules within it. These are remarkable findings. It would be difficult to overestimate the importance of Weber's and Fechner's contribution to psychology and physiology.

These then are some of the ideas and techniques which launched the new discipline of psychophysics, together with some of the areas which they have illuminated. But although we have described Fechner's aim of finding measureable links between the physical and mental worlds, we have as yet said nothing about any theory of the threshold. It was, after all, a consideration of threshold phenomena which inspired the whole enterprise of classical psychophysics.

THE CLASSICAL THEORY OF THE THRESHOLD

Fechner himself believed in the existence of actual thresholds. He held that the working brain is spontaneously active and therefore in order that a stimulus (or a stimulus change) be detected it must have an impact sufficiently large to raise a sensation above the threshold of consciousness (see Corso, 1970, ch. 11). In this, Fechner's view foreshadowed neural quantum theory, which will be described later in this chapter. Fechner was not a crude thinker, quite the reverse. If, however, for the purpose of exposition, we imagine the crudest possible interpretation of the above concept of a threshold—that it is an actual step between two states—then something like the following should hold. There will be a range of stimulus values which, being below threshold, elicit no response; then, as the threshold is crossed, there will be an abrupt change in performance such that all further increases in stimulus energy will be accompanied by perfect detection. Such a crude model of the threshold would predict that psychophysical data would take the form of the hypothetical function shown in Figure 2.2.

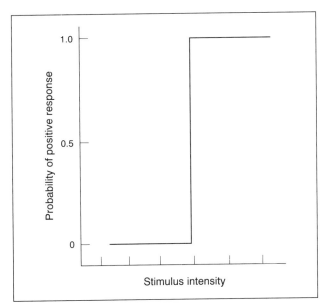

Figure 2.2 The psychophysical function implied by the definition of a threshold as an abrupt step between two states of sensitivity

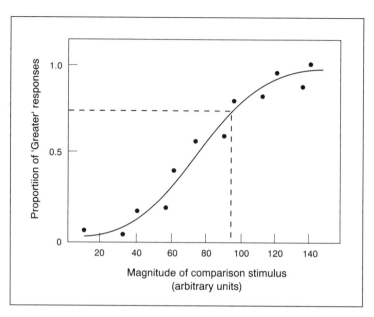

Figure 2.3 Typical threshold results (illustrative data) fitted by an ogive. In this case the measurement was of a different threshold. The standard stimulus was set at 80 units. The criterion of 75 per cent 'greater' responses was reached when the comparison stimulus was approximately 15 units above the standard. Compare this function with that in Figure 2.2

However, as what has been described as the classical theory of the threshold emerged, it was based upon assumptions which differed from this version. One reason for this was the nature of the data which emerged from early threshold determinations: they did not match the function shown in Figure 2.2.

Early psychophysicists discovered that typical threshold data most commonly resemble the function shown in Figure 2.3. Here, a difference threshold has been measured. It can be seen that the frequency of detection rises as stimulus intensity is increased, and that the function is curvilinear (similar functions are found when measuring absolute thresholds). The illustrative data shown in Figure 2.3 have been fitted by a *sigmoid* or *ogival* function. But the decision to fit such a function is not theoretically neutral, and the reason for its selection lies in the classical theory of the threshold. In order to explain this it is necessary to introduce some basic statistical notions. Readers who have some knowledge of simple probability theory and statistics should skip the next short section.

The curve shown in Figure 2.4 is known as the Normal or Gaussian probability distribution. The horizontal axis represents values of a random

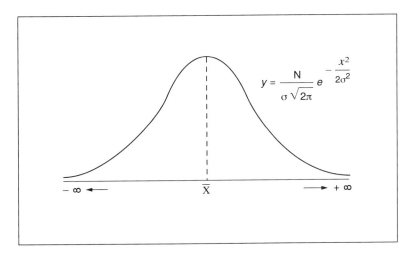

Figure 2.4 The Normal or Gaussian probability distribution. The figure shows the probability density function of a normally distributed random variable. N = total frequency or area under the curve, x is a deviation from the mean ($\bar{X}$), of the distribution, σ = the standard deviation

variable, x, and the vertical axis is the probability density value associated with each value of x. For the present purpose it is necessary to appreciate only four points: (a) as illustrated, the curve in Figure 2.4 is a mathematical abstraction; (b) the curve is designed so that its total area represents a probability of 1.0, and as it is symmetrical about a mean value, the areas to the left and right of the mean are equivalent to probabilities of 0.5; (c) the bell-shaped curve shown in Figure 2.4 is also found when a large number of independent random effects are counted. For example, when many coins are tossed repeatedly, then the trials on which every one fall heads or every one falls tails are found to be very rare—much more common are mixtures of heads and tails, and the most common of these will be around 50 per cent heads and tails. In fact, the distribution of 0, 1, 2, 3, . . . heads or tails matches the shape of Figure 2.4 more and more closely as the number of random events (coins) increases.

The normal distribution is interesting and useful because when we sample from populations in the real world and measure some aspect of the sample which is affected by many random factors, then the resulting frequency distributions commonly have a shape similar to that shown in Figure 2.4. For example, measuring the heights of people yields distributions very similar to the normal curve (there are few extremely short or extremely tall people—heights tend to cluster around the average). In such cases the horizontal axis will represent the values of the measure (length, height, weight, etc.) and the vertical axis will represent relative frequency. This relationship, between how things are and a theoretical probability distribution, is at the heart of many statistical techniques, for it permits powerful predictions to be made concerning the nature of populations which we know only from samples. Thus having shown that a sample of measures matches the normal distribution, it is possible to ask: What is the *probability* that an individual will exceed a certain height (or length, etc.)?

Suppose now that we select a value to the far left of the distribution in Figure 2.4 and record the *area* of the curve to the left of that value: the result will clearly be zero or thereabouts. Moving along the horizontal axis and recording successive area values yields a plot known as the *integral* of the distribution, or the *cumulative probability function*. As can be seen from Figure 2.5, the shape of this function *is very similar to that shown in Figure 2.3*.

This resemblance, between actual and psychophysical data and a theoretical probability distribution, was all that was needed to form the classical theory of threshold performance. The early psychophysicists were aware of the work of Gauss (who first constructed the formula for the normal curve), Laplace, Quetelet and others, all of whom had written on practical appliations of probability theory. When such applications were extended to the theory of the threshold, the classical theory emerged.

In the early version of the theory it was assumed that there are numerous random events occurring in the brain as a stimulus is presented. Some of these events are held to be 'disposed' towards, or favourable to, a particular category of response ('greater than', 'smaller than'). Although the events are not

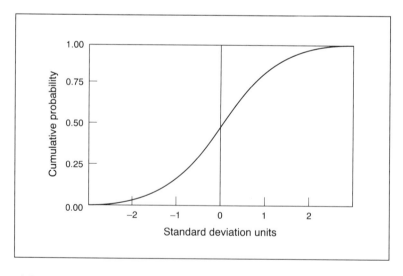

Figure 2.5   The integral of the normal distribution, or the cumulative normal distribution. Horizontal units are standard deviations from the mean of zero

caused by the stimulus, they affect detection as follows: if the comparison stimulus is of low intensity, the vast majority of events must be favourable if the positive ('greater') response is to occur; if the stimulus is strong, fewer favourable events need to coincide at that moment for the positive response. According to the theory, the cumulative odds in favour of the positive response when stimulus intensity rises will grow as the cumulative normal probability function shown in Figure 2.5.

The interpretation of the threshold outlined above became known as the *phi–gamma hypothesis*: a continuous but non-linear increase in the function relating discrimination (or detection) frequency to stimulus intensity. However, this interpretation too was to change.

The phi–gamma hypothesis implies that the ideal psychophysical function shown in Figure 2.2 has somehow been smeared by errors of measurement until it resembles that of Figure 2.3. But suppose that the truth is somewhat different, and that the real reason for the difference between Figures 2.2 and 2.3 is that there is a random component in thresholds which is not a measurement error but represents the basic fluctuating nature of the nervous system. It now becomes easier to understand why psychophysical functions are ogival: there is random, Gaussian, variability in the systems being investigated. And it is this belief which finally became the classical theory of the threshold. In essence, this is a *statistical* interpretation of thresholds.[2]

The state of knowledge described above had been reached by the start of this century. From then on we can discern three trends in theoretical and empirical work in psychophysics. First, there was an attempt to return to the concept of the threshold as a discrete step, as Fechner believed it to be; this is discussed below under the heading of 'The neural quantum theory'. Second was the development of a more sophisticated statistical model of the threshold, culminating in the theory of signal detection (TSD), to be described later. Third was an attempt to develop psychophysical functions for the growth of supra-threshold sensations. This will be described at the end of the chapter under the heading 'Direct scaling techniques'.

THE NEURAL QUANTUM THEORY

The statistical interpretation of the threshold is plausible and leads to successful ways of handling data which, it must be stressed, are among the most reliable and reproducible in experimental psychology. Why then should this interpretation be challenged?

---

[2] Gigerenzer and Murray (1987) give a very clear and interesting account of the way in which the concepts associated with probability theory eventually transformed the theory of the threshold.

It is widely accepted that observers in threshold determinations cannot maintain perfect attention, that they are likely to change over time, and that physical stimuli may vary slightly from trial to trial. But what if these extraneous 'nuisance' variables could be eliminated? Would the true nature of human sensitivity still appear to be essentially continuous, or would it reveal itself as abrupt and discontinuous? It was thoughts such as these that led some investigators to challenge the classical concept of the threshold.

The theory of the neural quantum was first formalized by Stevens, Morgan and Volkmann (1941). The theory assumes that the neural mechanisms underlying discrimination are functionally distinct or discontinuous: these are the neural 'quanta'. For the purpose of exposition we shall treat these hypothetical neural quanta as boxes, each triggered when it is filled by a certain fixed amount of energy associated with incoming stimuli. However, this discontinuous all-or-none part of the discrimination mechanism interacts with the inherent random variation in sensitivity which characterizes neural systems generally. The combination of these two functional components—the quantal reception of stimulus energy and the variability of sensory systems—determines threshold performance.

We may now re-examine difference thresholds in terms of the neural quantum theory. Presentation of the standard stimulus excites a number of quanta and the comparison stimulus is then presented. On the simplest possible quantum model the observer responds 'different' only when this new stimulation excites one additional quantum. (This is rather like a pair of scales in which containers of liquid form the weights, but only full containers may be so used.) Such an abrupt, discrete mechanism will generate a psychophysical function which is linear in form; in fact it will be the same as that shown in Figure 2.2, in which the probability of the response, 'different', rises abruptly from zero to one. As we have seen, actual threshold data never take this form, so this basic neural quantum model must be refined.

Two modifications to the model are necessary to enable it to generate sensible psychophysical functions. The first is the incorporation of the idea, described above, that there is moment-to-moment variation in the observer's sensitivity. Second, there is no need to constrain the model by assuming that stimulus energy (in a transduced neural form) will *arrive* in amounts exactly matching neural quanta. Why should it? It seems much more likely that the most common effect of stimulation will be to trigger a certain whole number of quanta, with some surplus energy left over. This surplus cannot, by definition, exceed one quantum's worth. Combining these assumptions leads to a very interesting deduction: the various possible amounts of this surplus energy, from just greater than zero to just less than one quantum's worth, will be distributed according to a *rectangular* distribution. This is because all amounts are equiprobable. And the integral of a rectangular distribution (its cumulative area) is a linear, not an ogival, function.

Thus the neural quantum theory states that when a standard stimulus is presented its energy excites a number of discrete quanta plus a variable amount of surplus. Under certain conditions of testing this surplus energy could still be available when the comparison stimulus is delivered. During all this time the observer's sensitivity is varying in a normal or Gaussian manner, so that stimulus energy is having a varied impact, as it were. Threshold task demands are such that the observer will wish to avoid responding 'different' when in fact there is no physical difference between standard and comparison stimuli: observers are usually instructed to 'take care', to 'concentrate', etc. But such an erroneous response must be a risk whenever a monetary increase in the observer's sensitivity coincides with an unusually large surplus from the standard to excite one extra quantum. A conscientious observer is therefore assumed to play safe by adopting a two-quantum criterion, responding 'different' only when the comparison stimulus energizes *two* additional quanta.

These various assumptions and deductions predict a novel psychophysical function: that shown in Figure 2.6, which is linear but with a definite slope. It is now possible to redefine the threshold in quantum terms. The smallest increment in stimulation which will always produce a 'different' response is assumed to excite two quanta; the largest increment which just never elicits a

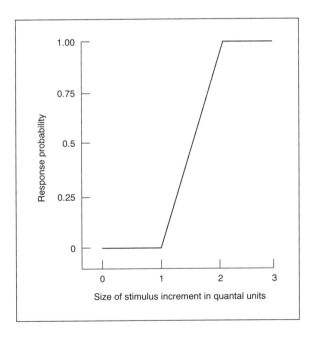

Figure 2.6 The psychophysical function predicted by the modified neural quantum theory

'different' response indicates the size of one quantum. The threshold is then calculated by interpolation from the psychophysical function of Figure 2.6 and is defined as the stimulus value associated with 1.5 quanta. Thus the neural quantum theory generates very precise quantitative predictions relating stimulus change and response probability. The trick, of course, is how to isolate the quantum aspect of performance from the random variability in sensory systems. This is where experimental technique becomes all-important.

One of the first technical innovations designed to examine the quantum alternative to the classical theory was in fact published before the formal statement of the theory by Stevens *et al.* This was a report by Békèsy (1930), who measured the difference threshold for hearing in the following manner. The observer was presented with a standard tone for 0.3 second immediately followed by a comparison tone of different intensity. By minimizing the delay between presentations it was hoped to eliminate the momentary random variations associated with changing attention, sensitivity, and so on. The results of this study were highly interesting. When the percentages of different judgements were plotted as a function of the difference between the standard and comparison stimuli, *linear* functions were obtained. Such linear functions were very different from the classical ogives typically obtained in psychophysical experiments, and they raised the possibility that the hearing system responds to intensity changes in a series of discontinuous steps.

Stevens, Morgan and Volkmann (1941) presented continuous tones to their observers, together with brief increments in frequency occurring every 3 seconds. The observer's task was to indicate whenever a change of pitch was heard. When percentage detections were plotted against amount of stimulus change, the result was a set of linear functions. Similar linear data were obtained by DeCillis (1944) for the detection of moving stimuli on the skin, and by Jerome (1942) for the olfactory detection of a certain smell. In several other published studies it was found that many (although not all) observers generated data which were essentially rectilinear rather than ogival in shape. The neural quantum theory seemed to be receiving a significant amount of empirical support.

Evaluation of the neural quantum theory

The main criticism of the neural quantum theory can be summarized very simply: the quantum theory can be tested only by quantum procedures. For example, to minimize variability in judgements (which would 'smear' possible linear psychophysical functions), it is necessary to display standard and comparison stimuli very briefly and to keep the interval between them as short as possible. Practised observers must be used for the same reason, and it is considered desirable by proponents of the theory that the standard and only one of the comparison stimuli be used in a block of trials. Equally important, nothing must intervene between presentations of standard and comparison stimuli; should there be extraneous factors at work, then tests of the theory are invalidated. With other psychophysical procedures one can attempt to replicate a set of findings obtained with one method by the use of another. With neural quantum methods, normal scientific procedures of validation are impossible. Finally, it must be stated that attempts to replicate the best-known findings in this area have not always met with success (see Corso, 1970, for an invaluable review).

The neural quantum interpretation of the threshold has been presented here because it is so different from much traditional thinking. As we have shown, the theory has received strong criticism, and at the time of writing it does not appear to have many active supporters. But the neural quantum theory is an impressive illustration of how simple but very clearly stated assumptions, combined with rigorous deductive reasoning, can lead to a novel and interesting theory.

THE THEORY OF SIGNAL DETECTION

We have shown how the idea of variability influenced early thinking about thresholds. Note that the pyschophysical procedures described earlier in this chapter typically yield a single value for the threshold. The procedures and their accompanying methods of data analysis were developed to enable psychophysicists to estimate such single values as accurately as possible. However, during the nineteenth and early twentieth centuries, leading statisticians such as Thurstone, Neyman and Pearson were developing statistical methods for testing scientific hypotheses which were eventually to influence psychological theory generally and psychophysical models in particular, as we shall show.

The background to the theory of signal detection (TSD), or theory of signal detectability, is a fascinating one and interested readers should consult the scholarly history of the subject in Gigerenzer and Murray (1987). These authors show that there has long been an interest in probability and the truth or otherwise of scientific hypotheses. In modern terminology this can be summarized as a concern with type 1 and type 2 errors in inductive reasoning. A type 1 error is the erroneous rejection of the null hypothesis[3] when it is in fact true. A type 2 error is a decision to accept the null hypothesis when it is false (in other words, to reject a true hypothesis). When choosing whether to

---

[3] The null hypothesis is the 'logical contradictory' of the hypothesis under test. For example, if the hypothesis adopted in an experimental design is that data from two conditions will show greater than chance differences, the null hypothesis is that there will be no greater than chance differences between the sets of data.

accept or reject a null hypothesis it becomes necessary to erect a *decision criterion*. Readers who have carried out statistical tests of significance have been engaged in making such decisions. In fact, as Gigerenzer and Murray remark, it is perhaps surprising that the TSD was so long in arriving.

Suppose that in a threshold situation the decisions that the observer must make are strictly analogous with those above: might observers somehow act as 'intuitive statisticians'? This was the idea that led to the TSD.

As an introduction to the TSD, one of the classical psychophysical procedures, the constant method, may be briefly re-examined. Suppose that one wishes to measure the absolute threshold for light. The observer is initially dark-adapted for about an hour. Then a warning signal sounds and the observer is presented with either a very faint light or a 'catch trial'—that is, a trial on which no stimulus is presented. On each trial the observer's task is to indicate whether or not a stimulus has occurred. Then a new intensity of light is selected and the next set of trials is run. The threshold is calculated on the basis of the number of stimuli detected at each intensity, but with a correction for guessing (this is because an observer responding positively on every trial will inevitably make correct detections). For this reason, the traditional method of calculating the threshold involves subtracting the observer's errors from his or her correct responses. There are, of course, refinements in the ways in which all this is done, but the essence of the procedure is as described above.

With very faint stimuli (stimuli around the threshold value, in traditional terms) it is obvious that even conscientious observers will be wrong on a proportion of trials. But note how their errors are treated: *they are weighed in the same way as correct responses*. That is, make 10 errors and the 'correct' score is reduced by 10. It is assumed that errors reveal nothing about the observer's sensitivity, and that they are directly (inversely) related to correct scores. It is for this reason that the observers used in the determinations of the main sensory thresholds are commonly given intensive practice and detailed instructions to be as careful as possible: errors are a nuisance.

However, think for a moment about what it would be like to be tested in the absolute threshold determination described above. All readers will have experienced complete darkness. Many will have noticed this interesting phenomenon: total darkness is not really black. After a short time small patches of light can be seen in the visual field, and the total experience is of pinky-grey rather than jet black. This phenomenon, once termed the 'self-light of the retina', is due to random firing of cells in the eye and optic nerve. Similar effects can be noticed in touch and hearing.

It follows that during the determination of the absolute threshold for light, some of the weaker stimuli presented will not be subjectively brighter than the 'light' which observers experience in total darkness. When this happens the observer will surely have to guess whether the experience he or she is having is due to internal or external causes.

TSD and its associated techniques are closely related to statistical decision theory (Wald, 1950), which is a set of formal rules for choosing between statistical decisions, in a manner outlined above. Initially, TSD was associated with the ideal detector, that is a (theoretical) agent showing perfect rationality by maximizing the options revealed by a formal analysis of a situaton: particularly the gains and losses. However, the theory was quickly applied to problems arising in electronics. Any electrical circuit (and any communication channel) will contain noise. The molecules in transistors, resistors, electrical cables and so on are never at rest. Turn on a television set in the small hours of the morning and any one may see, not a blank screen, but a dancing array of dots. Radios and telephones 'hiss'. Even digital players, if set to maximum gain, will emit a slight additional sound—the irreducible random activity of the amplifier circuit.

In the context of electronics it is obviously of great interest to know what effect such 'noise' will have upon the efficiency with which signals can be processed. Noise sets a limit upon the sensitivity of any channel for it shares some of the properties of signals, just as spontaneous retinal activity can occasionally be mistaken for faint lights. Thus, in any radar system, to use a real-life example, there must be a target size such that its representation on the display is no larger than the random noise of the equipment. At what point must we abandon attempts to detect small (or distant) signals? How can the probability of successfully detecting faint targets be optimized? What is the best strategy for maximizing the detection of real targets while minimizing the (erroneous) detection of spurious targets (or noise)? And if technical refinements permit us to improve a particular detection circuit, reducing the noise by some known amount, what will be the corresponding gain in the detection of signals? TSD raised the exciting possibility of solving these applied problems.

In 1954 Tanner and Swets published an extremely influential paper in which they claimed that certain psychological problems, including the detection of weak stimuli, might yield to the application of TSD techniques. We shall now outline their new approach to psychophysics.

Consider again the absolute threshold task. It is obvious that on each trial or presentation the observer has two choices to make: he or she can decide that the stimulus (or signal, in TSD terminology) is present, or that it is absent—and the signal may indeed be present or absent. This situation can be represented in the form of a matrix into which we shall insert the usual TSD terminology:

	Response 'Yes'	Response 'No'
Signal present	Hit	Miss
Signal absent	False alarm	Correct rejection

Thus there are two ways of being right and two of being wrong in this situation. In classical pyschophysics the erros would be interpreted as either failures of sensitivity (misses) or carelessness or response bias (false alarms). In practice, entries in the matrix take the form of relative response frequencies or probabilities.

In Tanner and Swets's application of TSD to psychological phenomena, a new model of the human perceiver is proposed. When applied to vision the model assumes the presence in the visual system of a physiological process, the value of which varies randomly over time. We need not define value too carefully, nor do we need to know exactly what the process is—it could be the closeness of a group of neurons to their threshold of firing, or it could be fluctuations at a synapse, or something else—it is necessary to assume only that (1) the process is involved in detecting stimuli and (2) its fluctuations form a random, Gaussian distribution.

Consider the left-hand curve of Figure 2.7. This represents the random process and is known as the *noise distribution* (*N*); it represents the activity of the system in the absence of stimulation. We now make the reasonable assumption that when the system receives external stimulation, energy from this is added to the momentary value of the noise distribution. This creates a second distribution (on the right in Figure 2.7) which is known as the *signal plus noise distribution* (*S+N*). (The two curves are also known as *probability density functions*.) If the incoming stimulation is strong, or if the system is

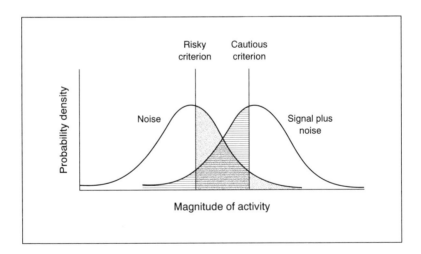

Figure 2.7 The two distributions of signal detection theory (TSD). The curve on the left is the noise distribution; the curve on the right is the signal-plus-noise distribution which arises when signals are added to the noise distribution

basically very sensitive (which amounts to the same thing) then there will be a correspondingly greater separation between the N and $S+N$ distributions.

This is the model of signal detection. Viewed in this way, the task of the observer in any detection situation is to form a criterion such that when the 'value' of the system (plotted on the horizontal axis in Figure 2.7) is exceeded a positive response is given, but not otherwise. The criterion, usually designated β (beta) is also known as the 'likelihood ratio'. Above any point on the horizontal axis are two values, that of the N distribution and that of the $S+N$ distribution. If the criterion is erected at a particular point, then it is expressed in terms of the ratio of the two values at that point. In any detection situation there will be one best position for the criterion. This criterion value is the one formally chosen by an ideal observer.

Referring again to Figure 2.7, it is obvious that another variable is the separation between the two distributions. As stated earlier, the stronger the incoming signal the greater will be the separation of the N and $S+N$ distributions. Equally, however, an estimate of this distance can be used as an index of the *sensitivity* of a hypothetical (or actual) observer. The index of sensitivity is known as d' (d prime) and is defined as the difference between the means of the two distributions divided by their variances. (More details are given in the notes at the end of this chapter.)

The attractiveness of this new model when it first appeared was partly due to the distinction it made between two aspects of an observer's performance. The criterion is clearly a subjective *response* effect, and as such may be affected by attentional set and instructions, including the payoff matrix. This is independent of the observer's sensitivity, which is clearly not under the influence of the payoff matrix.

Further interest stemmed from the fact that, in terms of the TSD model, shifting the criterion will not generally result in linear changes in hit and false alarm rates, as classical psychophysics would predict. In Figure 2.8 the probability of hits is plotted against that of false alarm for a given separation of the two distributions, that is for a given d'. To appreciate the origin of the curve, suppose that a criterion had been moved smoothly across the horizontal axis in Figure 2.7 and that pairs of hit and false alarm rates had been recorded at each position. The resulting figure describes the *receiver operating characteristic* (ROC) and is illustrated in Figure 2.8. Note that initial small rightwards shifts in the criterion lead to a disproportionate gain in hits as opposed to false alarms. This is a very important result.

Using methods which are basically simple, but tedious to describe, it is also possible to plot on the ROC curve the relationship between hits and false alarms which can be deduced from the traditional psychophysical model of the observer. Here it is assumed that stimuli below a given threshold value simply cannot be detected, that the observer can only guess (leading to the traditional correction for guessing), and that above the threshold there is a

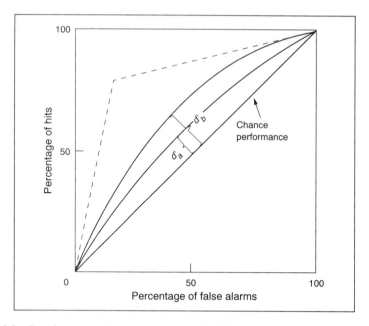

Figure 2.8   Receiver operating characteristic (ROC) curves. The greater the value of
d', the more sensitive the observer. The curve d'_a would be generated by a relatively
insensitive observer or (equivalently) from weak signals. The curve d'_b is that expected from a more sensitive observer, or the use of stronger signals. The broken line
represents the relationship between 'hits' and 'false alarms' predicted by a classical
model of the threshold when a certain proportion of blank or catch trials are used

smooth increase in the probability that signals will be detected. Note that this
function starts somewhere on the vertical hit axis and is linear and segmented:
it looks very different from the ROC curve and is shown as the dotted line in
Figure 2.8. It ought then to be possible to test between the classical and the
TSD models by actual experiment.

How does an actual observer decide upon the position of the criterion? The
answer, in TSD terms, is according to the task demands of the experiment.
More formally, this is described in terms of a *payoff matrix* which defines the
rewards and penalties associated with the four cells of the matrix printed
above. That is to say, the observer can be urged to be very careful (and
rewarded accordingly), or quite reckless. This in turn will decide the relative
frequencies of hits, misses, false alarms and correct rejections.

One of the strengths of the TSD is that it is able to predict the effects of
choosing different criteria. This is shown in Figure 2.9. For example, the
observer may adopt a very risky criterion, placed well over to the left of the
abscissa in Figure 2.9(a). Then all values which exceed this criterion will
produce a positive response. As a consequence, the observer will now detect a

high proportion of signals—the area of the $S+N$ distribution to the right of the criterion in Figure 2.9(a)—the hit rate will be high. However, the inevitable consequence of adopting this risky criterion will be that a large number of events which are part of the noise distribution will also trigger responses—the false alarm rate will also be high.

Alternatively, the observer can adopt a more cautious criterion, placed well over to the right on the abscissa in Figure 2.9(a). In this case, only high values will produce responses. The result will be a very low false alarm rate but many fewer hits.

More detailed accounts of the statistical basis of the TSD will be found in the references included in the notes at the end of this chapter. The present attempt to describe the theory of signal detection without using equations is rather like trying to swim with one hand tied behind your back: it can be done, but it takes longer. The preceding paragraphs are necessarily rather simplified; nevertheless, the reader who has persisted so far should now have a good idea of the thinking behind the TSD and will be able to appreciate how different this is from the classical threshold approach.

Conducting a TSD experiment

In actual practice, running a TSD experiment is similar to the orthodox psychophysical method of threshold measurement. In some auditory applications, for example, signals of different intensities are presented alone; in others they are presented together with actual noise, and these trials are randomly mixed with blank trials or with trials presenting noise alone. The first thing to establish is the observer's criterion or likelihood ratio (beta). This is done either by manipulating the observer's behaviour through instructions to be more or less risky, or by recording confidence judgements after each decision. Separate analyses are then made of hit and false alarms rates for decisions grouped as 'very confident', 'confident', 'less confident', and so on. Each run through a TSD procedure yields pairs of values of hits and false alarms from which the ROC curve may be plotted. Figure 2.9 will convey the essence of this procedure.

The sensitivity index d' can be estimated from the ROC curve by measuring the distance from its peak to the ascending left–right diagonal (as shown in Figure 2.8), or d' can be calculated from published tables of ordinates of the normal distribution. Other techniques employ special graphical solutions and there are even published tables from which d' values can be obtained directly, provided certain experimental procedures have been followed. In practice it is all much easier than it sounds.

The theory of signal detection was a major shift in thinking about psychophysics. The years following Tanner and Swets's seminal paper saw a rush of publications revealing a new interest in psychophysical phenomena. One

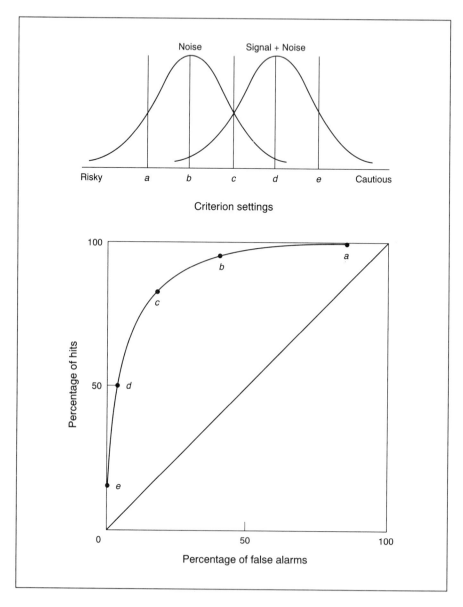

Figure 2.9 The effects of shifting the observer's criterion as predicted by the signal detection model. Note that although the riskier criteria (a, b) will ensure high hit rates (the large area of the signal-plus-noise distribution lying to the right of the criterion), there will be larger numbers of false alarm responses (the area of the noise distribution to the right of the criterion). The more cautious criteria (d, e) will produce fewer false alarms but also fewer hits

hundred years after Fechner there was a new, statistical, model of human sensitivity which rejected the classical concept of the threshold. In fact, according to the TSD, there is no such entity as a threshold, only an observer making statistical decisions.

The impact of the TSD was not restricted to sensory research. It seemed likely that the model would throw light on other psychological phenomena. For example, when trying to remember something we often find that we cannot recall the particular word required but have a strange feeling that we are just about to. Our intuitions are correct: people experiencing the 'tip of the tongue' phenomenon can in fact make very good guesses about the word they cannot recall; they often guess correctly its approximate length, even its syllabic structure (Brown and McNeill, 1966). However, as scored in traditional memory experiments, such failures to recall—and even the production of similar words—would be penalized as errors. By encouraging the use of payoff matrix methods of scoring, manipulating observers' criteria and then calculating indices akin to d', a new impetus was given to research in traditional areas such as recognition and recall. The TSD became a very stimulating addition to the psychologist's technical and theoretical repertoire.

Applications of TSD

The TSD was successful. In many detection experiments the results generated ROC curves of the form displayed in Figure 2.8 rather than that predicted from classical threshold theory (the dotted line in Figure 2.8). The sheer range of successful applications of TSD is impressive. It includes the study of brightness discrimination (Tanner and Swets, 1954); the detection of tones against noise (Tanner, Swets and Green, 1956); touch and warmth discrimination (Eijkman and Vendrik, 1963); time discrimination (Creelman, 1962); intelligibility of speech (Clark, 1960); memory (Swets, 1973); anxiety (Grossberg and Grant, 1978); eyewitness testimony (Wells, Lindsay and Ferguson, 1979); and even studies of the efficacy of acupuncture (Clark and Yang, 1974; Chapman, Chen and Bonica, 1977). What began as a formal application of statistical decision theory to the problems of the ideal observer became a widespread research technique in numerous areas of psychology and physiology.

An evaluation of the theory of signal detection

In offering an evaluation of the TSD, the first thing to be said is that it seems likely that that TSD techniques will have a lasting place in the sensory psychology. As promised, they do seem to offer a genuine way out of the problem of disentangling response and sensitivity effects in detection and other situations. The theoretical background to TSD is a rigorous one, and the concept of an ideal observer against which to measure actual human performance is appealing.

However, a few doubts have been expressed concerning the appropriateness of the TSD to psychology, some of which will now be outlined.

First, there has been debate as to whether the ROC curve always provides a best fit to detection task data. Remember that in Figure 2.8 results predicted on the basis of the classical theory of a sensory threshold led to a plot which was very different from the ROC curve predicted by the TSD and obtained in many TSD experiments. However, high-threshold theory (Blackwell, 1953), low-threshold theory (Luce, 1960), and two-threshold theory (Green, in Swets, 1964), are all attempts to preserve some notion of a classical threshold but with the observer seeking to maximize payoffs for detections of signals against noise above this point. The most elaborate of these, two-threshold theory, uses a three-segment plot on the ROC graph; it is clear that such a plot must be able to provide a fairly good fit to TSD data and thus the model represents a rival to the TSD. However, claims concerning these particular alternatives to the TSD do not appear to have attracted much subsequent support, as judged by published literature.

A second doubt concerns the plausibility of the TSD model in an actual setting. Familiarity with the concepts of the signal detection theory can be claimed when one can think in terms of the two-distribution model shown in Figure 2.7. But this very familiarity can cause one to accept too uncritically one of the main assumptions of TSD: that the observer has a model of the $S+N$ distribution available for decision-making during an experiment. This second Gaussian or normal distribution is a key assumption in arriving at ROC calculations, but how does the distribution form? There can be no objection to the assumption that noise is present in the nervous system and that its random character is modelled by the Gaussian curve. But in typical applications of the TSD, data are collected from very early trials. We must therefore ask how a sufficient sample of events could have been sampled for the $S+N$ distribution to have been formed; what evidence is available to the observer to permit him or her to optimize the setting of the maximum likelihood criterion during these early trials? In any statistical situation, Gaussian distributions do not take on their characteristic shape until hundreds, even thousands of data have been assembled.

Psychophysics is a practical as well as a theoretical part of psychology. The adequacy of any theory is measured in part by how useful its predictions turn out to be. It is fair to point out that during the past 10 years there has been a reduction in the number of publications in psychophysics (and other areas) which have employed TSD techniques. This conclusion is reinforced by an examination of the dates of key papers listed in this chapter. Threshold data continue to be reported, but many workers (including the present author) seem to have reverted to using classical procedures. It is as though the classical concept of the threshold is simply too useful to be lightly abandoned.

Whatever the eventual place of the TSD in psychophysics it can be asserted that it has been a stimulating alternative to the old concept of the threshold and it has afforded a valuable method of separating response and sensitivity effects. It may also be stated in conclusion that the TSD has played an important part in reinforcing the idea of perceivers as intuitive statisticians—an idea which will recur elsewhere in this book.

DIRECT SCALING TECHNIQUES

Since the introduction of psychophysical techniques and theories, many workers have assumed the truth of Weber's Law and the constancy of the Weber fraction across a major portion of each stimulus intensity dimension. Further, in most of the work we have described so far it has been generally accepted that sensations can be measured only indirectly, using indices such as the JND.

Concerning the constancy of the Weber fraction, it can be said that there has been some disagreement in the published literature. It is widely accepted that the Weber fraction does not hold over the entire intensity range of most senses (see, for example, Krueger, 1989, target article). On the other hand, it is also true that the common way of displaying difference threshold data—Weber fractions plotted against the logarithm of stimulus intensity—magnifies the relatively small range of intensities over which Weber's Law fails.

We may accept that JNDs are only indirect measures of sensation. However, it is then legitimate to ask how well they can predict performance. At this point we encounter other problems. To cite one of a number of similar findings, if one tonal stimulus is 10 JNDs and another 20 JNDs above the auditory threshold, the second should sound twice as loud (assuming the constancy of the Weber fraction). It will not: the second sound will be judged as much more than twice as loud (Stevens and Davis, 1938).

Two questions arise. First, might it be possible to measure sensations in a manner which is more direct than that associated with the measurement of difference thresholds and JNDs? Second, can Weber's Law (or Fechner's logarithmic amendment of it) be improved upon as psychophysical functions linking discrimination and stimulus variables such as intensity?

The first of these questions is not absurd. Most readers will agree that they could describe a 500 g weight as approximately twice as heavy as a 250 g weight in any direct comparison. Similarly, readers would not find it impossible to rank order, say, a number of cups of coffee in terms of bitterness. The point is that both these procedures involve primitive forms of measurement: perhaps direct measures of sensation are attainable after all.

In the remainder of this section most of the studies described employ stimuli which are (a) well above absolute threshold and (b) differ markedly from one another, being well above the relevant discrimination thresholds.

As a final introductory remark to the section readers should be warned that this is a highly controversial area of theory and research.

The work of S.S. Stevens and colleagues

The modern development of direct scaling techniques is closely associated with the work of S.S. Stevens and his colleagues (Stevens, 1957, 1959, 1961, 1962; Galanter, 1962; Stevens and Galanter, 1957), although certain similar techniques had been employed in the earlier days of psychophysics.

Early in his work Stevens drew a distinction between those stimulus dimensions where JNDs are not subjectively equal, and those where the JNDs remain fairly constant. Typically, it is along dimensions of *intensity* and *quantity* that JNDs are unequal (for example, brightness, loudness, warmth), and Stevens named these *prothetic* continua. Along 'qualitative' continua such as hue, spatial position and pitch, JNDs tend to be constant; Stevens named these *metathetic* continua. On prothetic continua changes in subjective intensity probably represent additional responses in the nervous system; on metathetic continua changes in the quality of the stimulus probably engage different regions of the nervous system (red receptors rather than blue receptors, for example).

Remember that at this point in the story the question being asked is: Can sensations be measured directly? In attempting to answer this question, it is necessary to use techniques which differ from the methods of classical psychophysics. Stevens and his colleagues developed and refined a number of what they believed to be more direct ways of measuring sensations. The two best known of these are *magnitude estimation* and *cross-modal matching* (see Engen, 1971).

In magnitude estimation the observer is presented with two extremes of the stimulus range and asked to assign a number to each of them. Then the entire range of stimuli is presented in random order and the observer assigns a number to each to match the resulting sensation. (Sometimes the range of numbers to be used is specified by the experimenter.)

In cross-modal matching the observer attempts to communicate the subjective intensity of a stimulus *via* another modality. For example, the perceived brightness of a light may be matched by adjusting the loudness of a tone or the force exerted on a lever. Perhaps surprisingly, observers find this novel cross-modal matching quite easy to engage in.

Stevens's investigations of the growth of sensation above threshold led him to propose a modification to the classical psychophysical law. Remember that the implication of Fechner's equation is that arithmetic (equal step) changes in sensation require equal *ratios* of stimulation (however, see the notes at the end of this chapter). This is why Fechner's basic law can be written as

$$\text{Sensation} = k \log (\text{Stimulus intensity})$$

Stevens argues that, particularly with suprathreshold stimuli, the relationship between sensation and stimulation is better expressed as: *equal ratios of sensation correlate with equal ratios of stimulation*. This is not to imply that the stimulus and response ratios are the same; rather that each time the intensity of a particular stimulus is multiplied or divided by, for example, 10, the sensation may double or halve. The relationship will not always be so clear-cut of course, but the essence is that it will always be between two ratios.

This claim implies that if, for example, observers' ratings in a magnitude estimation task are plotted in logarithmic form on one axis of a graph, and stimulus intensities are represented in logarithmic form along the other axis, then linear functions should emerge. The steepness of each function will indicate the rate at which sensation grows as a result of stimulation. This is what Stevens claimed to have discovered. Now the log–log relationship can be equally well expressed in an equivalent form:

$$S = aX^b$$

where S is the subjective response, X is the stimulus intensity, a is a weighting function which allows for different units of measurement, and b is the exponent indicating the rate of growth of sensation. This form of equation is known as a *power function*, and is the way in which most direct scaling data are presented.

Empirical findings

To explain how power functions are used and interpreted consider these two empirical findings. The exponent in the power function for brightness has been reported as 0.33; that for perceived strength of electric shock as greater than 3.0. To show what these mean we simply take the antilog of the numbers. For brightness, antilog 0.33 = 2.14, which means that when we raise the stimulus intensity by a ratio of 10, the sensation of brightness approximately doubles. For electric shock, antilog 3.0 = 1000; in this case a 10-fold increase in stimulation produces a 1000-fold increase in judged sensation. Readers may wish to satisfy themselves that if the intensity of the electric shock was doubled, then sensation would increase by a factor of 8. These results are typical of quantitative or prothetic continua. Functions for qualitative or metathetic continua are different: on these continua exponents of the power functions are frequently around 1.0; that is to say, a certain ratio change in stimulation causes the same proportionate change in sensation. When we consider metathetic continua such as spatial position, this linearity reflects the accuracy of our perception; in this case our mode of responding is clearly adaptive. Some typical power functions are shown in Figure 2.10.

The last of Stevens's findings to be reported here is implicit in some of the earlier sections. It is simply that subjective scales obtained by direct scaling appear to be consistent across situations. For example, one can scale

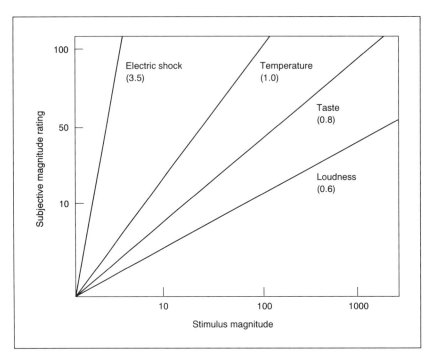

Figure 2.10 Power functions for four sensory modalities (logarithmic scales). The exponents (in brackets) indicate how rapidly sensation grows with increasing stimulus intensity. (Data from Stevens, 1961)

brightness by having an observer adjust the intensity of a vibrating stimulus. Then vibration can be scaled against loudness. Finally, loudness can be scaled against brightness. The claim is that power functions derived from these different procedures agree, and thus the procedure appears to be coherent.

An evaluation of direct scaling

In attempting to evaluate direct scaling, we can begin by stating something that must have been very obvious to the reader, namely that this approach differs greatly in theory and technique from much that is to be found in traditional psychophysics. The possibility of measuring sensations directly in this manner is an exciting one, but is this approach to psychophysics valid? There have been many psychophysicists who think not. Remember that the two major claims made by Stevens and his supporters are that (1) sensations can be measured directly, and (2) the power function is a better psychophysical law than either Weber's fraction of Fechner's logarithmic law. With these two claims in mind, we can offer a summary of some of the major criticisms of direct scaling.

First, doubts have been cast on the soundness of the work reported by Stevens and his collaborators. In the earliest papers by this group, explicit advice is given on how to ensure that clear-cut power function data are obtained. 'Even in Stevens's laboratory, the power law finding is not robust; it has been replicated many times only by keeping to a well-proven recipe' (Laming, in Krueger, 1989). Such advice includes encouraging observers to use ratios in their judgements; those who do not do this consistently are not encouraged to take part in further experiments. Further, Poulton (in Krueger, 1989) has claimed that the particular power function obtained in an experiment depends crucially upon the spacing of the range of stimuli presented; inserting additional stimuli near the top of the intensity range helps unpractised observers to generate linear functions in log–log plots of their ratings. And while it has been claimed that scaling techniques are free from context effects (see, for example, Stevens and Galanter, 1957; Galanter, 1962) this has been shown to be untrue (Poulton, 1968; Helson and Kosaki, 1968).

An important question arises when observers are given free choice over their use of numbers during magnitude estimation. What are they doing in this situation? What is the nature of the psychophysical function here? As Engen (1971) comments, when we use ratings in this manner we are making a large assumption, namely that observers respond to numbers in the same way that they do to sensory stimulation. And how are subjective and objective aspects of number related? The relationship is clearly not linear: many people, asked to pick a number approximately mid-way between 1000 and 1 million will suggest 100 000, at least until they have had time to reflect on the question. The point is, can we be sure that the use of numbers in magnitude estimation is valid?

Another problem concerns the interpretation of power functions. For example, we can say that two observers whose power functions are identical agree about the subjective difference between two stimuli A and B. But we cannot tell from the power functions whether both experience the same sensation arising from A; there is simply no way of knowing this and thus there is a limit to what direct scaling data can tell us about sensations.

As Stevens's power law is a modification of Weber's and Fechner's laws (it substitutes ratios on the response side but accepts the claim for ratios on the stimulus side), then there should be underlying relations between power law exponents and Weber fractions. Laming (in Krueger, 1989) tested this prediction by surveying published experiments in which both power functions and Weber fractions were measured, often using the same apparatus and the same experimenters. Laming found no evidence for any relationship between the two indices. This is a serious blow for proponents of the power law.

As a final criticism of the direct scaling approach, it is possible to question the need to discard the Weber fraction. In a review of published research, Laming demonstrated that the Weber fraction is in fact a good summary of the empirical relationship between difference threshold data and stimulus intensity. (As was stated above, a common way of plotting such data on logarithmic scales tends to exaggerate departures from linearity.) Why then discard the classical laws?

Direct scaling and associated power functions captured the imagination of a number of psychophysicists. Given the criticisms outlined above, we may ask whether there is any possible future for such an approach to psychophysics in general, and the measure of sensation in particular?

The first answer to this key question is that there are situations in which direct measures of sensation appear to have worked and to have practical value—a valuable test. Stevens (1957) showed that an average 10-fold increase in sound intensity (10 dB) lead to a doubling of subjective loudness. Translated into power function terminology, this means that the exponent for the subjective growth in loudness as a function of intensity is 0.3. Work following this discovery eventually gave rise to a new international standard— the Sone scale. Would this achievement have been possible if the ideas behind direct scaling and power functions were seriously misguided?

More recently, an attempt has been made to reconcile Stevens's ideas with earlier, more traditional ones. This is a major theoretical article by Krueger (1989) which, together with the accompanying published debate among contemporary psychophysicists, has been invaluable in the preparation of the present chapter.

Krueger considers psychophysical evidence obtained using a range of different psychophysical methods, such as magnitude estimation, partitioning (a direct scaling procedure in which the observer may be asked, for example, to set two stimuli so that one appears twice as intense as the other), JND scales and direct measures of neural activity in response to stimulation. He also carries out a detailed mathematical analysis of the various functions that have been proposed to link stimuli and responses in psychophysical research. In approaching the problem in this manner, Krueger is using the technique of *converging operations* in an attempt to discover the truth.

The interested reader should read Krueger's target article and the commentaries on it, in order to discover the technical and theoretical difficulties involved in assessing the value of direct scaling. Crudely summarized, Krueger states that:

(1) it is clear that psychophysical functions dealing with prothetic continua must include compression factors;
(2) we should abandon the assumptions that Weber's Law is valid across all stimulus intensity ranges and that the JND has the same subjective magnitude across modalities;
(3) it is not legitimate to use the numbers assigned to stimuli in magnitude estimation procedures as direct measures of sensation strength.

At the end of his analysis, Krueger asserts that the true psychophysical law may take the form of a modified power function. Its exponent will lie between the value of approximately zero (which is implied by Fechner's Law) and the much higher values claimed by Stevens and his co-workers. Krueger proposes that power function exponents will typically lie between 0 and 1. A number of different power functions are considered as possible candidates, all more complicated than Stevens's $S = aX^b$.

It is clear that Stevens's direct scaling studies gave an important impetus to psychophysics. His writings remind us that psychophysics was designed to illuminate the relationship between mind and body, in particular the relation between stimulation and sensation, and it seems foolish therefore to restrict our interest to threshold situations. Sensations are interesting, particularly when they are strong, and Stevens attempted to discover more about them. In doing so, he revived interest in one of the classical problems in psychology. The question remaining is, of course, were Stevens's methods really scientific?

GENERAL REMARKS ON PSYCHOPHYSICS

At the start of this chapter it was claimed that psychophysics was one of the undoubted successes of experimental psychology. We repeat this claim. To have discovered so much about the workings of the nervous system without penetrating that system is quite remarkable. In a later chapter on the neurophysiological approach to perception it will be possible to show how psychophysical data make sense in terms of what we now know about the neurophysiology of the nervous system and how elegantly these two different approaches have been combined.

The basic method of psychophysics, which, as we have shown, involves the careful presentation of calibrated stimuli and the recording of controlled responses, has been extended to other areas. It has been possible to record many important data from human infants and animals using clever combinations of psychophysical methods and training techniques. The basic methodology of psychophysics has also been widely adopted in other areas of experimental psychology, often with profitable results.

Psychophysics has therefore been of great importance in experimental psychology generally and the study of perception in particular. From the viewpoint of the present book, however, what is striking is not the technical achievements in psychophysics, but the interactions between research and theory.

The earliest nineteenth-century work in psychophysics believed in the existence of actual, fixed thresholds. These were defined, as in Weber's Law ($\Delta I/I = k$), in terms of physical stimulus properties. When empirical data showed variability, this was dealt with using statistical techniques designed to give a single 'best' value for the threshold.

Later, the idea that detection and discrimination were a function of inherent variability of neural structures became accepted. Thresholds were statistical concepts. We can see here the motive for the neural quantum approach: the desire to get samples of true sensory performance, with variability minimized or controlled during periods of measurement.

However, in the approaches summarized above, the observer is still viewed as an essentially passive receiver of stimulation. A paradigm shift in psychophysics occurred with the emergence of a different kind of model, one in which the observer is seen as active: an intuitive statistician following decision rules in a manner analogous to those used in testing scientific hypotheses. Gigerenzer and Murray describe this change as part of 'the inference revolution' in psychology. In psychophysics, it was resisted by the influential theorist S.S. Stevens, whose views on psychophysics are clearly not probabilistic—as we hope to have shown. The full impact of the revolution is seen in the emergence of the theory of signal detection. We shall see the wider importance of the inference revolution later in this book in discussions of empiricism and probabilistic functionalism.

We end where we began, with the problem of the threshold. It is a fact that any lay person entering a modern perception laboratory is likely to be dazzled by the array of modern scientific apparatus. Computer-driven experiments, precise timing and control devices and accurately calibrated stimulus generators abound. These are all available to those who would make new discoveries about the senses. Even Fechner, a visionary, could hardly fail to be impressed. But it cannot be said that his dream of linking the mental and the physical has been fully realized. Fechner's methods have allowed us to learn more about human processes, particularly sensory processes, than he could have imagined. But the theoretical concept of the threshold is still under debate 130 years after Fechner's pioneering work, and the true nature of sensation still eludes us. How strange that one of the first theoretical problems to be tackled by psychologists continues to provoke and perplex.

NOTES ON CHAPTER 2

The historical relationship between psychology and statistical theory, leading to the 'inference revolution' is described in an invaluable book, *Cognition and Intuitive Statistics* by Gigerenzer and Murray (1987). These authors show how the concept of the 'intuitive statistician' gradually entered psychology. Gigerenzer and Murray's account has been followed closely in the latter parts of this chapter.

Some of the calculations required in applications of signal detection theory are based on the following. First, it is commonly assumed that both the noise, N, and the signal plus noise, $S+N$, distributions are Gaussian, with equal variances. The N distribution is defined as having a mean of 0 and a standard deviation of 1.0. The distance between the N and the $S+N$ distributions is measured in z units (standard deviation units from the N distribution).

If x_n = the mean of the N distribution and x_{s+n} = the mean of the $S+N$ distribution, then

$$d' = \frac{X_{s+n} - X_n}{\sigma} \qquad (1)$$

where σ is the standard deviation of the N distribution.

The definition of β is in terms of the heights (ordinate values) of the N and the $S+N$ distributions above the selected criterion position. The height of the noise distribution (y_n) is derived from the formula for the Gaussian distribution:

$$y_n = \frac{\exp\left(-\frac{1}{2}z^2\right)}{\sqrt{(2\pi)}} \qquad (2)$$

where z is the distance of the criterion point from x_n expressed in σ units.

The height of the signal plus noise distribution (y_{s+n}) is given by

$$y_{s+n} = \frac{\exp\left[-\frac{1}{2}(z - d')^2\right]}{\sqrt{(2\pi)}} \qquad (3)$$

where $(z-d')$ is the distance of the criterion point from the mean of the $S+N$ distribution, again in σ units.

In practice, the required numbers can be obtained without solving the above equations by looking up published values of ordinates of the standard normal curve.

Most references to Fechner's work concentrate on his 1860 work, *Elemente der Psychophysik*. However, in a collection of his works, published posthumously, Fechner conceded that the basic psychophysical function linking stimulus intensity and sensation might in fact take the form of a power function (see the commentary by E. Scheerer in Krueger, 1989).

Since the first edition of this book was being written, an invaluable theoretical analysis of psychophysical functions has appeared Krueger (1987). This has been used extensively in the preparation of this revised chapter. Special thanks are due to Professor Krueger for detailed personal communications regarding errors of fact and theory which appeared in the first edition. Readers wishing to learn more about the relationship between the Weber–Fechner Laws and Stevens's work on power functions should read the Krueger article and its commentary. Corso (1970, ch. 11) provides a valuable discussion of the theory of the neural quantum and the present account owes much to Corso's exegesis.

3

The Gestalt theory

The first general theory of perception to be discussed, Gestalt theory, represents a fascinating paradox. As a formal theory of perception, it can be said to have failed. However, it can also be asserted that the Gestalt approach was, within limits, brilliantly successful, and that it continues to exert a significant influence on the psychology of perception. We shall attempt to show how this paradoxical situation came about.

As a preliminary, it can be said that the emphasis in the explanatory parts of Gestalt theory is very much upon brain processes. What needs to be explained, Gestalt theorists believed, is the relationship between the world and everyday experience: the world of meaningful objects and events. Their explanation was in terms of brain processes. From the point of view of our simple classificatory model, the relevant arc is that connecting the physical world to the central nervous system, and hence to mental experience.

Gestalt theory is closely associated with the work of three men: Max Wertheimer (1880–1943), Wolfgang Köhler (1887–1967) and Kurt Koffka (1886–1941). There were (and are) other Gestaltists but these psychologists pioneered the Gestalt approach which was to exert an important influence on the psychology of perception.

The remainder of this chapter will be organized under the following headings:

- The historical background to the movement
- A general outline of the Gestalt approach
- Köhler's brain model and the formal Gestalt theory
- An assessment of the Gestalt theory
- More recent developments
- General remarks on the Gestalt theory

We shall begin by tracing some of the historical origins of his important movement.

THE HISTORICAL BACKGROUND TO THE MOVEMENT

The benefit of hindsight allows us to discern some of the influences which made the development of the Gestalt theory almost inevitable.

Philosophy

The publication of Kant's *Critique of Pure Reason* in 1781 had a major impact on subsequent European philosophy. Nobody could do justice to this influential and difficult work in a few lines, but it is possible to take a single Kantian idea as an example of his thinking and show its potential importance for psychology. Imagine an object moving from left to right across the field of vision. The movement takes time and occurs through space. That we perceive the object's motion is something we take for granted; we can even guess about mechanisms which enable us to do this. But what about the framework within which the object moves? We cannot perceive space itself; there is literally nothing *to* perceive. Space is what the object moves through. Similarly, we cannot perceive time as such: it too is simply a framework within which events are ordered. But the perception we have had would clearly be impossible without our awareness of these frameworks. Where does the awareness come from? Kant's answer (stated here with some crudity) is that space and time are *a priori intuitions*; that is, they are 'givens', superimposed upon reality by our minds. Much of Kant's life was spent in justifying this claim and examining the consequences. For now we can say simply that there is one consequence which is of great psychological as well as philosophical importance if Kant's claim is true: perception must be innately determined. Mind imposes a structure on the perceived world and this world is the only one we are capable of perceiving. This leads to *Nativism*, which, as will be shown, became associated with the Gestalt approach. Gestalt psychology did not appear until one hundred years after Kant's death, but it was clearly influenced by his philosophical investigations.

Nineteenth-century ideas

There were other influences at work in nineteenth-century Europe. Many people, as a result of Darwinism, had abandoned their religious beliefs. If God was no longer to be seen at the centre of things, who was? The answer was, Man.[1] It is significant that the nineteenth century witnessed the great flowering of the Romantic movement in literature and the arts. Common to much of the creative work associated with this movement is the struggle of the individual—a hero or heroine—against fate. Think for a moment about the

---

[1] Historically, this was the common term.

great romantic poems of the period, the operas, the emotions induced by the music of Beethoven (for example, *The Eroica*: 'A heroic symphony . . .'), Wagner and Tchaikovsky. The themes which emerge repeatedly concern the heroic struggles of individuals. This was still part of the Zeitgeist at the time of the emergence of the Gestalt movement, where the emphasis was on the dynamic role of the perceiver in making sense of the world.

The Law of Least Action or the Minimum Principle

The ancient Greek geometers spent much effort in exploring what they considered to be ideal forms. They discovered that in the case of one such ideal form, the circle, an interesting shape is traced by a fixed point on its circumference as the circle is rolled along a straight line. This shape is known as a cycloid (see Figure 3.1).

The publication of Newton's *Philosophiae Naturalis Principia Mathematica* in 1687 led to a renaissance in which mathematicians strove to discover the general laws governing the physical world. Nine years after Newton's work appeared, the Swiss mathematician, Johann Bernoulli, wrote a letter in which he described what is now known as the brachistochrone problem:

> For two given points *A* and *B* in a vertical plane, find a line connecting them on which a moveable point *M* descends from *A* to *B* under the influence of gravitation in the quickest possible way.
>
> (Quoted by Hildebrandt and Tromba, 1985)

The reader will realize from Figure 3.2 that there are two aspects to this problem: first, how to make the 'best' use of gravity; second, how to get *M* from left to right. Common-sense but wrong solutions are shown in Figure 3.2(a). The correct solution, shown in Figure 3.2(b), is a *cycloid*.

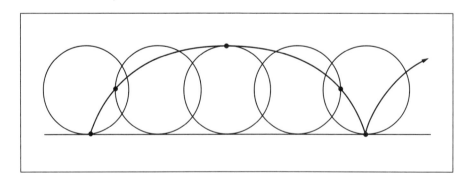

Figure 3.1   The shape generated by a point on a moving circle: a cycloid

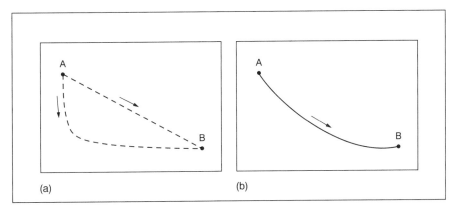

Figure 3.2 Bernouli's problem. What is the most economical path for the movement of *A* to *B* under the influence of gravity? Left: two incorrect solutions. Right: the correct solution—a cycloid

Interestingly, the seventeenth-century Dutch scientist, Huygens, realized that the inaccuracies of contemporary pendulum clocks were due to the fact that the time taken for a full period of a pendulum varies as a function of its amplitude—because the path of a simple pendulum describes an arc which is circular. In 1657 Huygens patented a solution to the problem—a way of causing the pendulum to swing in an optimal manner—which was to fit a collar around the flexible top of the pendulum, causing the swing to follow the path of . . . a cycloid.

In 1744, Bernoulli's pupil, the great mathematician Euler, applied the general principle of 'Least Action' to the motion of the planets around the sun. At the same time Maupertius announced his Law of Least Action: 'If there occurs some change in nature, the amount of action necessary for this change must be as small as possible.'

In the next century the existence of a general principle of minimum effort or action was demonstrated in a variety of phenomena, ranging from optics (light taking the shortest or quickest route) to the behaviour of chains suspended between supports (at equilibrium the chains adopt a curve known as the *catenary*). Particularly interesting was the application of the principle of minimum effort to soap films. Such films—when stretched across frames—assume equilibrium states of minimum potential energy. As potential energy is proportional to area, it follows that the shapes assumed by the films are *minimal surfaces*: they represent the smallest areas capable of spanning the frames. As the examples above demonstrate, this work had interesting practical as well as theoretical implications. The tradition continues: the remarkable Olympic Stadium in Munich, built in 1976, has a roof built with high steel masts connected by steel ropes and covered by a transparent membrane. The complex shape of this roof is in fact a minimal surface; its design was arrived at by building models in which the masts were connected by films produced from soap solutions.[2]

That was the historical background to Gestalt psychology. But the movement's beginnings were also a reaction against two contemporary approaches to psychology: structuralism and behaviourism.

Structuralism and behaviourism

Structuralism, which reached its peak between 1870 and 1910 with the work of Wundt in Germany and Titchener in America, was an attempt to explore the mind in a manner analogous to the chemical analysis of complex substances. Just as the chemist can consider compounds in terms of their basic chemical elements, Wundt, Titchener and others believed that the laws of the mind would be revealed by careful study of its elements and their relationships. In this case the 'mental elements' of the analysis were *sensations*. On this view, any rich subjective experience is essentially a blend of simpler, more basic experiences or sensations, and the job of the psychologist is to list these. But this reduction to sensations is not easy. There is a constant tendency to commit the 'stimulus error' in which the source of a sensation is confused with the sensation itself. For example, one frequently says that one hears *something*, say an engine. But the engine is not itself a sensation. One should say that one has certain sensations *like* those normally arising when one is near an engine. The technique for avoiding the stimulus error and for correctly identifying the sensations one is having is a difficult one which must be learned and practised, usually by the investigator who is the observer in the research. The technique is known as trained *introspection* and was the basic source of data in the experiments of Wundt, Titchener and others.

Reduced to its simplest formulation, structuralism leads to a view of perception in which the perceived world is a *mosaic*. Each stimulus element in a scene yields its own sensation and the totality of these sensations forms the percept. Stated baldly, it is obvious that such a scheme could not work. How do we explain, for example, why things remain the same size as we move away from them if our perception is tied to particular sensations, in this case those arising from the shrinking retinal image? To avoid this trap, the major theorist, Helmholtz (who was Wundt's contemporary and whose career overlapped with Titchener's), had been driven to an empiricism which asserted that experience and memory must correct and enhance the momentary effects of stimulation. This in turn suggests that much of perceiving must be learned. While

---

[2] The ideas so far described in this short section are taken from Hildebrandt and Tromba's *Mathematics and Optimal Form* (1985). The interested reader is urged to consult this fascinating book.

not denying the role of experience, the Gestalt theorists rejected both the mosaic view of perception and the emphasis on learning, both of which came under attack in their own writings.

Structuralist introspection as a method of studying perceptual phenomena is long dead and must strike the reader as somewhat unusual. It may help to finish with an example of the sort of thing which the Gestalt theorists attacked. Here is Titchener introspecting on the taste of two fairly familiar substances.

> Thus the 'taste' of lemonade is made up of a sweet taste, an acid taste, a scent (the fragrance of lemon), a sensation of temperature and a pricking (cutaneous) sensation. The 'taste' of limewater is made up of a weakly sweet taste, a sensation of nausea (organic sensation), a sensation of temperature and a biting (cutaneous) sensation.
>
> (Titchener, 1901)

Note that the phrase 'fragrance of lemon' implies that Titchener may not have fully succeeded in reducing the taste into its basic sensations: an analysis of the lemon fragrance is now required. The reader who would like to try this sort of thing is directed to the limewater problem; Titchener's use of the word 'nausea' is curiously apt.

The structuralists knew most of what there was to know about the experimental psychology of perception at the turn of the century. Their writings reveal close familiarity with the works of Helmholtz, for example. It is their philosophical approach to perception and their use of introspection which is unusual. Introspection failed (and with it, this type of structuralism) for a number of reasons: trained observers frequently disagreed in their introspections; introspective data cannot be easily quantified; most importantly, many mental processes are simply not available to self-observation. In fact, the influence of structuralism was probably at an end by the time the first Gestalt discoveries were announced. However, as we shall see, the approach made a useful straw man for the Gestalt theories, all of whom were gifted polemicists.

The second focus of the Gestaltists' attacks was behaviourism. Once again, it could be said that the Gestaltists exaggerated the influence of this movement, at least on contemporary work in perception (and it must be pointed out that the behaviourists were also hostile to structuralism). Nevertheless, it was true that behaviourists did attempt to explain behaviour in terms of a model derived from classical conditioning. This concentrated upon simple stimulus–response relationships, and tended to treat stimuli as essentially simple events confronting organisms. Further, the behaviourists had stated that the subject matter for psychology was objective behaviour, and only objective behaviour. Mental events, subjective experiences, had no place in this new, tough-minded scientific approach.

Gestalt theorists published lengthy rebuttals of the behaviourist case (see, for example, Köhler, 1947, ch. 1). One of the most telling criticisms is that which Köhler advanced against the objectivity which behaviourists aspired to. Köhler argued that this was a chimera, and that even in physics—which claims to deal with the objective world—the concepts and observations are never objective in the sense the behaviourists had assumed:

> How do I define my terms when I work as a physicist? Since my knowledge of physics consists entirely of concepts and observations contained in or derived from direct experience, all the terms which I use in this science must ultimately refer to the same source. If I try to define such terms, my definitions may, of course, refer to further concepts and terms. But the final steps in the process will always be: pointing towards the locus of certain experiences about which I am talking, and hints where to make certain observations. Even the most abstract concepts of physics, such as that of entropy, can have no meaning without a reference, indirect though it may be, to certain direct experiences.
>
> (Köhler, 1947)

It is worth noting that these remarks of Köhler's would have carried extra weight as it was known that he had trained originally as a physicist.

To summarize, the Gestalt theorists were opposed to sensations as data and the accompanying mosaic view of perception, to crude atomism, to introspection as a method, and to the search for a bogus objectivity in psychology. These objections will acquire more force when we outline what Gestalt psychology offered in place of the approaches and assumptions to which it was opposed.

A GENERAL OUTLINE OF THE GESTALT APPROACH

The start of the Gestalt movement

This is one of the best-known stories in the history of psychology. It should be said at the outset that two important Gestalt principles had been published prior to the formation of a separate Gestalt school of thought. Ehrenfels (1890) had drawn attention to the fact that many groups of stimuli acquire a pattern quality which differs from the parts when seen in isolation: a tune is more than the sum of its notes; in a square something emerges which has a quality not present in a random assembly of the component lines—the 'squareness'. Ehrenfels named this emergent property, *Gestaltqualität* (form-quality), a name which was adopted by the Gestalt movement. A second precursor of the Gestalt movement was Rubin (1915), who published an important paper on the distinction between 'figure' and 'ground' in perception, a distinction which later found an important place in Gestalt thinking.

In the summer of 1910 the person who can be said to be the true founder of Gestalt psychology, Max Wertheimer, broke a journey to buy a toy stroboscope. He then carried out some investigations of the illusory movement which such devices can create. If one exposes two stimuli alternately in rapid succession then a number of strange things can happen, depending on the exposure times, the rate of alternation and so on. At low rates of alternation two separate stimuli are seen; at higher rates one sees a displacement of a stimulus from one position to the other (this can be seen at British Rail unmanned crossings where pairs of red warning lights flash alternately): this is stroboscopic movement. But there is an optimum rate at which what is seen is not a moving stimulus, but simply movement *per se*. Obviously, this movement cannot be explained in terms of the behaviour of either of the two stimuli—each simply appears and disappears at its own location. The experience of pure movement, which Wertheimer later called Phi-Movement, arises as the result of temporal and spatial *relationships* between stimuli: something new has arisen which differs from (is over and above) the sum of the parts acting in isolation, it has *Gestaltqualität*.

Wertheimer continued to work on the phi phenomenon at Frankfurt university using as subjects two young psychologists, Wolfgang Köhler and Kurt Koffka. This trio were to create a new approach to the study of perception and a major theory: the Gestalt theory. It is perhaps unfair to single out one member of the movement for a biographical sketch. However, a few remarks concerning Köhler's career will convey something of the academic life of the period. Köhler was educated in three German universities and was at the Psychological Institute in Frankfurt when Wertheimer started his work on the phi phenomenon. Köhler worked from 1913 to 1920 on Tenerife studying problem solving in chimpanzees. After directing the Psychological Institute in Berlin, he fled Nazi Germany in 1935 and spent the rest of his academic career in the USA. His last post was at Dartmouth College.

Phenomenology

There is a special way of looking at the world. To experience it, follow this simple procedure: take a piece of paper and punch out a small hole in the middle about half a centimetre in diameter. Examine any nearby surface and note its colour. Look again, this time through the hole, with the paper held about six inches from the face. Two things may become apparent. First, the colour seen through the hole (which has the fancier name, 'reduction screen') no longer appears to belong to the surface; it seems to float just behind the hole as a film. Second, colours may appear different from those seen when looking normally: for example, someone sitting by a wall may have a portion of his or her face tinted in the wall's colour; grey shadows may now appear coloured.

Using a pencil in front of one eye as a referent (a trick commonly used by artists) one can quickly come to see that objects subtend smaller visual angles as they recede from us. And, once it is pointed out to us, we can experience this troubling fact: the nose is always visible in our field of view—if we choose to notice it.

The procedures above are not simply tricks. It is a fact that careful analysis of what is to be seen when we look in a special way differs from what we normally experience. Introspectionists believed that demonstrations such as the reduction screen reveal the raw material of perception, namely sensations. And it is undeniably true that retinal images of objects do in fact shrink with distance, and that we can become sensitive to these changes.

The question the Gestalt theorists raised was: Which of these two modes of perceiving should be explained in perceptual theory? Their answer was unhesitating and forceful: everyday experience. To this end Koffka asked what has become the most famous question in the history of perception:

'Why do things look as they do?'

In other words, what must be explained by perceptual theories is the stability and coherence of the world of everyday experience, the world in which surface colours are stable under different illuminants and familiar things do not change size as they recede. This is a world of objects, not sensations, and the proper approach to this world is that of the phenomenologist.

> There seems to be a single starting point for psychology, exactly as for all the other sciences: the world as we find it, naively and uncritically.
> (Köhler, 1947, opening paragraph)

The decision to try to understand the world of the unself-conscious perceiver shaped Gestalt research and led to the distinctive *style* of the movement. Gestalt workers concentrated mainly upon strong effects in perception, a legitimate approach, but they went further: whenever possible their readers are not offered a table of experimental results, but a compelling illustration. The emphasis is upon experience rather than data. The reader is not to be convinced by the results of some obscure experiment, but by what he or she actually sees while reading the text. The unusual power and clarity of Gestalt writings owes much to this tactic.

Perception as a dynamic, organized process

Whenever we open our eyes we see, not sensations of light, but objects and surfaces. There is a tendency (most easily noticed in vision) to organize our

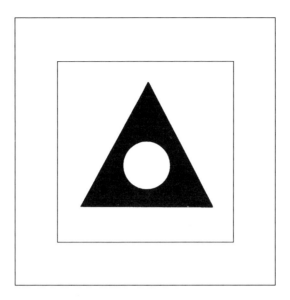

Figure 3.3 Ambiguous figure–ground relationships. Is the white disc superimposed on the triangle, or is it a hole through which the underlying white ground can be seen? (From a demonstration by Miller, 1964)

percepts in a certain manner during all perceiving: we effortlessly distinguish between the *figure* in a field of view and the *ground* against which it is seen. The figure–ground distinction is highly important evidence for the dynamic character of perception. Figures tend to be complete, coherent and in front of the ground, which is seen as less distinct, is attended to less readily, and is often seen as floating behind the figure. When figure and ground share a contour (as they commonly do), then the contour is usually seen as belonging to the figure.

In Figure 3.3 the immediate organization leads us to see a black triangle (the figure) in front of a white ground. But the printed page affords trickery. Is the white disc on the triangle a figure (in which case it will be seen as over the black, which is now ground) or an aperture (in which case we appear to be looking through the triangle at the white ground on which the original triangle is superimposed)? Notice the subtle change in the status of these figure–ground relationships when we change our attention in this way. Figure 3.4 shows how figure–ground relationships can be made entirely ambiguous: which is the figure in this case, the profiles or the vase?

Figure–ground separation occurs in all sensory modalities—for example, when we abstract the voice of a speaker from the background sounds of a noisy party, or when we feel an insect crawling over our skin. And it seems that we do not have to learn how to achieve this valuable economy in

Figure 3.4   Figure–ground reversal: the face–vase illusion

perceiving. When people recover their sight after many years of blindness they commonly experience many difficulties in seeing the world as it is. But, almost without exception, the case reports say that figure–ground separation is achieved from the outset. Are we built to see in this way?

So powerful is the tendency to organize vision into figure and ground that we take it very much for granted—hence the Gestaltist's use of ambiguous material such as Figure 3.4, which is intended to shake us out of our normal habits. The magnitude of the figure–ground achievement becomes apparent to those attempting to make machines which can perceive. How could a computer be programmed to ignore everything but the people in a complex scene? What rules would enable it to attend only to the left-hand performance of a jazz pianist?

The laws of grouping

In one of the early discoveries in Getalt psychology, Wertheimer (1912) demonstrated several principles by which groups of stimuli organize themselves in perception. Looking at the arrays illustrated in Figure 3.5 reveals a spontaneous tendency to organize the stimuli into wholes or *Gestalten*. For example, stimuli which are adjacent tend to be grouped together: in Figure 3.5(a) the stimuli could be seen as unconnected, as rows, or as columns. But the Adjacency or Proximity Principle guarantees that we see them as paired

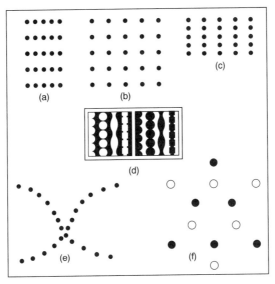

Figure 3.5 Some of Wertheimer's laws of grouping. (a) Proximity induces grouping by rows; (b) proximity is equal and there is no dominant direction of grouping; (c) proximity induces grouping by columns; (d) groupings by symmetry (after Bahnson, 1928); (e) groupings by continuation; (f) grouping by similarity

columns. The figure illustrates some other laws of grouping such as Good Continuation and Similarity. If a subset of the stimuli in Figure 3.5 were to move in the same direction then this movement would cause them to separate phenomenally and take on organized figural properties, illustrating the law of common fate.

These spontaneous groupings in perception are fascinating and reliable phenomena and are still being researched 80 years after Wertheimer's demonstrations (see, for example, Restle, 1979). It is difficult, having experienced such effects, to return to any view of perception which ignores its dynamic aspects. Note once again the power of demonstrating rather than describing phenomena.

Goodness or Prägnanz

The Gestalt theorists concluded that there must be a general underlying principle behind the numerous examples of organization which they discovered. It was as if perception tended, wherever possible, towards simplicity, symmetry and wholeness—a tendency summarized by the German word *Prägnanz*. As applied to perceptual phenomena, the concept of Prägnanz is in fact rather complex. In modern German the word can mean clear-cut, concise or succinct. But as Arnheim (1987) states, Prägnanz can imply not only a tendency towards regularity and symmetry—the cleansing of the stimulus of distracting detail—but also the intensification of characteristics. For example, when we suddenly see a face in the amorphous configuration of a cloud or a dying fire, this is change towards perceptual simplicity. However, once the face appears, the details become emphatic. If anything, this is a tension-enhancing, rather than a tension-reducing process.[3]

We now call the process of seeing novel similarities 'lateral thinking'. Remembering that Köhler had trained as a physicist helps us to understand the next stage in the development of Gestalt theory. Where else do we find processes which tend towards simplicity? The answer, as was demonstrated earlier, is in the physical world. Perception appears to be analogous to certain processes which we can observe in nature. It is an exciting step to wonder whether essentially similar physical forces are the cause of Prägnanz in perception. Later we shall show that this is the conclusion which Köhler eventually arrived at.

Wholes and parts

The claim that in perception the whole is different from the sum of its parts acting in isolation is one of the most important tenets of Gestalt theory. This simple idea, elegantly illustrated in numerous demonstrations, has great significance for perceptual theory. If correct, it rules out the possibility of developing adequate theories of perception which treat stimuli as single, isolatable events.

As was stated earlier, Ehrenfels (1890) introduced the concept of *Gestaltqualität* prior to the emergence of Gestalt psychology. The importance of this concept cannot be exaggerated and it was elevated to a major principle in the Gestalt theory. When we hear a tune, the experience of the tune itself (the *Gestaltqualität*) is something more than the aggregate of the notes. It is not reducible to individual notes and is not an adding together of simple sensations. For example, the last three notes of 'God Save the Queen' are the same as the first three notes of 'Three Blind Mice', but how many people who know both tunes well would ever realize this? The notes do not sound the same because they are not in the same context. And there is an interesting paradox here: although the notes form the context, the context shapes the notes. Similarly, when a tune is transposed an octave, or played in a different key, we recognize it as the same tune, even though each individual note is different. Because the *relationship* between the notes is the same, they exhibit the same *Gestaltqualität*.

---

[3] The author is indebted to Professor Lester Krueger for advice about the subtle meanings associated with the term Prägnanz.

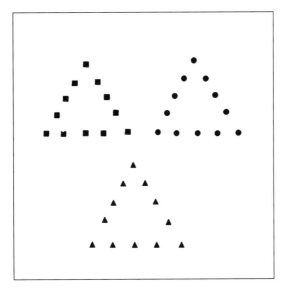

Figure 3.6   Triangularity Gestalten

Historically, the most influential demonstration of part/whole interactions was Wertheimer's use of the phi phenomenon, which has been described earlier. Phi movement is something new, something not predictable from the behaviour of each light in isolation, but emerging as a function of the spatial and temporal *relationships* between the lights.

In Figure 3.6 the triangles have been formed from different elements, and yet 'triangularity' is evident in each display. None of the parts in isolation possesses triangularity'; this emerges only in relationships. The Müller–Lyer illusion in Figure 3.7 is another example of this important point: the shaft lines are objectively the same length, but their relationship with the arrows creates an illusion, an illusion which could not have been predicted from knowledge of the individual components. Once again we see that the whole is different from the parts studied in isolation.

The constancies

The tendency for perception to be veridical, summarized by the term 'perceptual constancy', was seized upon by Gestalt theorists. When objects recede they commonly do not shrink; white paper in shadow does not look greyer; objects remain the same colour despite changes in illumination; shapes do not change when seen from new positions.

All these are examples of perception going beyond the local effects of isolated stimuli. In these cases, Gestalt theories likened the environmental

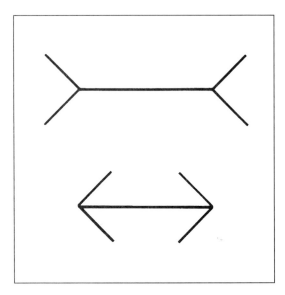

Figure 3.7   The Müller–Lyer illusion

context in which stimuli are lodged to a dynamic *field*, a term synonymous with that currently being developed by the physicists of the period:

> The constancy of brightness, for instance, depends on the relation of the illumination and brightness of the surrounding field to the brightness of the object under observation.
>
> (Köhler, 1947)

We shall return to the idea of a field later in this chapter.

The main perceptual phenomena which shaped the Gestalt theory have now been outlined. During the history of the Gestalt movement the work was extended to other areas. It was found, for example, that when a chicken is trained to peck at the darker of two greys, and this is now paired with an even darker grey, it is to the latter which the animal now responds—suggesting that the original learning involved a relationship rather than an absolute stimulus value. Monkeys solving problems which are more closely related to their natural lives than the laboratory mazes used by the early behaviourists do not engage in constant trial-and-error, but show periods of inactivity followed by sudden solutions of the problems. This suddenness following a latent period is also characteristic of much human experience when, for example, we suddenly see a face in a fire which we have been staring at for a long time, or we equally suddenly solve a crossword clue. In a very different context, Gestalt theory has been applied to artistic phenomena (Arnheim, 1949, 1956, 1969), and some have tried to relate it to psychological therapies. However, it is in the field of perception that the theory has had its major impact.

It must be remembered that the ideas we have outlined above became known partly as a result of the flair and conviction with which they were announced. As has been said, Gestalt phenomena were often demonstrated on the printed page. The Gestaltists were good writers and enjoyed polemics. The success of the movement is hardly surprising, and readers are urged to consult some of the original Gestalt writings listed at the end of this chapter to experience more directly the power of this approach to perception.

KÖHLER'S BRAIN MODEL AND THE FORMAL GESTALT THEORY

So far, we have used the term 'theory' very loosely in describing the Gestaltists' work. We have used it to describe (a) a movement in the history of perception, (b) some beliefs about the nature of perceivers and the ways in which their abilities should be studied and (c) a set of laws describing the behaviour of stimuli during various interactions. What is missing from all this has been an account of the Gestaltists' views as to *why* perception is as they claim. This is an appropriate place to turn to the explanations which Gestalt theory advanced to explain the Gestalt laws. The explanations comprise the formal Gestalt theory.

If the word 'failure' can be applied to any part of Gestalt psychology, this is it. Historically, the actual theoretical account of Gestalt phenomena has never achieved the status and acceptance afforded to the empirical parts of the work, and it is instructive to consider why this should be so.

Why is perception dynamic? What causes the degree of organization which we have described? How shall we predict the behaviour of stimuli in new situations—i.e. how do we know what something will look like? A set of descriptions cannot answer these questions. What are required are explanations. Not surprisingly, the Gestalt theorists, particularly Köhler, went to considerable lengths to meet this challenge.

With hindsight we can consider the problem facing Gestalt theorists as a choice between three alternative ways of explaining perceptual phenomena: introspection, physical Gestalten, or physiological mechanisms within the central nervous system.

An introspectionist approach to the explanation of Gestalt phenomena would have been essentially psychological or mental in flavour. However, as we have seen, the hostility of the Gestalt movement to introspection rules out any explanation of this type.

Physical Gestalten and the Minimum Principle

Köhler, a trained physicist, considered the possibility that perceptual Gestalten were manifestations of a wider set of phenomena which included physical Gestalten. The reader will remember from an earlier section that studies of physical phenomena over the centuries had accumulated a mass of evidence to support a general principle of least effort—the *Minimum Principle*. It is hardly surprising that Köhler, as a trained physicist, should have been familiar with the Minimum Principle and the resulting tendency of physical systems to settle into equilibria involving minimum energy, minimum surfaces and so on. Köhler's detailed knowledge of magnetic and electrical fields led him to suppose that if such fields behave in dynamic ways, exhibiting tendencies to closure, balance and Prägnanz, then perception might obey the same laws—given that it arises from the action of neural (physical) systems in the brain. In this way, Köhler attempted to attain 'scientific citizenship' (Petermann, 1932) for the concept of the Gestalt. Thus in his work, *Physical Gestalten*, Köhler (1920) states that when two electrolytic solutions are in osmotic contact the electrical potential which arises is a new property of the system as a whole: '. . . the communicating system of solutions has Gestalt characteristics'. It should be obvious what Köhler was trying to do in his discussions of these physical analogues.

Unfortunately, this approach cannot be fully sustained. It is possible to collect many instances of Gestalt-like phenomena in the physical sciences, but it is only too obvious that there are many situations in which assemblies of things, including chemicals, do not show Gestalt effects. Is a pile of coal a Gestalt? What about a mixture of salt and sand—where are the Gestalt interactions here? It seems unlikely that physical Gestalten have sufficient generality or relevance to permit extrapolations to psychological phenomena; they cannot carry the theoretical weight.

Even if the idea of physical Gestalten had seemed more plausible as the basis of a theory of perception, this would not have solved all the problems facing the Gestalt theorists. When we attempt to analyse a particular pattern, what can we say about its components? The Gestalt movement (at least after 1929) opposed any form of reductionism, believing that theoretical explanations in psychology should be 'from above' rather than 'from below'. More seriously, we find in Köhler (1925) the statement that in completion phenomena, which are excellent examples of the dynamic aspects of perception, '. . . a part will suggest a whole only if it is a genuine part'. But, as one commentator has remarked, '. . . it is difficult to see how [this definition] can finally avoid the tautology that what produces a genuine whole is a genuine part' (Staniland, 1966).

The Gestaltists found themselves forced into an even more extreme position than this. Replying to a critic, Koffka was driven to say:

. . . in characterizing a real object as a stimulus we do not refer to an absolute property of that object, in and by itself, *but only to the object's relationship* to a living organism.

(Koffka's *Reply to Benussi*, 1915; italics added)

Later, Koffka adds:

Hence even if there were no physical Gestalten, there might nevertheless be stimuli for Gestalt presentations.

(Koffka, 1915)

As Staniland (1966) goes on to comment:

If the perceptual experience cannot be inferred from the physical data and the stimulus data are not available to introspection, the only correlation left is with the processes of the central nervous system, and it was towards this that Gestalt theory deeply committed itself.

And in doing so the Gestalt theorists lost their chance of bringing about a permanent change in the ways in which psychologists approached the problem of explaining perceptual phenomena.

Isomorphism

Köhler attempted to lay the theoretical foundations for an adequate account of Gestalt phenomena (see, for example, Köhler, 1940, 1947). His writings placed a major emphasis upon physiological/neural mechanisms as the required level of explanation. To this end he announced a 'general leading principle', that of *psychophysical isomorphism*, in which it was assumed that there is a correlation ('coordination') between psychological experiences and physiological events in the central nervous system: 'Experienced order in space is always structurally identical with a functional order in the distribution of underlying brain processes' (Köhler, 1947).

For example, if the organization of a visual display leads one to group stimuli into, say, a triangle, then the stability and Gestalt-character of the triangle is due to underlying processes in the visual cortex. These preserve the essential relationship between the components of the figure—in other words, their triangularity. If the triangle is formed from three sets of dots, then the underlying processes must preserve (a) the ordering of proximities and (b) the angular relations between the sides thus formed. Similar principles relate temporal ordering of experience to temporal sequences of brain processes.

The representation, it must be stressed, is *topological* rather than *topographical*. Just as the London Underground map indicates the correct sequence of stations, but would be of little use when navigating one's way through the streets above, we must not expect that when someone reports that an array has become organized into a triangle, an actual triangle of neural responses has formed in the visual cortex. What has come into existence is a neural process underlying the spatial essence of the organized figure experienced as a triangle. It is important to recognize that Köhler did not suggest that there were pictures in the head, although many commentators have falsely accused him of this (see Henle, 1984, for a review of the many erroneous interpretations of Köhler's position). He knew that this merely displaces the problem (who, or rather what, perceives the pictures?). Gestalt isomorphism was that existing between organized experience and processes in the brain.

Köhler had been struck by the tendency of some stimulus patterns to reverse after a period of prolonged inspection. It was as if perceiving involved a process in the brain which caused its own termination. What sort of process could this be?

Köhler knew about the behaviour of chemicals in solutions. Most readers will be aware that many substances decompose in solution into particles that have (opposed) electrical charges. Water itself forms positively charged hydrogen ions and negatively charged hydroxyl ions: H^+ and OH^-. Common salt (NaCl) forms Na^+ ions which have lost an electron, and Cl^- ions which carry an extra one. Hydrochloric acid forms H^+ and Cl^- ions. Collecting differently charged ions at two spatially separated sites forms the basis of the electrical cell, which, when short-circuited, will cause a current to flow. This is the key to the Gestalt brain model. Köhler therefore speculated that the following chain of events follows visual stimulation (we shall modify one of his own examples).

Consider a stimulus array comprising a light disc on a darker background. The disc is seen as an organized figure against a ground. The neural processes associated with the perception of the disc and the background terminate in the visual cortex. The final neurons in the causal chain between the retina and the visual cortex discharge chemicals into the fluid medium surrounding them and ionic decomposition takes place. The stronger discharges associated with the disc lead to higher ion concentrations at certain sites compared with those induced by the darker ground. But both figure- and ground-induced discharges are part of the larger liquid environment surrounding the visual cortex. Thus electromotive forces will arise between the figure, the darker ground and the internal environment. These forces will maintain a current, the intensity of which will depend upon the intensity of the original visual stimulus. Further, *the currents in the visual cortex will come under the influence of physical laws.* For example, they will distribute themselves spatially according to the laws of electrostatic vectors and therefore tend towards Prägnanz (Figure 3.8 illustrates this type of analysis). Thus the dynamic tendencies

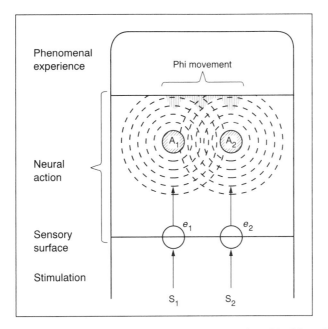

Figure 3.8 Köhler's field forces and the phi phenomenon (modified from Petermann, 1932). S_1 and S_2 are events at the two retinae. A_1 and A_2 are points on the visual cortex from which the induced electrical fields spread. The overlap of the two fields yields a unitary percept: phi movement

which we can observe inside ourselves when perceiving reflect the influence of physical forces in our brains. Here we see the influence of the Minimum Principle (described earlier in this chapter) on Köhler's ideas: dynamic physical systems tend to stability and minimum work; perception tends towards Prägnanz; the brain is a dynamic physical system.

The reader should now have a good impression of the style of Köhler's thinking. It is clear that his brain model is quite a gross one, in the sense that it involves large areas of the visual cortex. (Towards the end of his career Köhler was starting to speculate that the fields which he had postulated to account for the Gestalt nature of perception might be smaller in scale, involving activity around single synapses: see Henle, 1984.)

The implications of Köhler's model are as follows.

First, context effects are explained because the electrical processes in the brain are not local and discrete but behave as *fields*; thus the impact of a stimulus is determined in part by the nature of the surrounding array—a fundamental Gestalt principle.

Second, the effects of stimulation can outlast a stimulus. Köhler does not claim that we can be aware of neural processes directly, but that we can adopt

certain procedures which give us a clue to their nature. For example, prolonged fixation of patterns may give rise to *after-effects* in which it can be seen
that one's perception is changed for relatively long periods. Thus when one
fixates a rotating spiral for several minutes, the after-effect (which is an apparent rotation of the spiral in the opposite direction) may last for hours or even
days.

Third, the behaviour of the fields in the visual cortex explains the tendency
of perception towards Prägnanz: it is because the underlying electrical distributions follow minimal principles, and therefore tend towards balance and
symmetry, that perceptual experience does the same.

Finally, the dynamic processes in the visual cortex have an existence of their
own—they are physical events. If electrical charges can cross gaps and distribute themselves around resistance networks in a dynamic, holistic manner,
we should not be surprised to discover that perception can fill gaps or show
field-like effects: the two sets of phenomena are directly related.

The temptation to look back disparagingly at Köhler's psychoneural model
should be resisted. Köhler was searching for an explanation of perceptual
phenomena in terms of neural activity. There are still those, a quarter of a
century after Köhler's death, who believe that the ultimate explanation of all
psychological phenomena will be written in the language of physiology. His
attempt was not absurd; remember, too, that when Köhler first described his
model, knowledge of the workings of the living brain was sketchy, to say the
least. It has been said that early neurophysiological attempts to probe the
brain were like trying to understand people in the street from the top of a
skyscraper, armed only with a giant needle. Köhler had to make the most of
the knowledge available at that time. He wanted his model to be scientific.
What could be more reasonable than to link it to some of the best science of
his day—namely, that associated with physics and chemistry?

To end this section on the Gestalt explanation of perceptual phenomena it
must be stressed that it stands apart from the main contributions of the
Gestaltists. Other Gestalt psychologists were less concerned with Köhler's
psychoneural model. Koffka, for example, was more content to describe and
discuss Gestalt phenomena than to try to find a sound physiological explanation of them (see Koffka, 1924, 1935). To repeat a point made earlier, the
wider meaning of Gestalt theory includes the phenomena described by Gestalt researchers and the psychological laws which they advanced. All this
needs to be assessed. But for many who have supported the Gestalt approach
over the years, the truth about the wider aspects of Gestalt psychology does
depend upon the correctness or otherwise of Köhler's model. We must respect this distinction when examining the Gestalt contribution to perception.
Incidentally, the special nature of Köhler's model, which we have called the
formal Gestalt theory, explains why the theory was described at the start in
terms of only two regions of our general classificatory scheme (described in

Chapter 1). What we shall subsequently refer to as the Gestalt theory is broad, but Köhler's model is narrow: it links experience and the brain.

AN ASSESSMENT OF THE GESTALT THEORY

This assessment will attempt to look at the more general Gestalt contribution to perception (which may now be referred to as the Gestalt theory) rather than limit itself to the brain model, although this will be mentioned.

We shall begin by describing some work which has challenged Gestalt ideas to varying degrees, then a brief selection of more recent work will be presented to show some of the directions in which research in this general area has gone since the earlier days of the movement.

As has been shown, the Gestalt theorists held that there are certain phenomena which reveal the basic laws of perception, that perceptual processes are dynamic rather than passive, and that the perceptual world is organized into patterns or configurations rather than a mosaic of sensations. They argued for a phenomenological rather than an introspective approach to perception, and preferred strong demonstrations to statistical descriptions. Their explanation of perceptual and related phenomena took the form of hypothetical brain processes which were part of a psychoneural isomorphism, an explanation which is inherently nativist in its implications concerning the origins of perception in the individual perceiver. We shall now look at some of these topics.

The brain model

Earlier in this chapter an attempt was made to give as sympathetic an account as possible of this aspect of the Gestalt theory. Even so, the reader must have felt that we were drifting into science fiction. In truth, apart from Köhler, few have taken this account of perception very seriously. It is now possible to assert that it is probably wrong. (However, see Henle, 1984, for a vigorous defence of the general principle of isomorphism.)

First, while it is true that the disturbance of activity in the central nervous system following sensory stimulation often outlasts that stimulation, it is not true that this involves very large fields or areas of the brain (Sperry, Miner and Meyers, 1955). Second, and more seriously, experiments have cast grave doubts on the existence in the brain of anything like the direct currents proposed by Köhler. Placing connected metal pins in the visual cortex of experimental animals should surely short-circuit such currents if they exist; the insertion of insulating mica plates into the same regions of the brain would be expected to block the spread of electricity. Both of these experiments have been performed and in neither case was the visual performance of the subjects seriously disrupted (Sperry and Miner, 1955; Sperry, Miner and Meyers, 1955). We must conclude that this important part of the Gestalt theory, in fact the basic explanation of Gestalt phenomena, is likely to be incorrect. (Once again, see Henle's (1984) paper for a criticism of these direct attacks on the Köhler model of cortical functioning.)

The inadequacy of two-dimensional displays

Because they wished to convince their readers through dramatic illustrations, and (presumably) because drawings are simpler to make than three-dimensional objects, the Gestaltists obtained many of their effects from flat patterns. Under these conditions, Wertheimer's laws of organization have not been seriously challenged: none has been shown to be actually wrong. Nor is the general phenomenon of figure–ground organization recognized as other than very important. However, the two-dimensional drawings which have been most commonly used to investigate these phenomena are not charac-teristic of all our daily experience: they are not what our eyes evolved to see. It is not surprising, therefore, that when three-dimensional arrays have been studied the results have sometimes cast doubt upon the adequacy of the Gestalt laws (Kaufman (1974) provides an excellent introduction to this more recent work). And there is at least one rival to the Gestalt view of figure–ground phenomena which places much more emphasis upon learned rather than innate factors (Hochberg, 1971).

In the next chapter, and elsewhere in this book, the concept of *ecological validity* will be discussed. For now, it suffices to define the phrase as meaning the naturalness of stimuli, how representative they are of the objects and events which organisms must deal with in order to survive. It must be said that many of the displays which the Gestaltists used in their work had very low ecological validity. This does not prove that Gestalt generalizations are invalid or that Gestalt claims about the laws of perception are seriously wrong, but simply that their choice of stimuli was often unfortunate and should have made them cautious about over-generalizing their findings. This criticism can be extended to the Gestalt work on illusions, which are fascinating and reliable phenomena, but how often do we experience strong illusions in everyday life?

Stimulus ratios in perception

The Gestalt movement was correct in stressing the role played by ratios between stimuli as determinants of how things will appear. Paper always looks white and coal black across a wide range of normal light intensities. What is the basis of this veridical perception? One answer, adopted by the Gestaltists, was that in this case the paper will always reflect *relatively* more light than coal no matter what the level of illumination. Similar arguments were advanced to explain other forms of perceptual constancy. Stimulus ratios appear to be important in perceiving.

Let us develop this further by adding some numbers to a possible case involving brightness (or lightness) constancy. Suppose that one surface reflects 25 per cent of light falling onto it, another 50 per cent, and that light of, say, 200 units intensity illuminates both surfaces. They will reflect 50 and 100 units respectively. Now double the illumination strength to 400 units: the surfaces will now reflect 100 and 200 units to the eye—although the illumination has doubled, the *ratio* of reflected light to the eye has not changed. This is the basis of the classic explanation of constancy which the Gestalt psychologists adopted to explain the unchanging lightness or brightness of surfaces under conditions of changing illumination.

Generally, there will be few real-life situations which differ markedly from the hypothetical example above. Reflectance is a property of surfaces: no change in illumination will alter ratios of reflection. The explanation of brightness constancy seems secure. There is, however, one situation in which ratios of reflected light can be altered, this is when additional light is added, not to the surfaces but to stimulus energy on its way to the eye. This can happen when we look at things through a glass surface when that surface is reflecting additional light from other sources—one example is looking through the reflected glare of a shop window. To illustrate this point, consider again the numerical illustration above: adding 100 units to the light which has already been reflected from the two surfaces will produce intensities at the eye of 200 and 300 units. The ratio has now changed from 1 : 2 to 2 : 3. So when we look *through* a reflection the ratio basis of brightness or lightness constancy has gone.

Gilchrist and Jacobsen (1983) noticed something which any Gestaltist could have seen: things do not seem markedly different when see them through reflections. They describe an elegant experiment in which scenes were viewed through a sloping glass surface onto which additional light could be projected, thus altering the ratios of lights coming from objects in the scenes. This additional light is known as a *veiling luminance*. The experiment showed that, provided the scene is real (that is, it contains three-dimensional objects) *perception is veridical through a veiling luminance*. In other words, lightness constancy remains even though the ratios of reflected lights from the surfaces have changed. Thus, while the Gestalt emphasis on ratios is probably close to the truth, this cannot be the whole story. We still do not know exactly *how* perceivers use ratios to achieve constancy in perception, or how they cope when the ratios are corrupted, as in the above example. Similar conclusions have been arrived at by those who have examined the role of ratios of wavelengths of light in the perception of colour (see, for example, Land, 1985). Generally, we can suggest that most students of perception accept the importance of stimulus ratios in perception, particularly in the perceptual constancies. However, there are cases in which it seems that there must be other effects at work in everyday perception, some of which are dependent upon more cognitive, knowledge-based processes involving judgement, familiarity with objects and surfaces, 'allowing for illumination', and so on (see Rock, 1995, for a lucid discussion of some of the theoretical problems in this area).

Stimulus ratios in learning

The discovery that an animal trained to go to the darker of two grey stimuli will subsequently transfer this learning to an even darker grey was held to be an important extension of a Gestalt principle from human perception to animal behaviour. It was claimed that the demonstration was particularly embarrassing to stimulus–response theories of animal discrimination learning. It suffices to say that in fact stimulus–response theories can be made to account not only for this result but for those instances when the phenomenon does not occur (when, for example, the differences between the various stimuli are very large). This was demonstrated by Spence 1956).

Nativism

If perceptual experience is a direct reflection of underlying (electrical) brain forces, and if these forces obey physical laws, then it follows that this experience should be as fixed and rigid as the laws of physics demand. Gestalt theorists might have been willing to concede that Köhler's field forces have not been confirmed by subsequent research, but it seems very likely that they would have clung tenaciously to some form of nativism, given the philosophical origins described at the start of this chapter. Thus the Gestalt view must be that while perception can be influenced by attentional processes and the effects of such variables as familiarity, practice and learning, it is basically fixed in nature. Two tests of this position are possible: first humans and animals should not be able to reorganize their perceptions; second, there should be perceptual competence at birth. Both these issues have been addressed in experimental investigations.

The obvious theoretical importance of these questions—whether perception is rigid or flexible, and the degree to which it is innate rather than acquired—has led to much research. Animals and humans have been subjected to a number of procedures in which their sensory inputs were distorted or blocked. The severity and bizarreness of these manipulations has varied greatly.

Distortion and deprivation studies

1. *Mild sensory distortion.* This has frequently been employed as a test of the flexibility of perception. Such mild distortion has taken the form, for

example, of having people wear tinted lenses for long periods. After a time (as any wearer of sunglasses knows) the tinted world reverts to normal: one has adapted to the slight change in the nature of the light entering the eye. Those who have worn prisms which tilt the world in a certain direction also report complete adaptation to this distorted input.

2. *Severe sensory distortion.* This can be achieved by lens or mirror systems which completely invert the world. Here reports of adaptation must be treated with extreme caution. It is obviously difficult to know just what complete reorganization of inverted vision would look like, and many reports are extremely ambiguous. Certainly there is *adjustment* to severe distortion: in one famous experiment (I. Köhler, 1955) the subject was eventually able to ride a bicycle while wearing inverting lenses—but it is not clear whether this is accompanied by phenomenal reinversion of the world.

Many animals are able to recover from moderate sensory distortion, but in extreme cases, such as when the eyeball of an amphibian was loosened, rotated through 90 degrees and then replaced in the socket, no adaptation took place. Flies with their heads rotated 180 degrees fail to show any adaptation to the consequent inversion of their visual inputs. (For an account of some of these dramatic experiments see Sperry, 1951.)

The experimental literature in this area is too large to review comprehensively. At this point we shall simply assert that (a) animals and humans can adapt to many forms of mild sensory distortion, (b) 'higher' animals such as monkeys and chimpanzees are better at adapting (are more flexible) than 'lower' animals such as flies, amphibians and chickens, and (c) it is doubtful if any species can completely adapt to very severe distortion (although such a statement risks being tautological). Readers wishing to make their own assessments of this literature should consult some of the original publications cited above and at the end of this chapter.

Our overall assessment of the evidence from distortion studies is that it suggests that basic perceptual organization is relatively inflexible. This accords with the nativist stance taken by Gestalt theorists, although it must be added that some contemporary workers might disagree with this conclusion; many would argue for the old Scottish verdict, not proven.

Animal deprivation experiments

These no longer seem to hold the promise they once did. Rearing an animal without, say, vision, and then testing its visual perception is probably not the way to discover whether visual capacities are innate: the animal is an abnormal animal; suddenly acquiring vision may be frightening; the animal may not be motivated to do well with its new sense. These problems may be insuperable.

Human deprivation studies

Such studies have been used to compare the visual abilities of those who have recovered from blindness with those of the normally sighted. Here, too, problems of adjustment and motivation are to be expected, and this is borne out in many reports. Here is a tentative summary of the literature.

The newly sighted are not simply people who have lacked vision, but people who have learned to live with their other senses. In this they are atypical perceivers when their vision is restored. What does seem to be generally true is that such people have great difficulties in organizing and making sense of their new visual world. A nativist would not be dismayed by this discovery, for reasons such as those outlined earlier. However, the nativist position gains some limited support from these studies in the general finding that most subjects who have been studied appear to perceive lines, edges, brightness and colours without difficulty (see, for example, Senden, 1960; Gregory and Wallace, 1963; Valvo, 1971). Equally striking is the fact that in most reports it appears as though the organization of the world into figure and ground takes place quickly and spontaneously, as the Gestaltists would have predicted. This evidence suggests that at least some of our visual capacities are innately organized and require little or no learning.

Infant vision research

This, in our opinion, is currently the best way of examining the relative importance of innate *versus* acquired factors in perception. To the student of the history of perception this is a fascinating area. If one looks at the literature of the 1940s and compares it with contemporary work, one becomes aware of a steady swing from the empiricist emphasis of the early workers such as Hebb (1949) to a growing belief that the newborn is amazingly competent. It is not the infants who have changed in this 40-year period, it is the skill of experimenters. The great difficulty has always been how to communicate with the newborn. As the techniques for doing this have improved—using conditioning methods, measuring eye-movements, habituating the infant to one stimulus before presenting a different one, recording changes in heart rate—so the age at which infants can be shown to have certain perceptual abilities has moved inexorably downwards. Newborn infants show shape constancy (Slater and Morison, 1985); they prefer their mothers' voices (DeCasper and Fifer, 1980); they will follow with their eyes a head shape bearing normal features more intently than one with the features scrambled—this within five minutes of birth (Goren, Sarty and Wu, 1975; Dziurawiec and Ellis, 1986); their colour vision resembles that of adults (Bornstein, Kessen and Weiskopf, 1976).

None of these studies proves that the world of newborns is the same as ours. It must certainly lack associations, meaning and familiarity. Perhaps their experience resembles ours during those first few moments when we awaken in a strange room: we see everything, but nothing makes sense. And it is likely, particularly from animal studies and from studies of children born with visual defects (see, for example, Blakemore and Cooper, 1970), that there are *critical periods* following birth during which experience of the world moulds the developing senses. For example, if an infant is born with a squint and this is corrected immediately, normal stereoscopic vision will develop. But if there is a delay in treating the squint, then when the deviant eye is brought into line surgically the child's visual performance may be permanently impaired: it looks as though those cells in the visual cortex which are binocularly driven must receive appropriate input in the first 18 months of life if they are to develop correctly.

But even if the existence of critical periods is recognized, there remains a mass of evidence to show the existence of perceptual abilities shortly after birth. This throws doubt on the claim that we must learn to perceive and is strong evidence in support of the nativist position adopted by the Gestalt theorists.

Conclusion

Clearly, the above reviews have been biased to studies of humans and the 'higher' primates, for obvious reasons. It is important to say at this point that a very strong version of nativism can be defended if discussion is restricted to the perceptual abilities of simpler organisms. Many creatures show complex behaviour the moment they emerge into the world, and as this may involve things as complicated as flying through the environment, it is clear that their visual powers must be intact from the start: insects mostly do not bump into things. There is no doubt that perception can be innately organized, but the interesting question is whether this is the case in us and species similar to us.

Given the amount of evidence described above, we can assert that there are good reasons for believing that a major part of our ability to perceive is innately determined. While this evidence could be marshalled to support *any* nativist theory, it remains true that it is the Gestalt theorists who put forward the most explicit and influential version of nativism and provoked much of the stimulating research which we have attempted to outline.

MORE RECENT DEVELOPMENTS

It is impossible in a short chapter to do justice to all the research into Gestalt phenomena which has been published since the pioneering work by the founders of the movement. This section will offer a brief review of a selection of subsequent researches, with a greater emphasis on the most recent work.

The review will concentrate on those findings which, we may guess, would have seemed exciting or important to the pioneers of the Gestalt movement.

Grouping by similarity

Beck (1966) subjected one of Wertheimer's laws, grouping by similarity, to an ingenious test. Simple shapes were used to generate textures. A display comprised three sections, each formed from multiples of a simple shape. The observer's task was to indicate which of the two boundaries between the textures was the most natural or salient. An example of one of Beck's displays is shown in Figure 3.9. Note that in this case, the stronger boundary is that between the upright and slanted 'T's. However, observers' choices of boundaries did not strongly agree with their judgments of the relative degrees of similarity between the three sets of elements. Grouping in terms of lightness or colour is easily predictable from relative similarity; grouping in terms of shape is unfortunately not as simple as this: we may conclude that this important rule concerning grouping is still not fully understood.

Symmetry and information

The concept of symmetry is important in Gestalt theory, and is another of Wertheimer's laws. Attneave (1955) brought a new way of thinking to the problem of symmetry, namely the application of Information theory. Attneave's idea can be described by referring to the familiar game of 'battleships', in which contestant A draws a shape on graph paper and opponent B attempts to discover the shape by naming squares and asking whether each

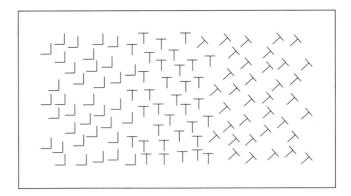

Figure 3.9 Grouping by shape similarity. Two boundaries form between the three textures: which is the more natural break? (From Beck, 1966. Reprinted with permission)

does or does not contain a fragment of the shape. The game is to find the shape in as few moves as possible.

Information theory links amounts of information with degrees of uncertainty. Thus the final word in the sentence, 'God save the . . .', is associated with relatively little information as it is so predictable. The next digit in the sequence 301265 . . . is associated with a relatively large amount of information because it is so hard to predict. The advent of a theory of information was an exciting one as it offered the possibility of quantifying information capacities in systems as diverse as television channels and neurons.

Returning to the Attneave research, one reason why symmetrical shapes may be easier to recognize and remember than asymmetrical ones may lie in the fact that the very existence of symmetry means that the shape contains less information. To illustrate this point, imagine again the game of battleships. Once one has hit enough correct squares to form half a symmetrical shape—such as an ink bottle—guessing the remainder is easy. Attneave was thus able to link the ease of recognition of shapes and symmetry by means of an informational analysis. This was a very interesting result.

Research interest in symmetry has persisted and has led to some very interesting ideas and discoveries. A number of theorists have approached the perception of symmetry from an evolutionary point of view. The fact is that many living things show symmetry, particularly bilateral symmetry. This is as true of humans as it is of trees. Further, many objects in the world—fruits, for example—are approximately rotationally symmetrical. As a result, they will give rise to images on the retina which are bilaterally symmetrical. In contrast, non-living things may be highly asymmetrical: think of rocks, lumps of ore, piles of scrub, clouds and cascades. A perceptual system tuned to symmetry might have considerable survival value.

Symmetry and genetics

Some of the most interesting and provocative recent findings concerning symmetry are those reported by the Danish biologist, Anders Pape Møller.

Møller has argued as follows. In a symmetrical organism, perfect symmetry is optimal in the sense that its development represents the ability of the individual to generate the same phenotype under the varying conditions of the environment. In this sense, degree of symmetry represents the genetic fitness of an organism. If this idea is correct, then we might expect that highly symmetric organisms should be favoured in sexual selection. A selection of Møller's findings will show how research tends to confirm this prediction.

The tail feathers of the swallow (*Hirundo rustica*) show differences in symmetry in different birds. The symmetry of these sexual ornaments was manipulated. Møller then found that females prefer those males having greatest symmetry (Møller, 1992). Other studies of the swallow showed first that the more symmetrical females laid their eggs earlier (an advantage) and were preferred by males; similarly, the more symmetrical male swallows were more successful in acquiring mates (Møller, 1994). The bumble bee (*Bombus terrestris*) prefers symmetrical flowers, as these produce more nectar, providing better rewards for the bee. Experimental manipulation of symmetry in flowers also affected the behaviour of the bees in the predicted direction (Møller, 1995a).

Although these findings are highly interesting, the species studied are very different from humans in structure and complexity. Is it possible to demonstrate any comparable relationships between genetic fitness and preference for symmetry in humans? The answer is, yes. Consider the case of the female human breast. For a given age group, breasts clearly vary in size. More interestingly, for our purpose, measurements show that breasts also vary significantly in symmetry. Following the animal studies above, it might be argued that maintaining breast symmetry through variations in the environment provides a 'health certificate'. Is this true? The answer appears to be yes. It has been found that women in two different cultures, Spain and New Mexico, who possess higher degrees of breast symmetry have a greater chance of having children and show greater fecundity overall.

> Males that acquire mates with low levels of breast fluctuating asymmetry will thus tend to sire daughters with little breast fluctuating asymmetry. This will provide choosy males with a sexual selection advantage because their daughters may experience higher mating success, earlier reproduction, and higher fecundity.
>
> (Møller, Soler and Thornhills, 1995)

It is obviously not easy in modern times to defend the idea that there is any evolutionary selection currently occurring, as Møller would surely agree. The basic selection described above may have taken place in our distant evolutionary past. And yet, how interesting to find symmetry and its possible evolutionary advantage appearing in such a markedly different context from that in which Wertheimer worked 70 years ago.

Work by Gaetano Kanizsa and colleagues

One of the present author's great pleasures is to reread the selection of papers by Gaetano Kanizsa, *Organization in Vision* (Kanizsa, 1979). Kanizsa was a distinguished experimental psychologist at the University of Trieste. He was also an artist. This adds to the appeal of his work, much of which is illustrated with fascinating perceptual demonstrations—maintaining the Gestalt tradition. He was not, however, a rigid adherent to all aspects of the general Gestalt theory, mainly because he saw perception as a constructive process

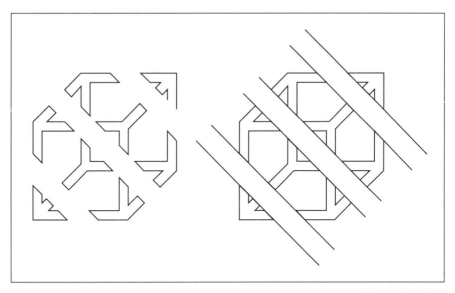

Figure 3.10 Kanizsa's demonstration of the difference between thinking and seeing. The cube on the left can be imagined, but it is hard to see it as such. In the cube on the right, amodal completion takes place and the perception of a cube behind the three stripes is effortless. (From Kanizsa, Gaetano, *Organization in Vision* (Praeger Publishers, an imprint of Greenwood Publishing Group, Inc., Westport, CT, USA, 1979. Reprinted with permission.)

capable of going beyond the information given by stimulation (a theoretical position which will be examined more fully in a later chapter on empiricism). Although Kanizsa believed that seeing and thinking are related, he recognized that they must be distinct processes. Using the familiar Gestalt tactic of the striking demonstration, Kanizsa provides direct evidence to support his position. Note the different impression given by the two cubes represented in Figure 3.10.

A single example from the numerous researches published by Kanizsa and his colleagues will suffice to show the style of this approach.

The original Gestaltists rarely sought to quantify the phenomenon which interested them. Here is an example, by one of Kanizsa's colleagues, of how the earlier Gestaltists might have quantified something of interest to them. The effect relates to figure and ground separation, which has a prominent place in Gestalt theory.

Note the two upper patterns in Figure 3.11. In the left-hand pattern the circle is generally seen as lying in front of the rectangle; in the right-hand pattern, the circle appears to be behind the rectangle. What causes this change?

Petter (1956) discovered the ruling governing this phenomenon: it is delightfully simple and deserves the name 'Petter's Law'. The fact that we can

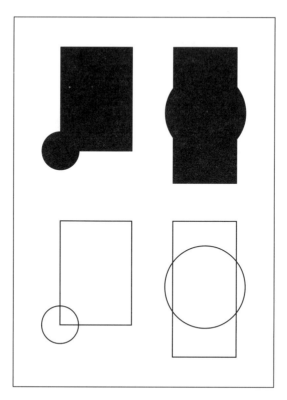

Figure 3.11 Petter's Law. It can be seen that the direction of overlap favours the shorter amodal contour length required by completion

see such displays as *overlapping* separate figures implies that we have supplied something extra to the displays. Kanizsa would call the conceptually necessary but perceptually invisible lines needed to complete the figures, *amodal contours*. Measuring the lengths of these contours is all that it takes to demonstrate the operation of Petter's Law. For what is found in examples such as Figure 3.11 is that *the figure requiring the smaller length of amodal contour for its completion will appear in front.*[4] What an elegant finding, and how exciting to discover yet another example of a minimum principle at work in visual perception. With hindsight, we can regret that the early Gestalt workers did not do this simple piece of measurement. It was all that was needed to find a quantitative relationship between figure and ground, and might have given impetus to further quantification.

---

[4] This law can be overriden by meaning: if the amodal contour would complete, say, the tail of a cat, it will tend to be seen in front whatever its length.

Coding theory and the Minimum Principle

Restle (1979) set out to quantify some effects discovered by Johansson (1950, 1977). Over a number of years, Johansson has examined the ways in which subjects see simple moving dot displays. In a typical experiment three or more dots move smoothly and rhythmically back and forth across a display. The dots may move at different speeds, in various directions, and may be in or out of phase. Johansson found that the perception of these displays is dynamic in the sense that the dots are seen to be connected in some way, or to represent, say, the ends of rigid structures. In one display, for example, two outer dots move up and down in opposite directions while a central dot remains stationary. What one sees in this case looks like a rigid rod swinging around a central pivot. When a row of dots move different distances, the inner ones moving furthest, one sees something like a skipping rope swinging in and out of the plane of the display. The effects are very beautiful and very compelling.

The questions Restle asked were: How can the movements of the dots be described or coded *objectively*?' and 'How do these descriptions correlate with what viewers see?' For example, one way of coding the displays would be to treat each dot as independent. Then one parameter will be required for a dot's starting position, one for its amplitude of movement, one for its phase (when it starts to move compared with other dots), one for its angle of tilt relative to the vertical, and so on. In such a manner one can produce a completely objective description of the movement of the dots, one which could be used, say, to program a computer to drive the displays. But it is also possible to treat the dots as combinations. For example, if a number of dots move together in phase and across the same distance then a single set of parameters will code the motion of one of them and additional parameters will code the spacings and repetitions. This alternative way of coding will be equally objective, but it will of course be different.

Restle did an exhaustive coding exercise in which the various hierarchies of dot clusters used in the Johansson displays were coded, the dots treated as independent or linked in some manner. The results of this exercise are highly intriguing. Not surprisingly, the coding of dots as independent events requires the maximum number of movement parameters. When dots are treated as groups the number of parameters required to code the movement drops, and the more intimate the grouping the fewer the number of coding parameters required. The exciting finding is this: if one wishes to predict how the moving displays will be seen, then the movement configuration requiring *the fewest objective parameters* is the best bet. And the greater the discrepancy between the number of parameters needed for independent coding and for the coding of a particular grouping, the stronger is the tendency for observers to report the latter.

But the tendency to see the displays as simple, grouped and coherent is exactly what the Gestalt theorists meant by Prägnanz. The difference is that the Gestaltists proposed the principle (and gave examples) but offered no means of quantifying it. Here is an example where Prägnanz, operating as a minimum principle, is clearly at work. But now we are offered an objective measure of its effects. This is an important development.

Shepard's apparent motion experiment

This review of modern research relating to the Gestalt theory will end with a brief description of a remarkably interesting experiment by the American psychologist, Roger Shepard.

Some of Shepard's best-known researches have been into the nature of internal representations. This has led him to ask certain questions concerning Gestalt principles of organization. Shepard agrees with the idea, described earlier in this chapter, that visual systems attuned to symmetry and other principles of perceptual grouping have survival value. He goes further, however. The world is in three-dimensional Euclidean space. Objects move in this world, but their movement is constrained by an associated kinematic geometry. For example, a pair of gloves lying on a flat surface are mirror images of each other. No rotation in the plane of the surface can make them *congruent*, so that their outlines exactly match when one is placed over the other. Either the left or right glove must be rotated in the third dimension for congruence to be achieved.

Early humans would not have survived without the ability to manipulate objects, and in doing so they would have been constrained by the laws of kinematic geometry. Shepard's intriguing idea is that this evolutionary past led to the constraints associated with these laws becoming internalized in our visual systems.

There is an infinite number of ways in which a rigid object at position A can be moved to position B in three-dimensional space. However, there is one simplest, most economical way of effecting this displacement, and this was published as a theorem by the mathematician Chasles (1830). This theorem proves the existence of '. . . a unique axis in space such that the object can be moved from A to B by a rotation about that axis together with a simultaneous translation along that same axis: a helical twist or "screw displacement"' (quoted from Shepard, 1984). At this point the reader should be reminded of some of the material included earlier in this chapter in the review of the Law of Least Action or the Minimum Principle.

From these theoretical ideas Shepard designed an experiment on apparent motion (see Shepard, 1984), one form of which was described earlier in our discussion of the phi phenomenon. Pairs of outline polygon shapes were presented in rapid alternation. In each pair, one polygon represented a different view of the other after it had gone through various transformations and combinations of transformations. For example, one member of the pair might

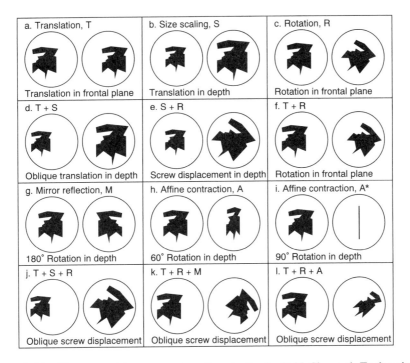

Figure 3.12 Shapes used in apparent motion studies by R.N. Shepard. Each pair of shapes represents a type of transformation. When the shapes are alternated, the apparent motion follows the minimum paths predicted by Chasles's theorem. (From Shepard, 1984; copyright American Psychological Association and R.N. Shepard)

represent a rotation of the other in the frontal plane; a rotation and a change of size—representing a shift in the third dimension; or a mirror reflection; and so on. These different transformations are shown in Figure 3.12.

The question now, of course, is: What path will observers see the object take during its apparent movement? The answer is,

> . . . in each of these cases, if the rate of alternation is not too great, the motion tends to be experienced as the rigid transformation prescribed by Chasles's theorem.
>
> (Shepard, 1984)

Once again, here is a very important and thought-provoking result.

Petter's Law and Shepard's discovery suggest that the search for other examples of the Minimum Principle at work in perception may prove to be a highly fruitful enterprise. All credit to the Gestalt pioneers.

GENERAL REMARKS ON THE GESTALT THEORY

Subsequent research in perception owes a great debt to the movement started by Wertheimer, Koffka and Köhler. Each of these men had a good eye for important phenomena. Little of what they researched seems trivial in retrospect. Indeed, many of the phenomena which they uncovered are now seen to present some of the major challenges to perceptual theory. The Gestalt theorists had breadth. They wrote well and with conviction. Their phenomenological programme—to explain everyday perceiving—was a valid one. Their belief in the innate basis of much of perception may well prove to be true. The recognition of similarities between perceptual processes and aspects of problem solving may prove to have been an invaluable insight.

What, then, of the flaws in the Gestalt approach to perception? In the first place the central explanatory device, the brain model, is almost certainly incorrect. Had the contemporary knowledge of neurophysiology been more advanced Köhler would probably have avoided this trap. But the remainder of the Gestalt theory (in contrast to Gestalt research) is also faulty by modern standards, and it is worth trying to explain why this should be so.

At the start of this chapter it was stated that the Gestalt psychologists were motivated by a philosophical conviction that perception must be a centrally organized dynamic process. The rate at which supporting evidence for this position was accumulated is a very impressive achievement. Most of the key Gestalt phenomena had been described and explored within 20 years of the first statements of the theory: figure–ground, relational effects, whole–part interactions, the constancies, laws of grouping and the tendency towards Prägnanz had all been presented to a wide readership in lucid books and papers.

But too much of a scientist's time can be spent demonstrating the correctness of a theory. We have already listed some of the inadequacies of the Gestalt theory: experimental results which should have provoked further research rather than argument—the investigation of Prägnanz being a good example. The Gestalt psychologists were fine polemicists, but debating skilfully is not the same as being right.

Much of Gestalt theory is circular; for example, having demonstrated the powerful tendency to organize perceptual inputs into simple, coherent experiences, the Gestaltists allowed descriptions of this phenomenon to serve as explanations. The concept of Prägnanz is a good example: that is, perception tends to be as good as conditions allow. Why? Because of Prägnanz (a tautology) or field forces in the brain (speculative and untestable at the time).

Gestalt psychology contains few references to Darwin. As a result there is little concern in Gestalt theory for what we would now term the ecology from which stimuli arise. The dangers of this have been outlined earlier. In terms of the general model offered in Chapter 1, it can be said that the Gestalt psychologists should have included more regions in their theory; they might then have been forced to think more about the real-life stimuli which shaped the evolution of perception. We have shown how profitable such an approach can be in our descriptions of the work of Møller and Shepard.

Finally, the Gestaltists tended to concentrate upon strong effects which can be reliably demonstrated. This was a successful tactic. But much of perception may not be like this. In the real world—the world of unreliable, uncertain stimuli—perceiving may involve processes of a statistical nature (as will be asserted in the next chapter). This is an unfortunate complication for the researcher, but if it is the truth it must be handled by an adequate theory. Gestalt theory did not find a place for such ideas.

These then are some of the criticisms which occur to one who looks back over the Gestalt movement. But the importance of this body of work cannot be doubted. Gestalt psychologists exerted a permanent influence on the psychology of perception. All who follow are indebted to the theory in some manner. And, despite what now look like strategic errors in the Gestaltists' approach, their movement still stands as a model of the literate, enthusiastic and creative approach to the problems of perception.

NOTES ON CHAPTER 3

We have occasionally expressed regret in this chapter over the fact that Gestalt psychologists did not pursue certain research problems more vigorously. One of the reasons was the tragic circumstances of their time. Several key figures in the movement suffered under the Nazi regime; some were forced to emigrate, to the detriment of their careers. Otto Selz, who worked on thinking, died in a concentration camp. Karl Duncker, famous for his ingenious studies of problem solving, committed suicide at the outbreak of the Second World War. Mandler and Mandler (1969) give an account of this tragic history.

Gestalt writings on perception are clear, accessible and very interesting. Readers wishing to learn more about this approach should start by reading original Gestalt documents, particularly the Köhler and Koffka references given in the text. (It may seem strange that a number of the references given below appeared so long after the start of the Gestalt theory. Many of these are English translations which appeared after the Gestalt theory became more widely known and the Gestalt psychologists had moved to the United States.)

Köhler's field theory of neural action is described in his book, *Dynamics in Psychology* (1940).

The source book by Ellis (1938) is invaluable and contains some of the best-known replies of Gestalt theorists to their critics. See particularly Koffka's *Reply to Benussi* and Köhler's *Reply to Müller*.

Petermann (1932) provides a useful description of Gestalt work on dynamic aspects of perception. Part 1 of this book contains a description of Köhler's views on physical Gestalten and his brain model.

Haber and Hershenson (1980) is a valuable introduction to studies of the development of perceptual mechanisms. (See their Chapter 13 for a discussion of infant studies.)

A central theme in this chapter has been that of perceptual organization. There is in fact a book with this title written by Michael Kubovy and James T. Pomeranz (1981). The work described therein (and in other publications by Kobovy) should now be read by interested readers. As this important work cannot be described briefly, it was decided to omit it from the present chapter rather than offer an inadequate account. It is, however, of the greatest interest and relevance.

One Gestalt psychologist who has not been referred to in the main text, but whose work deserves mention, is David Katz. See, for example his book, *Gestalt Psychology* (1951).

Readers who enjoy the style of the best Gestalt writings will also enjoy reading Michotte's work on the perception of causality (Michotte, 1946). This shares some of the characteristics of Gestalt research and the demonstrations, which are easy to set up, are extremely compelling.

The Johansson (1964) reference describes experiments which would have been of great interest to Gestalt theorists.

The distinguished contemporary psychologist, Julian Hochberg, has attempted to extend and improve some Gestalt ideas on visual perception. See Hochberg (1968, 1973) for an account of some highly interesting perceptual researches.

Interesting applications of Gestalt theory to the arts are described by Arnheim (1949, 1956, 1969). Arnheim has also written interestingly on the precise meaning of the term *Prägnanz* (see Arnheim, 1987).

For a defence of Gestalt views on brain processes see Henle (1984).

We have run the risk of overemphasising the Gestaltists' nativism. In fairness it should be pointed out that, for example, Koffka (1924) was willing to consider the possibility that experience and language could influence the development of colour vision in children. In the same book, Koffka takes a very moderate position when discussing human development from empiricist and nativist viewpoints.

Applying the Minimum Principle to visual phenomena is not as straightforward as we may have suggested. Is 'simplicity' phenomenal, descriptive, or related to economy of process? See Hatfield and Epstein (1985) for a thorough analysis of this problem.

The enduring validity of Gestalt laws is demonstrated by a display to be seen with increasing frequency in public buildings in Britain. The reader may care to say which laws of organization underlie the way we perceive Figure 3.13.

Figure 3.13

4

Brunswik's probabilistic functionalism

The second theory to be described is 'probabilistic functionalism', which was essentially the work of one man, Egon Brunswik (1903–1955). Brunswik left no school of followers, his work is rarely cited in modern writings, and no subsequent group of workers has ever assumed the label, 'probabilistic functionalist'. There are, however, good reasons for including this short chapter on Brunswik's work. We shall attempt to justify this claim by describing Brunswik's theory as sympathetically as possible, before offering a number of criticisms.

The remainder of this chapter is organized as follows.

- Egon Brunswik
- A general outline of Brunswik's work
- The terminology of probabilistic functionalism
- Brunswik's lens model
- Brunswik's empirical research
- An evaluation of probabilistic functionalism
- General remarks on probabilistic functionalism

EGON BRUNSWIK

Egon Brunswik was born in Budapest in 1903. As a child he spoke Hungarian and German. His university education took place in Vienna, where he worked under Karl Büller. It was there that Brunswik came to know the Vienna school of logical positivists, whose views were to influence his later career as experimenter and theoretician. In 1937 he moved to the University of California at Berkeley. He died in California at the age of 52.

Brunswik's work on perception is described in a number of papers in English and German. Detailed statements of his theoretical position are to be found in *The Conceptual Framework of Psychology* (1952) and *Perception and the Representative Design of Psychological Experiments* (1956), which was published posthumously.

A GENERAL OUTLINE OF BRUNSWIK'S WORK

In terms of our informal model or scheme in Chapter 1, we shall see that Brunswik concentrated upon the relationship between distal and proximal events and what the brain must do when the correlation between these is less than perfect.

It may be useful to begin with a general outline of Brunswik's thinking and its historical context before considering the details of his work.

Brunswik and the inference revolution

What Gigerenzer and Murray (1987) have called the inference revolution was nearing completion by the time Brunswik arrived in the United States for the final stage of his career. The inference revolution had two effects. First, it became increasingly natural to interpret a number of psychological processes in terms of statistical decision making, in a manner analogous to that involved in testing the truth or falsity of scientific hypotheses (we have illustrated this point in Chapter 2 when discussing changes in the concept of the sensory threshold). Second, by the 1940s the work of Fisher, Neyman and Pearson was beginning to provide psychologists with powerful tools for analysing data: the various tests of significance, such as the *t*-test and analysis of variance, are obvious examples. Between the mid-1930s (when Brunswik moved to America) and 1940, the total number of articles published in the psychological literature reporting tests of statistical significance was a mere 17. By 1960, five years after Brunswik's death, such reporting had become the norm. We shall show later how the lack of statistical sophistication among psychologists (including Brunswik) reduced the impact of Brunswik's novel and interesting ideas and made it difficult to refine and extend them.

The statistical nature of cues

One of Brunswik's most important achievements was to extend the notion of uncertainty within the individual perceiver, and ascribe it also to the physical world. Brunswik maintained that it is not just among sensory processes that the need for statistical evaluation and decision arises, but that the world itself is an uncertain place. He showed how the cues arising from objects and events in the world are commonly less than perfectly reliable. However, these imperfect cues seldom arise in isolation. Objects and events are frequently complex, and because of this they generate not one but many cues. The problem for the perceiver is how to arrive at rapid and generally valid perceptions of the world based on uncertain information conveyed by these varied cues.[1]

Brunswik's functionalism

Brunswik's functionalist approach convinced him that perceivers do in fact usually get things right; they would not survive if they did not. And they often get things right very quickly, which has obvious survival value. The question is, of course: How does all this happen? Brunswik's answer was that in order to understand perception we must begin by studying the environment or ecology from which perceptual processes evolved and in which they continue to function. And we must study this ecology in its full complexity, avoiding the artificiality of the controlled, single variable laboratory experiment. We shall only discover how perception functions if we observe it under complex, life-like conditions. His programme therefore called for 'representativeness' to replace control and artificiality, and was designed to allow observers to display the flexibility and subtlety which they needed in their dealings with the everyday world. Whether or not Brunswik's aims were achieved will be the focus of this chapter.

THE TERMINOLOGY OF PROBABILISTIC FUNCTIONALISM

An economical way to introduce Brunswik's approach is to explain some of the most important concepts and terminology which appear in his writings. Brunswik's writings can be difficult to follow on first reading, as will be shown. One source of difficulty is his difficult terminology: once this has been mastered, the writing becomes much easier to follow. A picture of the general approach will emerge via a description of the particulars.

Distal and proximal cues and the achievement of stability

As we study a perceiving organism it becomes increasingly obvious that its behaviour is directed, not to the pattern of stimulation on the sense receptor, but to the world beyond. Although it is possible to list *proximal* variables or *cues*, such as the sizes and shapes of retinal images, behaviour is directed not to these but to the actual properties of things and events out in the world, to *distal* variables. The researcher's main task is to discover the basis of this

---

[1] Hammond (1966) points out that, as a schoolboy, Brunswik studied the history of the Austro-Hungarian empire in both German and Hungarian and noticed discrepancies between the accounts, and that he may have remembered this later when thinking about the probabilistic nature of knowledge, cues and the environment.

achievement. Further, all that we know about our own perceiving (and what we can infer about perceiving in other species) tells us that the central achievement of perception is *stability*. For example, although images on the retina are constantly shifting because of head and eye movements, the phenomenal world is stable.

The probabilistic nature of cues

The environment, to use Brunswik's term, 'scatters its effects'. The cues which arise in the external world are only *probabilistic* and not fully dependable. But if this is true, what possible basis can there be for the achievement of perceptual stability? An example (not Brunswik's) will reinforce this important point. Suppose we are searching for edible fruit. Let us assume that edible fruit is in fact generally (a) darker, (b) redder, (c) softer and (d) sweeter. Obviously, darker and redder are visual cues, softer is tactile, sweeter is gustatory: the environment is scattering its effects. And these cues, the only ones available, are all imperfect—they all carry some risk. Not all ripe fruit is red, nor is all red fruit edible. Sweetness often indicates edibility, but some poisonous fruits are sweet. Some fruit is less edible when soft, and some soft fruit will be rotten.

Vicarious functioning and the perceiver as an intuitive statistician

What can the perceiver do, faced with such uncertainty? We must remember that for millions of years such problems were, literally, a matter of life or death. Brunswik's answer was that in order to survive, the perceiver must be able to act as an *intuitive statistician*. It is necessary to weight and combine cues and shift from those which are not available to others which are. As cues are varied and commonly have reliabilities of less than 1.0, the environment is described as being *vicariously mediated*. The response to vicarious mediation is *vicarious functioning* in the perceiver. Thus flexibility in perception must be accompanied by flexibilty of response: organisms are clearly goal-directed. An experimental animal, prevented from gaining access to reward in a usual manner, will find another solution to the problem. A rat which has learned to run through a maze will swim if the maze is flooded.

Perception, then, is *uncertainty-geared*. It aims for '. . . smallness of error at the expense of the highest frequency of precision'. And as perception involves the evaluation of evidence from different sources, the estimation of relative probabilities and decisions about the attainment of goals, it clearly shares many of the properties of thinking. There are differences, however. Thinking aims at definite answers, it is 'certainty-geared'. Thinking is deterministic and discontinuous; it is characterized by 'sudden attainment', often following lengthy pauses. These qualities are sufficiently different from perception for the latter to require a special term: *ratiomorphic*. Thus a clever person will not necessarily be a better perceiver. And illusions commonly persist even when they have been 'explained' to us (Brunswik once referred to this as 'the stupidity of the senses').

The validity of cues

Validity is an important concept in Brunswik's theory. The nature of the physical world, and the structure of the various sense organs, creates relationships between distal and proximal variables. For example, one impressive aspect of vision is its stability. Researchers can measure the size, distance and position of any object in a field of view. From this list of distal variables we can calculate the sizes and positions of retinal images (or, more conveniently, we can take photographs from the observer's position and use these as substitutes for the retina). These new values tell us about proximal variables. In Brunswik's opinion, the task remaining for the researcher is to discover the relationship between the distal and proximal variables, for here must lie the key to the achievement of perceptual stability. The relationship will seldom be perfect and simple, of course: distant objects usually form smaller images than near objects, but very small objects form small images even when they are near.

How might the relationship between distal and proximal variables be quantified? Brunswik suggests that the *correlation coefficient* is the most appropriate measure. The magnitude of the coefficient offers a useful index of the *ecological validity* of a particular cue—retinal image size in the example above. Ecological validity will seldom be perfect, as we have shown, but obviously some cues will be better than others and this will be reflected in higher correlations.

The ecological validity of a cue indicates its potential usefulness for an organism, but does not reveal whether or not the cue is actually used. The researcher must now ascertain whether or not a potential cue has *functional validity*. Consider, for example, the role of the two eyes in stereoscopic vision. It is known that this form of depth perception is based upon the small differences between left- and right-eye views which exist because of the lateral separation between the eyes. The resulting retinal disparity is a powerful source of information concerning an object's position in the third dimension: it has high ecological validity. But it is of no help to a small minority of people who lack the ability to fuse information from the two eyes. For these 'stereo-blind' individuals the ecologically valid cue has no functional validity. In contrast, people have been shown to base their judgements of the intelligence of others on aspects of their appearance. For example, wearers of spectacles tend to be judged as more intelligent; but as this is not in fact true, we can say that spectacle wearing may have high functional validity (it is used as a cue) but low ecological validity (don't trust guesses about intelligence based on appearance).

To summarize so far. Brunswik's writings suggest an analogy between a perceiver and a boxer who is fighting to survive. On no account must the boxer take a hard punch to a critical area, but he must always be ready to seize his own opportunities to attack. It is vital to anticipate the opponent's moves: which is the real threat and which is the feint? The boxer needs clues, ways of predicting what will happen in the next fraction of a second. The opponent will inevitably give some hints—movements of the arms and legs, changes of expression, shifts of gaze—but none of these is entirely to be trusted. A well-matched fight is in part a gamble: the first fighter to predict accurately will survive; errors will be punished. And there is no set of rules, no textbook of boxing, which can guarantee success. It all depends on getting things right at the time, with speed rather than precision.

BRUNSWIK'S LENS MODEL

Brunswik considered this to be an important part of his theory. The model was meant to illustrate how perception involves a kind of focusing: the scattered and mutually substitutable cues arising from the environment must somehow be gathered together for possible use. Perception involves a focusing of cues, it 'achieves' distal objects and it is towards these that responses are directed.

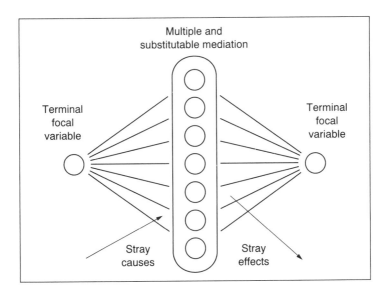

Figure 4.1   Brunswik's lens model (from Brunswik, 1952)

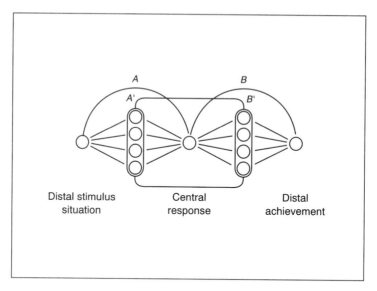

Figure 4.2   A double-lens version of Brunswik's model. *A* and *B* are functional areas. *A* ' and *B* ' are central processes which mediate between substitutable stimuli. High correlations between responses (verbal reports, pointing, button-pressing, etc.) suggest that they too are substitutable and arise from central goal-directed processes, represented by a circle in the figure. (From Leeper, 1966)

In its original form, the lens model treated perception as analogous to a single bi-concave lens (Figure 4.1). Later versions reflect Brunswik's increasing recognition of the importance of central, ratiomorphic processes: habits, evaluations, and predispositions can all influence behaviour. And it is (trivially) true that central factors must underlie mutually substitutable responses: we can respond to a stimulus by speaking or pushing a button if asked to do so. For these reasons a pair of bi-convex lenses may be more appropriate as a model of perceptual processes (Figure 4.2).

Brunswik believed that his lens model could guide the quantitative assessment of particular perceptual achievements and thus assist researchers. In an illustrative exercise (Brunswik, 1956, Figure 10) data from a study of size constancy are summarized in a lens model. Photographs of a real scene were taken and the actual and proximal (or photographic) sizes of objects compared. Other cues to distance were recorded. Observers then judged the sizes of objects from the photographs. Correlations between object and image sizes yielded values for ecological validities, and correlations between cues and judgements yielded functional validities. The various cues available in the photographs (for example, size and vertical position) could then be ranked in terms of their relative importance. Although Brunswik did not do this (he did elsewhere), it was now possible to use the correlation coefficients to trace 'principal rays' through the lens, revealing the basis of the form of perceptual stability represented by size constancy. In other words, people can judge the sizes of familiar objects in naturalistic photographs—the overall reduction in size does not greatly hinder them—and the lens model can reveal the basis of this attainment.

The lens model will not be discussed further. As a way of conceptualizing various aspects of perception it can be useful; it shaped the opening parts of this book. As a means of gaining deep insights into perception, the lens model appears to have little to offer; a conclusion which is reinforced by experience with students who appear to gain little understanding even of Brunswik's own work by concentrating on this single part. It should be said of the lens model, however, that it is one of the earliest examples of this type of thinking in the history of perceptual research. And Brunswik himself thought it important.

BRUNSWIK'S EMPIRICAL RESEARCHES

Brunswik's style of thinking can become more understandable when his own empirical investigations are studied. Some of these are less valuable for what they achieved than for what they attempted. This review will omit Brunswik's earlier, more orthodox researches and will concentrate on some of his most original publications.

Brunswik's experiments are unusual. They cannot be described as systematic explorations of a group of phenomena. Nor do they constitute critical tests of a theory. Rather, they are demonstrations which allow some of Brunswik's ideas to be presented in ways that make them more understandable and memorable. We shall describe only three examples of Brunswik's researches, which will give a fair impression of his originality. The reader should be reminded that, at the time they were published, there was almost nothing like these experiments in the research literature.

Judging coins

In many currencies, coins vary in both size and value; commonly these two variables co-vary—larger coins are worth more.

Brunswik assembled some roughly circular clusters of Turkish coins (he was working in Anakara at the time). The standard cluster comprised 40 2½-cent coins with a total area of 16 units and a total value of four Turkish units. Observers who were familiar with the coins were then asked to judge a series of comparison displays and compare them with the standard in terms of (a) area, (b) numerosity or (c) value. What emerged was that judgements in terms of one variable were affected by others (the results are described in Brunswik, 1956). For example, perceived area increased with increased value. This was also true of perceived numerosity.

Similar results were found in another experiment where observers adjusted the height of an elongated rectangle in order to match the area of a standard. Here, observers selected heights which were too great: the long thin shapes were perceived as having smaller areas.

These results supported Brunswik's claim that in perceiving the complex world, from which numerous proximal cues arise simultaneously, what is perceived is a *perceptual compromise*. This idea was later refined by Helson (see Helson, 1947) who showed that, for example, the perception of coloured surfaces can be biased systematically by controlled changes in context and illumination. Most recently, perceptual compromise has been invoked by Day in his attempts to explain certain geometric illusions (see, for example, Day, 1989). Thus the distortions occurring in the perception of the Müller–Lyer illusion may represent perceptual compromises between the perceived length of the shafts and the perceived extents of the entire configurations, which vary according to the direction of the arrow lines—inwards or outwards.

Perceptual compromises are not the same thing as the powerful stimulus interactions demonstrated by the Gestalt psychologists. They do tell us one thing however: if the perception of certain stimulus dimensions can be affected by the presence of others, this must be taken into account in experimental research. This is clearly a complicating factor of great importance. If Brunswik's views are generally correct, the study of perception will become increasingly complex and difficult.

Size constancy under real-life conditions

The traditional psychophysical method of measuring size constancy requires the observer to adjust a near stimulus until it matches the apparent size of a distant one. Typically, the measurement takes place in a large room or a long corridor. The variables manipulated include the attitude of the observer, the distance of the far stimulus, the use of one or two eyes, and so on. This, of course, is the type of design to which Brunswik objected because of its artificiality—its failure to sample the real environment.

In an experiment published in 1944 and reworked in his 1956 book, Brunswik describes a very different approach to the phenomenon. A student was followed outdoors for a period by a psychologist who asked her to estimate the size of that object which was currently dominant in her field of view. From the resulting sample of 174 estimates a number were selected for further analysis, which involved measuring the actual sizes and distances of the judged objects.

The size range of the objects was very large, 105:1, much greater than any that had ever been used in a laboratory study. (Brunswik was clearly correct about the unrepresentative nature of much of the research in this area.) Brunswik's reporting of his main results leaves much to be desired; however, the main finding is of some interest: the correlation between object size and image size (expressed in this case as the angle subtended at the eye by an object) was only 0.7 over all objects, dropping to 0.1 when small objects were excluded from the analysis. Thus the ecological validity of image size is low. But the overall correlation between object size and judged size was extraordinarily high: 0.99. Clearly the observer had achieved true and valid distal focusing despite the relatively poor utility of one well-known cue to size constancy.

At this point we await a lengthy discussion by Brunswik on how the sizes of objects in the real world are 'attained': his work has uncovered an important paradox and we await his speculations on this with interest. Disappointingly, we are offered only a brief description of distance cues in general and reference to a proposed experiment using photographs.

This is not the place for a lengthy discussion of the perception of size: interested readers should consult the admirable review in Kaufman (1974, Ch. 9). But there is a problem here which Brunswik does not face up to. A common technique used in the study of size constancy is to provide the observer with a variable stimulus within arm's reach. The observer looks at a distant target and adjusts the variable to match it. Various instructions are used: the observer may be instructed to try to achieve a 'retinal match', that is, to make the two stimuli subtend the same visual angle, or he or she may be asked to match the actual size of the distant object. Interestingly, it is difficult to achieve true retinal matches because of the tendency to respond in terms of true object size: in other words, because of size constancy. Also, we all notice in daily life that people do not shrink when they walk away from us; that is, there is phenomenological evidence to support the claim that size constancy is a basic tendency in visual perception.

Brunswik's outdoor observer could not, however, be given a variable stimulus with which to match real distant objects, as this would have had to be extendable to 20 metres or more. So she gave a verbal estimate of perceived size. But is this what we mean by size constancy? To the author, a high-flying 747 looks very small indeed: his size constancy is clearly breaking down when looking upward through empty space. But asked to judge the size of the aircraft (rather than set a retinal match on a variable display) he would reply that it was about 50 metres long. This could be taken as evidence of size constancy, but it is not. It does not agree with phenomenal experience. It seems a pity that someone with Brunswik's research aims did not think this particular problem through more thoroughly. In fact, a convincing account of the basis of size constancy, this very important aspect of vision, did not emerge until 20 years after Brunswik's death.

Grouping and spatial proximity

This study is a rarity in psychological research in that it did not employ an experimental observer.

An important principle in Gestalt psychology is that of *nearness* or *proximity*. Wertheimer's (1923) classic demonstration revealed that stimuli arranged like those in Figure 3.5 in the previous chapter become organized patterns. For example, it is conceivable that Figure 3.5(a) might be seen as a widely spaced inner pair of lines flanked by additional lines, or as four independent vertical lines. But neither of these organizations occurs: the figure is seen as two adjacent pairs of lines.

The Gestalt theorists explained this powerful tendency to group elements according to their proximity by postulating underlying fields in the brain which followed principles of attraction and repulsion. Thus grouping is seen as a basic property of experience caused by lawful brain processes.

Brunswik's novel question, arising out of his functionalist approach was: Might grouping by proximity occur because it has survival value? Is it the case that in the real world adjacent parallel lines tend to be associated by forming the boundaries of objects? The question can be answered by a simple analysis of parallel lines in a sample of the environment.

As an approximation to a representative sample of the 'existing ecology', Brunswik and Kamiya (1953) obtained several stills from a popular motion picture. The number of adjacent straight (or nearly straight), parallel (up to a deviation of five degrees) pairs of lines was counted and their separations in the photograph measured. The pairs of lines were then classified by what they represented in the photographed scenes.

The results of this study are quite revealing. The (geometric) mean distance in the photographs between pairs of lines common to actual objects was 1.2 mm; that between lines representing 'ornamental divisions' (that is, regular markings on surfaces) was 1.3 mm; lines delineating holes, gaps or spaces between objects had a mean separation of 2.8 mm. A correlational analysis restricted to separations of lines representing objects and those representing spaces between them yielded a coefficient of +0.34. This significant result confirms Brunswik's guess: *proximity has ecological validity*.

Wertheimer's discovery can now be seen in a new light: the law has functional value. Grouping is useful because it will commonly lead to the delineation of objects. It works because of the way the world is. A valuable insight has been gained by examining the relationship between perception and the environment in which it takes place. This is one of Brunswik's most original and successful contributions. Notice, too, how this pioneering experiment foreshadowed some of the modern examinations of Gestalt ideas that we described in Chapter 3.

AN EVALUATION OF PROBABILISTIC FUNCTIONALISM

Brunswik's approach to perception has been presented as clearly and as convincingly as possible. If this attempt has been successful, the reader may agree that Brunswik had some stimulating and novel ideas, ideas which are the more impressive when one considers how long ago they were formulated. Why then has he had so little subsequent influence on theory and research? Those who knew Brunswik testify to his originality and cleverness, and yet his influence has been slight. A number of factors seem to have led to this state of affairs, and the main ones are listed below.

Brunswik's style

Brunswik's first languages were Hungarian and German. His English, while always correct, is often difficult and even turgid. Compare the opening of Köhler's highly influential *Gestalt Psychology*, which was written by one whose first language was German, with the ending of Brunswik's best-known work, *Perception and the Representative Design of Experiments*.

> There seems to be a single starting point for psychology, exactly as for all the other sciences: the world as we find it, naively and uncritically.
>
> (Köhler, 1947)

> Perception, then, emerges as that relatively primitive partly autonomous, institutionalized, ratiomorphic subsystem of cognition which achieves prompt and richly detailed orientation habitually concerning the vitally relevant, most distal aspects of the environment of the basis of mutually vicarious, relatively restricted and stereotyped, insufficient evidence in uncertainty-geared interaction and compromise, seemingly following the highest probability and smallness of error at the expense of the highest frequency of precision.
>
> (Brunswik, 1956)

The Brunswik paragraph is in fact a remarkable summary of an original theory, achieved in 68 words. And it is hoped that anyone who has worked through the present chapter will find it entirely comprehensible. It is, however, a hellish sentence.

The style of Brunswik's English would matter less had he been more considerate in his reporting of experiments. Several diagrams in his publications are all but incomprehensible. It is commonly very difficult to know what exactly happened in his experiments. The choice of symbols is often unfortunate and sometimes quite surreal. In one case, U-variables are so named because u is a vowel in the middle of the word 'population'; S represents the environment in the lens model, U now standing for individual differences. For every reader who learned to cope with this sort of thing there must have been dozens who decided that Brunswik was not for them.

Brunswik's view on experimental design

Brunswik was opposed to 'classical psychophysics' in which all variables save one are controlled. The history of perception suggests, however, that such designs can be very fruitful ways of discovering the laws of perception. For example, much of what we know about colour vision has come from experiments using carefully controlled beams of monochromatic light; major researches into hearing have used only pure tones. We have not discussed this, but Brunswik was interested in the perception of faces and ran a multivariate experiment using schematic face patterns. His complicated design and the failure of the subsequent statistical analysis to reveal anything of real importance is in marked contrast to the much later work of Hess (1965, 1975), who showed that simply enlarging the pupil in a photograph of a face makes that face seem more attractive, even when the alteration remains unnoticed. This very simple (classical) experiment yielded a result as intriguing as any of Brunswik's in this area.

Brunswik's experiments

Brunswik often strayed from the ideal course he advocated for perceptual research. Consider his experiments, described earlier, which supported the idea of perceptual compromise. What, we may ask, is representative about an ensemble of Turkish coins or simple elongated rectangles? Brunswik's study of the phenomenon of grouping by proximity was a good idea and provided a critical test of the Gestalt explanation of the phenomenon, and hence of a whole aspect of Gestalt theory. The aim was clear: look at the disposition of adjacent lines in the world and see whether there is a functional basis for the grouping tendency in perception. But how representative were the photographs? They were not from the real world but from a film studio. They were pictures of constructed film sets. It is not necessary to labour the point, but anyone who reads Brunswik's experimental work after learning his views on the importance of ecological sampling will be surprised by the frequently contrived and artificial nature of his visual displays.

Some general criticisms

We shall not offer an exhaustive examination of all aspects of Brunswik's work. Interested readers may consult the Hammond (1966) reference cited at the end of this chapter. But it is proper to ask the extent to which Brunswik's programme for perceptual research is feasible.

   Brunswik emphasized the need to sample the environment or ecology of the organism. But here we meet a major difficulty: what is 'the' ecology? Are outdoors and indoors part of the same niche? We evolved in one and came to inhabit the other, so should we perceive them in a common way? Brunswik is silent on this point and it is clear that he greatly underestimated the problems associated with 'representativeness'.

The idea of the perceiver as intuitive statistician is one of Brunswik's most important assumptions and one which he shared with many other perceptual theorists. Perception involves making the best bet from imperfect information. Cues are weighted according to previous success or failure—a claim which emphasizes learning. Of course, certain cues such as pain-inducing stimuli might be responded to reflexively, but generally the weighting of cues must depend upon experience. Brunswik wrote at a time when much of American academic psychology was engaged by the problems of animal learning, and the 1940s produced several major theories in this area. At the same time workers such as Hebb (1949) were stressing the role of learning in perception. Not surprisingly, Brunswik's theorizing reveals the influence of this Zeitgeist. However, subsequent research has shown that organisms, including humans, are surprisingly capable perceivers very soon after birth (evidence for this was reviewed in Chapter 3). If this shift of emphasis towards the innate aspects of perception continues, approaches such as Brunswik's will require important modifications.

GENERAL REMARKS ON PROBABILISTIC FUNCTIONALISM

The desire to communicate complex ideas clearly and convincingly should be strong in any theorist who wishes to influence others. The neglect into which Brunswik's writings has fallen is partly his own fault. We wish to assert once again that Brunswik's view of perception is stimulating and original and that any reader who is now prepared to work through his writings will find that the ideas therein amply repay the effort.

Throughout this chapter we have maintained a fairly critical attitude towards Brunswik's work, particularly his empirical researches. Why, if there is so much to criticize in probabilistic functionalism, have we included Brunswik's difficult theory in the present selection?

The answer to this question is that Brunswik should be valued less for what he achieved than for what he attempted. We believe that he was the first researcher to face up to the true complexity of perceptual processes, to recognize what a great achievement is represented by perceptual stability in an inherently uncertain world. The workings of our senses have been shaped by a successful evolutionary past, just as their structures have. And this shaping has been done by the complicated rich environment in which evolution took place: we must take this into account when thinking about perception.

Brunswik's assertion that to simplify stimulus situations in the classical psychophysical manner was to ignore the properties of real-life stimulation, is convincing and well-argued. The alternatives he offered—ecological sampling of stimuli, factorial designs, correlational assessment of performance—led to problems which he could not solve. But that does not detract from the originality of his ideas and the wisdom of his advice. And the complexity of his writing reflects not the confusion of a fool, but the vigorous efforts of someone who is trying to capture the complex truth as he sees it. Anyone who takes the trouble to read *Perception and the Representative Design of Psychological Experiments* will finish the book puzzled, but with a new and valuable perspective.

The emphasis which Brunswik placed on the study of the ecology is re-emerging in contemporary work in perception. Workers who have adopted the direct perception paradigm have, as we shall show later, followed J.J. Gibson's lead in claiming that light and sound reaching the perceiver are rich in information. The task for the psychologist is to find, within this richness, invariant patterns which are capable of specifying a stable, external world. Attention must be directed to the environment and its relationship to the perceiver. Indeed, Gibson's last book was entitled *The Ecological Approach to Visual Perception*. And when we describe the computational approach to vision we shall show that it is by carefully studying the environment that theorists can arrive at plausible constraints on their models of perceptual processes, a discipline which has been particularly fruitful.

At the start of this chapter, mention was made of the 'inference revolution' described by Gigerenzer and Murray (1987). Two facets of this revolution may be singled out: first, the idea of humans as statistical decision makers—an idea of central importance in Brunswik's work; second, the incorporation into experimental psychology of the new statistical techniques pioneered earlier in the twentieth century by Fisher, Neyman and Pearson.

It is very important to stress at this point that the new statistical techniques were not adopted by psychologists as soon as they appeared. One route, which took some time, was via the work of agricultural scientists in the USA. Only then did statistical testing start to enter experimental psychology.

The fact is that, when he was reporting the results of his experiments, Brunswik lacked advanced statistical competence—as did all experimental psychologists at that time. The techniques for the analysis of results from multivariate experiments may have been known to some scientists; but they were not part of the training of psychologists. Thinking about the lens model and the various correlational 'rays' running through it, suggests very strongly that one technique which could have helped Brunswik to handle his data more adequately is that of multiple regression. Although this is now taught to psychology undergraduates; Brunswik may never have heard of it.

We see then that the time-worn phrase 'ahead of his time' is the truth in Brunswik's case. He was insufficiently expert to manage the analyses of the complex experiments he wanted to do. And even had he been able to do so, the number of readers with the competence to understand and further develop his experimental programme would have been very small. In Chapter 3, we described the plight of some of the Gestalt psychologists who were forced to leave their home countries after the rise of the Nazi movement. Brunswik, too, was a refugee and he also had a short life. It is a cruel irony that by the time of his death academic psychologists were beginning to absorb the important ideas of inferential statistics and were mastering the new statistical techniques which could have supported Brunswik's research programme and led to experiments as rich and as complex as those Brunswik aspired to.

NOTES ON CHAPTER 4

Brunswik's *Perception and the Representative Design of Psychological Experiments* (1956) is a difficult book, but contains the core of his ideas and is thus essential reading.

Hammond (1966) is a useful source book, containing essays by a number of psychologists who were contemporaries of Brunswik. Some evaluate parts of Brunswik's theory and others attempt to relate his ideas to their own researches. The modification to the lens model shown in this chapter is explained more fully in Hammond's collection (see Chapters 2 and 3). Part 3 of the book is a reprint of some of Brunswik's papers. All Brunswik's publications are listed in an appendix.

The following references are not cited directly in the text but may be useful in understanding Brunswik's approach: Brunswik (1938, 1939, 1948, 1955).

Petrinovich (1979) contains valuable discussions of some of Brunswik's ideas.

Brehmer (1984) attempts to show the relevance of Brunswik's approach to modern perceptual theory and research.

Once again, the book by Gigerenzer and Murray (1987) may be strongly recommended for its description of the inference revolution and its comments on Brunswik's work.

5

The neurophysiological approach to visual perception

This chapter will describe some areas of perceptual research in which it has been suggested that psychological hypotheses can be replaced by known neural mechanisms. There are good reasons why a significant number of perceptionists have always been in favour of this shift. In the first place it is manifestly true that neural mechanisms underlie all behaviour. In an important sense *they* wrote these words and are now reading them. And there are those who believe that psychological knowledge is more secure when it can be linked to known physical structures. For example, the acuity of the eye falls off dramatically as one moves away from the central (foveal) region. The function linking falling acuity with degree of eccentricity is known sufficiently precisely to allow the prediction of visual performance in the periphery. But the reason *why* this falling-off takes place is now known: it is because of the increased ratio of rod to cone cells in the peripheral retina. The high degree of connectedness of the rod system results in high sensitivity through summation of outputs, but the price for this is the lowered resolution of the system. For many this is satisfying knowledge.

A final reason for preferring neurophysiological explanations is simply that some researchers find it easier and more satisfying to think in terms of neural mechanisms rather than in more abstract psychological terms.

The fact that perception, memory and thought are all mediated by the central nervous system does not, however, force us to accept reductionism. The neural structures underlying mental events may be interacting in ways of which we cannot conceive and which could never be described using only the language of neurophysiology. This is said simply to warn the reader against too ready an acceptance of some of the claims to be outlined later in this chapter.

The approaches to be described have one thing in common: they invoke neural mechanisms in explanations of perceptual phenomena. We, have of course, met such an approach in the earlier chapter on the Gestalt theory. But this modern work differs from the Gestalt approach in two important ways. First, Köhler's physiology was highly speculative, and largely incorrect; modern theories are much more securely based. Second, the Gestaltists, as phenomenologists, wanted to explain the richness of everyday perception; modern neurophysiological theories of perception are usually more modest in their aims. Typically, what they try to explain are basic sensory discriminations: how perceivers process some of the basic information contained in, say, the visual image; how this is coded; and in what form it is sent onwards into the higher regions of the visual pathways. Such questions are very different from asking, for example, how familiarity affects our perception of objects or why blue is almost certainly the world's favourite colour. Thus, in terms of our basic model the areas of interest are joined by a very short arc—one connecting that which arrives at receptor surfaces with peripheral and (sometimes) central processes of the nervous system.

The remainder of this chapter will be organized under the following headings.

- An outline of neural function
- Examples of the neurophysiological approach to perceptual theory
- Some problems arising from the neurophysiological approach
- A new type of model: the connectionist network
- General remarks on the neurophysiological approach to perceptual theory

AN OUTLINE OF NEURAL FUNCTION

None of the theoretical work to be described would have been possible without the remarkable gains in the understanding of the nervous system which have been achieved during the past 150 years. This is clearly not the place to undertake a history of neuroanatomy and neurophysiology, although this is a fascinating story and well worth reading about. However, for those readers who are unfamiliar with neural structure and physiology and who lack easy access to specialist libraries, the following very brief treatment may be of some help. Other readers will skip the next section; those wishing to learn more about the workings of the nervous system should consult the basic references given at the end of the chapter.[1]

---

[1] It will greatly assist the understanding of this and further chapters if readers can familiarize themselves with the basic stages of the visual pathway, from retinal cells, via the lateral geniculate nucleus, to areas 17 and 18 of the visual cortex. Modern textbooks describe this pathway in a very clear manner.

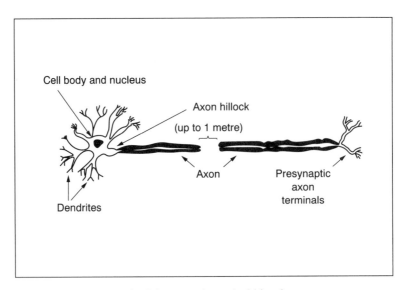

Figure 5.1   Diagram of a typical bi-polar neuron

The nervous system

The term 'nerve' is used somewhat loosely. Major nerves are in fact bundles of nerve fibres: each human optic nerve, for instance, actually comprises approximately one million separate fibres. But 'nerve' is sometimes used to describe the basic unit of the nervous system, the neuron.

Neurons are specialized cells having a variety of shapes and sizes. Basically, each neuron comprises a cell body with a nucleus, a complex arrangement of branching structures or dendrites, and one or more long processes or axons which run either to other neurons or to muscles or glands. The neuron receives stimulation via its dendrites and passes on stimulation via the axon. A typical neuron is shown in diagrammatic form in Figure 5.1.

The connection between two neurons in a sequence is not physically direct. Activity in the first leads to temporary changes in a minute gap or *synapse* between neurons. Whether or not the stimulation from the first neuron is passed on depends upon the strength and timing of the changes at the synapse. Many neuronal endings may terminate on the dendrites or cell body of a single neuron.

When a dendrite receives sufficient stimulation the characteristics of its membrane at a local site suddenly change. As a result of rapid chemical processes, the permeability of the membrane alters in such a way that ions pass into and out of the cell. This results in a wave of electrical disturbance, or depolarization, which spreads away from the site of stimulation. This wave of electrical disturbance is decremental, tending to diminish with distance. But if several stimulating events occur within a short time, or within a small area, the electrical wave may be strong enough to reach the site where axonal conduction begins.

Once a disturbance reaches the axon it is propagated according to a different principle: now the wave of electrical conduction is no longer decremental but all-or-none. That is to say, if an impulse begins to run along an axon it will continue to the end. And the size of the impulse is independent of the strength of the original disturbance—just as the speed of a bullet is independent of the strength of the trigger pull, provided this exceeds the threshold of firing. Neurons tend to code strength of stimulation as frequency, the stronger the stimulus the more impulses per second. From the end of the neuron, activity spreads into the next synapse and, of course, this can lead to graded stimulation of the next neuron. Thus the rapid all-or-none conduction down an axon fibre can be seen as a means of conveying graded information, translated into a frequency code, to another site in the body.

The preceding account of the causal sequence between adjacent neurons has omitted an important phenomenon. We have described the pattern by which one neuron excites another, increasing the chance of the latter's firing. But neurons can also interact in an *inhibitory* manner. Thus one neuron's activity, rather than inducing a wave of depolarization in another neuron, may actually cause a *hyperpolarization* of the next membrane, thus lowering the probability that the second neuron will fire.

When we put these basic facts together, we can see that the activity between successive neurons permits (i) threshold effects resulting from summation over space and time and (ii) positive (excitatory) and negative (inhibitory) interactions between these basic units of the nervous system. These facts are very significant for it means that groups of neurons can behave in ways directly analogous to *logical gates* (see Figure 5.2).

Logical gates

In engineering terminology, an AND gate, for example, is a switch-like device which produces an output only when both its inputs are positive. An AND-NOT gate will not give an output if both inputs are simultaneously positive; an EXCLUSIVE-OR gate will give an output if either of two inputs occurs, but not if both occur. With such simple switching devices it is possible to build elaborate logical networks.[2]

It is now possible to link these facts and draw an exciting conclusion:

1. Neurons interact in various ways. One neuron can excite or inhibit another, increasing or decreasing the chance that the latter will fire.

---

[2] Philosophically trained readers will recognize the connection between logical gates and truth tables.

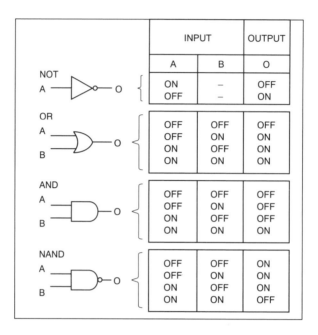

Figure 5.2 Four common logical gates. The function of the OR gate, for example, is to give an output if either or both of its inputs are active; the AND gate gives an output only if both its inputs are active. Combinations of various gates can be used to build computing devices

2. Logical gates are switches and can be used to build computing devices.
3. Because of the ways in which they interact, neurons can simulate logical gates.
4. Therefore neurons can do something akin to computing.

This is a very important development in the history of neurophysiology. Some of the implications of this idea will be described later in this chapter.

It should be remembered that neural processes take time. The discovery by Helmholtz in 1850 that the speed of conduction down a sensory nerve was in the order of 100 metres per second was vitally important. Neurons do not conduct with the speed of light (as some had believed), they are relatively slow. 'The speed of thought' is not instantaneous, but is commonly slow enough to be measured, as is the speed of perceptual processes. Were this not so, psychologists would not have been able to discover nearly as much as they have about perceptual processes, and neurophysiologists would have had a much more difficult time trying to understand the ways in which neurons respond and interact.

Responding to change

This necessarily brief review of neural action may be completed by stating a final major principle which researchers have discovered: a large proportion of the various sensory neurons seem to have evolved to deal with *change* (see Figure 5.3). In numerous regions of the afferent nervous system it has been found that the onset or offset of stimulation produces a rapid and marked increase in neural firing. But should the stimulation continue then, typically, the neural response returns to a value close to the resting baseline. We know that change is important in vision: if one looks into a completely homogeneous volume—for example, if the head is placed inside an illuminated white sphere (known as a Ganzfeld)—then vision will fade within seconds; the surface of the sphere softens to a fog, and eventually the sensation of seeing is lost completely (interested readers may experience the Ganzfeld effect by placing half a table tennis ball over each eye and looking towards a source of illumination). A similar fading occurs when the eye is effectively prevented from moving: this is known as the 'stabilized image' phenomenon. Analogous effects occur in touch: an object placed on the skin is felt very clearly at first,

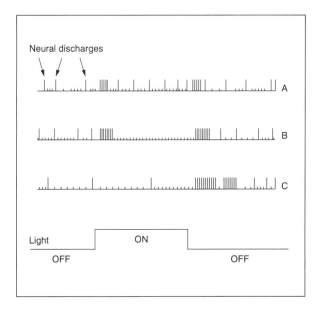

Figure 5.3   Three types of response from neurons in the optic nerve of the frog. Each spike represents a single neural discharge. Fibre A responds to light onset and maintains a steady discharge rate. Fibre B responds maximally to light onset and offset. Fibre C responds maximally to light offset. The combined effect of these responses is that the visual system responds most strongly to *changing* illumination. (Diagrammatic, after various authors)

but within a few seconds the tactile impression fades. These effects seem to reflect an underlying basic principle of economy of response. Change is always potentially important and there is an obvious evolutionary advantage in concentrating neural resources so as to maximize responses to it.

The questions asked in this chapter are: How far can the knowledge outlined above be employed in the solution of perceptual problems? Can one bypass psychological theory and go straight to a causal, mechanical account of sensory and perceptual phenomena? There are those who believe that this may be possible and it is to their work that we now turn.

EXAMPLES OF THE NEUROPHYSIOLOGICAL APPROACH TO PERCEPTUAL THEORY

To date, neurophysiological explanations in visual perception have been of various kinds. We shall draw examples from three areas of research: (i) the direct substitution of known neural/physiological mechanisms for hypothetical constructs, (ii) the discovery of neural feature detectors, and (iii) work which reinforces the growing belief that structures in the visual system can perform elaborate syntheses as well as analyses of incoming sensory data. This three-fold classification is somewhat arbitrary, but it does provide a structure within which to describe a selection of modern researches.

Although elegant neurophysiological work has been done in other sense modalities, all the following examples are drawn from visual studies. The neural region of the eye, the retina, is actually an outgrowth of the brain and is thus a region of formidable complexity. We should not be surprised by some of the extraordinary processes which neurophysiologists have discovered there in the past few decades.

Neurophysiology and colour vision

The following examples of this substitution of known mechanism for psychological hypotheses are both drawn from the area of colour vision. They are good illustrations of the successful application of neurophysiological knowledge to classical psychological problems.

The two most important facts about colour vision in humans (and some other species) are, first, that our colour vision is trichromatic and, second, that we experience highly predictable contrast and fatigue effects.

Trichromacy

The trichromacy of human colour vision means simply this: most of the hues which a person is capable of perceiving can be matched by suitable mixtures of three wavelengths of light. These primary wavelengths need not be precisely specified, provided that (a) they span the visible spectrum—there is a wide range of choices among the blues, greens and reds—and (b) no two primaries should be exactly complementary. For each hue in the visible spectrum there is a complementary hue which, when added to the first, yields an achromatic mixture. Such complementary pairs must be avoided when choosing the primaries.

Most people are greatly surprised when their trichromacy is first demonstrated to them. It is a memorable experience, particualrly when it is seen that equal amounts of the three primaries mix to produce white: as the intensity of the third light is increased, all colour simply fades away. Moreover, the matches made are highly stable. For example, if one produces yellow by adding red and green light, the yellow can be made indistinguishable from that seen in the 'yellow' portion of the spectrum (a wavelength of approximately 560–580 nanometres). If one then biases colour perception by fatiguing the eye with, say, orange light, *both yellows change in exactly the same way*. The stability of the match is also maintained when an additional coloured light is added to both yellows.

Colour contrast and fatigue effects

These are equally remarkable phenomena. If a red square is placed on a grey ground and fixated for a few moments, one comes to see a greenish tinge surrounding the red. An intense green light induces a reddish after-image; blue light induces yellow, and *vice-versa*. (Note that red and green and blue and yellow are complementary hues in that they mix to form neutral greys.) Anyone can experience these effects by simply staring at a coloured light (*not the sun*) for a few moments and then looking at a white surface. A related phenomenon may be observed on brightly lit snowscapes where it can be seen that shadows are blue (this was first brought to general attention by the Impressionists).

The Young–Helmholtz theory

In the nineteenth century these very reliable and interesting phenomena gave rise to a number of theories of colour vision. The first, known now as the Young–Helmholtz three-factor theory (Helmholtz, 1909–1911, translated 1924–1925) attempted to explain trichromacy as follows. Suppose that the eye contains three types of receptor, each maximally sensitive to a portion of the spectrum (Young originally proposed three pigments; Helmholtz three types of retinal cones. Historically, the difference is not important). Then if the eye is illuminated by a particular hue the type of cell whose sensitivity is closest to the wavelength of the hue will fire strongly while other types of receptor will

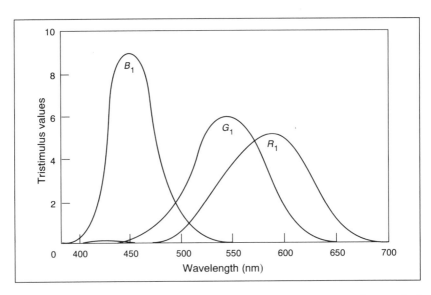

Figure 5.4 A diagrammatic illustration of a typical three-component theory of colour vision. B_1, G_1, R_1 describe the hypothetical short- medium- and long-wavelength receptors postulated in the Young–Helmholtz theory. The vertical axis can be interpreted as the relative absorption efficiency of each receptor as a function of wavelength. (From Judd, 1951. Copyright 1951, John Wiley & Sons Inc., reproduced with permission)

respond less vigorously. Yellow light will stimulate the cells sensitive to the red and green parts of the spectrum about equally. White light will stimulate all three types of receptor, evoking the achromatic response (see Figure 5.4).

The Young–Helmholtz theory of colour vision does have weaknesses. It does not readily explain the stability of yellow, a hue which is still seen in intensely strong light when all other hues apart from blue vanish. How can the yellow remain when the contributing receptors (in the red and green regions) do not appear to be functioning? And the theory has some difficulty over certain forms of colour vision deficiency. Nevertheless, the Young–Helmholtz three-factor theory has proved to be very useful and durable. It is the most widely cited theory in the history of colour vision research.

Hering's opponent-process theory

Historically, the major rival to the Young–Helmholtz theory was Hering's opponent-process theory (Hering, 1890). This theory postulated the existence in the optic nerve of three processes capable of functioning in, as it were, opposite directions. In the 'anabolic' direction the processes give rise to the sensations of red, yellow and white; in the 'catabolic' direction these same

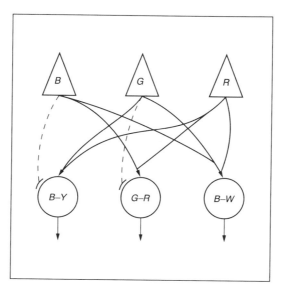

Figure 5.5 A modern three-pigment/opponent-process model of colour vision. Three types of receptor (*B, G, R*) responding to short-, medium- and long-wavelength light sends outputs to opponent cells (*B–Y, G–R, B–W*). These outputs may be excitatory (—>) or inhibitory (- - ->). For example, the *B–Y* receives an inhibitory signal from the short-wavelength receptor and this rusults in a 'Blue' output from the cell. Yellow light will stimulate the *G* and *R* receptors equally; they excite the *B–Y* cell which then produces a 'Yellow' output. (After various authors)

processes give rise, respectively, to green, blue and black (see Figure 5.5). Thus the phenomenon by which complementary hues mix to grey is accounted for in terms of a balanced neutral point in the relevant opponent process. Fatigue and contrast effects are handled just as easily, as is the fact that one cannot see, for example, blue and yellow at the same time in the same place. And while there are bluish greens, there is no blue-yellow sensation; nor are there any reddish greens or blackish whites.

Hering's opponent-process theory also has its weaknesses. For example, it predicts a form of yellow-blue colour blindness which has never been found, and the theory does not yield an entirely satisfactory account of the brightness of colours. Nevertheless, it provides an explanation of some very important phenomena.

The debate between these two very different theories (or their more recent counterparts) has been lengthy. And one can see why: each explains some of the data of colour vision but not others. But the theories are very different: how could they both be right?

We now know that both the Young–Helmholtz and the Hering theories are essentially correct within limits. Our confidence that this is the case is one of the triumphs of visual research. An account of the work which confirmed both three-factor and opponent-process theories will demonstrate the way in which actual neural mechanisms can displace hypothetical constructs.

Human (and animal) data from colour vision experiments have led to the construction of quantitative models of colour vision in which various triads of hypothetical pigments are evaluated. By constructing absorption curves for these hypothetical pigments one can test whether it is possible to account for various aspects of colour performance—particularly matching tasks, the colour confusions made by colour deficient judges, and the relationships between hue and other aspects of colour, such as lightness, brightness and saturation. As a result of many years of careful measurement there are now good data which can be used to predict various colour phenomena. However, the hypothetical pigments in this research are selected to give the best fit to the performance data: there is no direct evidence that pigments in the eye exactly match them. How satisfying it would be to locate the real pigments and to know once and for all what underlies human trichromacy. This is a goal which eluded visual researchers for many years.

The discovery of the three cone pigments

No single researcher can be given the credit for solving this classic problem. However, many would agree that an important breakthrough came when Rushton (1964) perfected a technique which made it possible to search for pigments in the living eye.

In essence, *microspectrophotometry* entails shining a narrow beam of pure, monochromatic light onto the cells of the retina, trapping the returning beam and measuring the difference between the two. In this way it is possible to assess the absorption properties of retinal cells. Described so baldly the work sounds relatively simple; in fact perfecting the technique took many years of intensive research.

Rushton's work was extended by MacNichol (1964) and Dartnall, Bowmaker and Mollon (1983) who worked with isolated cone cells. When these various researches were combined, it became certain that the cone cells of the retina do in fact contain three different pigments. Each has a wavelength to which it is maximally absorbent and the three peak sensitivities are at 420, 530 and 560 nanometres (see Figure 5.6 and compare it with Figure 5.4). This is a most satisfying result. It enables us to call cells containing the pigments the short-, medium- and long-wavelength colour receptors of the eye. This is exactly what is required by trichromatic theories, such as the Young–Helmholtz theory outlined earlier. Helmholtz was essentially correct (that he chose cone types, rather than pigments, does not matter). The basis of visual trichromacy has been discovered.

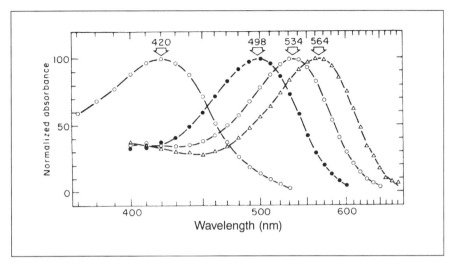

Figure 5.6 Actual absorption data obtained from isolated cells from a human retina. Microspectrophotometry has revealed the presence of three distinct cone pigments with absorption maxima at 420, 534 and 564 nm (the filled points are absorption data from the rod pigment, rhodopsin). The basis of trichromacy has been discovered. (From Bowmaker and Dartnall, 1980. Reproduced with permission of the Psychological Society)

The story just told represents a remarkable gain in our knowledge of colour vision. It is not, however, an adequate explanation of all the basic sensory colour vision phenomena. The existence of a cone type containing a long-wave (red-absorbing) pigment does not by itself explain how we distinguish between different reds, how our colour discrimination is so good, nor does it readily explain those phenomena which prompted the opponent-process theory outlined earlier.

The discovery of opponent processes

The goal of finding opponent processes was achieved with the success of Svaetichin (1956), who discovered an electrical potential in cells of the fish retina which responds differentially to coloured light in the following manner: at short wavelengths the potential responds positively, at long wavelengths negatively (see Figure 5.7). Other cells in the retina produce a similarly selective response to blue and yellow light. Then DeValois (1960) found cells in the lateral geniculate nucleus (a relay station between the retina and the visual cortex) of the monkey which also respond in an opponent manner to wavelength. These cells respond by increasing their firing when the eye receives light from one end of the spectrum and decreasing their firing when the light is from the other end of the spectrum. Refinements in this research have now uncovered +Blue –Yellow, –Blue +Yellow, +Red –Green, and +Green –Red lateral geniculate cells, *all behaving in a manner suggested by opponent-process theory.* Once again, neurophysiological work has demonstrated the essential correctness of an abstract theory of colour vision, and has yielded a satisfying explanation as to why the theory works and also complements very different three-factor theories. That is to say, retinal cone cells in the eye do absorb light by the action of three pigments and these three pigments underlie trichromacy. At the same time, cells in the visual pathways located inwards of the cone cells use the outputs of these cells and respond differentially to them, producing the sharpening postulated by opponent-process theory.

Taken together, these two sets of researches justify the claim that theoretical constructs at this level of colour vision research can be replaced by known neurophysiology mechanisms. This in turn allows research to be directed to new problems: how the various pigments and opponent-process cells are

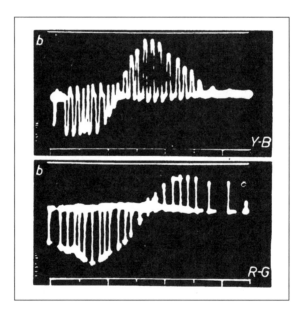

Figure 5.7 Svaetichin and MacNichol's discovery of opponent-process responses in cells of the fish retina. The slow electrical potential (the S-response) changes its polarity according to wavelength. In this figure the vertical axis shows the direction of the S-response, the horizontal axis represents the wavelength of the stimulus. Note the differential effects of Red versus Green and Yellow versus Blue light. (From Svaetichin and MacNichol, 1958. Reproduced with permission of the Annals of the New York Academy of Sciences)

arranged in other species. What is lacking in those people who have impaired colour vision? And so on. Of course, the discoveries do not signal the end of colour vision research and theory. Many questions remain, in particular how we perceive coloured surfaces where texture and hue interact; how the 'true' colours of things can be perceived when illumination is changing; why some animals, such as the cat, have cone cells and visual pigments in the retina but find it difficult to learn colour discriminations. But at the basic sensory level of trichromacy and contrast and fatigue effects, neurophysiology has given us definite answers. Small wonder that some believe this to be the eventual fate of many other perceptual phenomena.

Feature detectors in the visual system

As an example of another type of neurophysiological theorizing in perception, some modern research into the perception and recognition of shape will be described, with particular emphasis on the search for feature detectors.

Recognition of the importance of shape perception and discrimination came early in the history of psychology. Mach (1836–1916), aware that contours play an important role in delineating shapes, solved some of the psychophysical problems of contour extraction. He established that contours appear whenever a gradient of lightness or brightness changes suddenly (technically, this is the second differential of the intensity gradient). The Gestaltists demonstrated how shapes emerge from ground, they stressed the importance of shape constancy in perceptual stability, and they showed how priority appears to be given in perception to balanced, simple, symmetrical shapes according to the law of Prägnanz.

By the early 1950s there were enough facts to fuel a theoretical controversy. Some workers, for example Hebb (1949), claimed that there was evidence to support a learning interpretation of shape perception. Hebb's theory assigned an important role to eye movements in the creation of 'cell assemblies' mediating subsequent shape recognition. But at the same time ethologists, studying animal behaviour under natural conditions, found evidence for the innate recognition of certain shapes. For example, compound shapes comprising only large and small discs induce unlearned gaping responses in nestling thrushes (see Tinbergen, 1951) which are the same as those induced by parent birds. The ethological literature contains many other examples of this kind of innate responsiveness to shapes.

Another development in the 1950s was the advent of digital computers capable of some restricted pattern recognition. This encouraged the development of psychological models of shape perception and recognition (generally subsumed under the heading 'pattern perception'). What eventually emerged were two main types of model: template matching and feature detection.

Template-matching models

Models designed by Selfridge and Neisser (1960) and Uhr (1963) recognize patterns or shapes by noting their similarity to canonical forms. Such an idea is illustrated by those educational toys for infants in which solid shapes can be posted only through the correct apertures in a box. However, such template-matching models have major flaws: how is it, for example, that we can recognize a certain letter when it is presented in an unusual typeface, or in a different size, or at a different retinal location? Our ability to do all these things presents serious problems for this type of model.

Feature detection models

These were designed to avoid the difficulties described above. They work by analysing shapes into component parts or features. For example, Selfridge's well-known 'pandemonium' model (Selfridge, 1959) postulates peripheral, low-level feature detectors, many of which are triggered by shapes falling onto a receptor surface. The outputs of these detectors are weighed at higher levels of the system, with the detector (actually called a demon) which 'shouts' loudest having the best chance that its output will be accepted for further processing. The shape finally arrived at is based on combinations of features detected by the demons.

In a different context, Sutherland (1957) claimed that those shape discriminations of which the octopus is capable can be explained by assuming that visual stimuli are analysed in terms of horizontal and vertical features, but not by oblique ones. In yet another context—human perception and thinking—Bruner (1957) suggested that patterns are examined for key attributes which are then related to categories created by the perceiver beforehand. Hence some cognitive activity is believed to precede actual shape recognition.

A valuable discussion of much of the work described above will be found in Neisser (1967). For now it suffices to say, first, that the importance of shape perception and recognition has long been recognized by psychologists; and, second, that this is still a live issue. For example Marr, whose important work will be the subject of Chapter 8, stated quite explicitly that he was attempting to formulate a theory '. . . in which the main job of vision was to derive a representation of shape' (Marr, 1982).

These, then, are some of the theories which have arisen in response to the challenge of shape perception. We shall now attempt to show how such thinking is being influenced by discoveries in neurophysiology.

The discovery of receptive fields

In a pioneering study of the responses of the nervous system to stimulation, Adrian (1928) found that tactile sensory fibres in the limb of a monkey respond whenever a region of skin is stimulated. Adrian coined the phrase *receptive field* to describe the relationship between a region of a sensory surface, such as the skin, and neural cells inwards of the surface which receive messages from it. The concept of the receptive field is now centrally important in visual neurophysiology.

Adrian's work on the tactile receptive fields was quickly extended to other areas. From the work of such distinguished researchers as Hartline (1938, 1940), Barlow (1953), Kuffler (1953), Lettvin *et al.* (1959) and Maturana *et al.* (1960), knowledge of receptive fields grew rapidly. It was found, for example, that receptive field organization exists in the frog retina and in the optic nerve fibres of the cat (whose visual system shares many important characteristics with our own). Many visual receptive fields have a circular organization. In some of these fields central excitatory areas are surrounded by concentric inhibitory regions. The result is that stimulation in the centre of a visual area results in increased neural activity, but this can be inhibited by stimulation of the surrounding area—the on-centre/off-surround fields. The opposite organization is found in what are described as off-centre/on-surround fields. The quality of these researches was recognized in the award to Hartline and his colleagues of the 1967 Nobel Prize.

The possible relevance of this research for the psychology of perception was further demonstrated by the work of Lettvin *et al.* (1959) and Maturana *et al.* (1960) on the frog's visual system. Recordings from fibres in the optic nerve produced a very exciting discovery: the frog's visual system appears to respond in a very limited but selective manner to stimulation at the retina. Some cells produce a prolonged response to edges. Others respond when small dark objects are moved across the visual field (hence their name, 'bug detectors'). There are cells which respond maximally to changes in contrast in the visual field. Others respond when their visual fields are darkened. Finally, there are cells which respond inversely to light intensity and thus appear to be dark detectors.

These remarkable findings are doubly significant. First, they show that the visual world of the frog must be very different from our own. It appears to be a simple world, restricted to those stimulus attributes which are vital to the frog's survival: the presence of small prey, the shadows of possible predators, the safety of darkness. Second, these aspects of the world which the frog must perceive in order to survive are extracted automatically.

Neural mechanisms in the frog retina extract features from the visual image. That this processing is thus peripheral rather than central may be explained in part by the fact that the frog does not have a very complex brain—for example, it lacks a cortex. But warm-blooded vertebrates do have complex central nervous systems. When some of the researchers listed above turned their attention to the visual system of the cat (which, like many other warm-blooded vertebrates, has a well-developed visual cortex) they found that receptive fields can also be found in more central regions of the nervous system.

We shall now describe what has become a classic set of experiments. The work by Hubel and Wiesel (1962, 1977) to which we now turn has been described by some psychologists as the most important set of discoveries in the history of physiological psychology. The quality of this research was recognized in the award to the authors of the 1981 Nobel Prize.

Hubel and Wiesel (1962, 1977) succeeded in recording the electrical responses of living cells in the visual cortex of the cat and the monkey to various patterns of stimulation. To appreciate the magnitude of this achievement one must realize that cortical cells are microscopically small, so that to record from them without destroying the cells requires the use of exceedingly fine microelectrodes. (These are so fine that the tip is invisible, even under a microscope.) Then the electrode must be positioned very carefully in the cortex using precision stereotactic instruments. The aim is to make contact with the outer wall of the cell without puncturing and destroying it. The researchers must be certain that they are actually recording from a living cell—which, of course, they cannot see. Finally, the experimental animal must be kept alive and well under anaesthesia while the retina is stimulated in a controlled manner. It took researchers many years to overcome these formidable technical problems.

Hubel and Wiesel have described how one day, while trying vainly to induce a response in a cortical cell, they accidentally moved the slide in their projector so that the *edge* of the slide moved across the experimental animal's visual field. The cortical cell immediately responded to this moving edge. Subsequent experiments showed that what had been discovered was a receptive field organization in the cat's visual cortex. However, unlike the simple, circularly organized receptive fields found previously in the retina and lateral geniculate body, these cortical fields are thinner and more elongated in shape. They respond to the presence in the visual field of moving edges or contours having a particular orientation. Some cortical cells respond to vertical lines and their response falls off as the lines are changed away from the vertical. Other cells respond to horizontal or oblique lines and edges. Figure 5.8 summarizes some of these discoveries.

Not all the cells explored in the cortex by Hubel, Wiesel and others have receptive fields, but subsequent studies of those that do uncovered some remarkable facts about the visual cortex of the cat and, later, the monkey. For example, some cells in the visual cortex exhibit a vertical, columnar organization. As one penetrates deeper into the cortex below a particular site the column of cells produces subtly changing responses to stimuli, but all cells in the column exhibit a preference for the same orientation of the stimulus. Cortical cells show different types of responsiveness. In some the receptive field is an elongated area with excitatory and inhibitory regions. Others respond positively to appropriate stimulation anywhere in the relevant portion of the retina and have no inhibitory regions. Still other cells are indifferent to the orientation of the stimulus but respond selectively to patterns of a particular height and width. Many cortical cells are binocularly driven and can be induced to fire by stimulation of either eye.

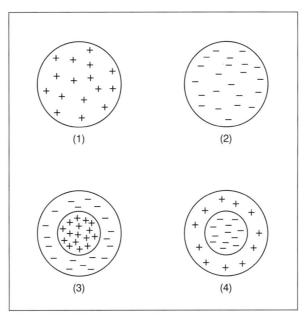

Figure 5.8 Examples of types of receptive field organized in the vertebrate visual system. Each diagram represents an area of the retina monitored by a retina ganglion cell. The signs represent the responses of the ganglion cell (+ = excited, – = inhibited) when light falls onto the receptive field. (1) and (2) represent the simplest forms of receptive field; (3) is an on-centre/off-surround field; (4) is an off-centre/on surround field. Receptive fields are also found in more central regions of the visual system. Not all fields have such clearly circular arrangments. (After various authors)

The responsiveness of some cells is bizarrely specific: for example, Gross, Rocha-Miranda and Bender (1972) found cells in the macaque monkey's inferotemporal cortex (a region of the brain at a distance from the visual cortex which is implicated in certain forms of visual recognition) which respond selectively to the image of a hand.[3] It is important to stress at this point that the discovery, through microelectrode recording and other techniques, of a cell responding specifically to, for example, the image of a hand, is not interpreted by neurophysiologists as being the brain's only response to that hand. It is likely that adjacent cells, from which recordings are not being taken, are also responding to the image, but in these cases the responses may be to subtly different aspects of the hand. It is probably closer to the truth to conceive of groups of neurons acting in loose confederations, with each group

---

[3] Some more modern researches employ different techniques when exploring the specificity of cortical cells. For example, radioactively labelled 2-deoxyglucose can be used as a marker, showing which cells respond most to particular stimuli.

showing some specialization (visual areas of the cortex versus auditory areas, motion detectors versus colour detectors, and so on) rather than any complete function being performed by a single specialized neuron.

Receptive fields are present at birth, a finding which gives some support to the nativist view of perception advanced by Gestalt psychologists. However, early experience can modify the nature of the fields. For example, Blakemore (1974) reared kittens in artificial environments comprising either vertically or horizontally striped surfaces. After varying periods of time in such environments the kittens were examined in two ways. First, their ability to discriminate contours was tested. It was found that kittens reared in a vertically striped environment showed impaired acuity to horizontal stripes, and *vice versa*. The animals were not blind to the unfamiliar stripes, but their performance made it obvious that the stripes were not perceived as clearly as those in the familiar orientation. Second, when receptive fields were examined in the visual cortex of these animal cells were found which respond normally to stripes in the familiar orientation, but the cortical responses to stripes in the other orientation were severely reduced. It was not that the cortex had actually lost a number of functional units, but rather that an abnormal number had developed to match the orientation of the striped rearing environment.

Thus overt behaviour and the cellular responsiveness of the visual system both indicate that some early experience is needed for normal development of receptive fields, and that abnormal experiences can bias them. There is, moreover, a *critical period* during which experience is particularly important and this exists between approximately three weeks and three months after birth. Similar conclusions emerge from variants on this work in which, for example, animals are reared with one eye permanently closed for a period to see the effects this has on binocularly driven cortical cells. Thus, this neurophysiological research seems to support a modified nativism, in which the elements of perceiving are present at birth, but not in a rigid or unmodifiable form. To date, it is not yet safe to extrapolate this important conclusion to human perception (although the evidence is very suggestive): the obvious experiments are rendered impossible by ethical and technical considerations.

Readers wishing to learn more about this important research will find excellent accounts in the source books listed at the end of this chapter. We shall now attempt to show how the discovery of receptive fields has influenced psychological theory.

One obvious interpretation of the discoveries by Hubel and Wiesel and subsequent researchers is that *the feature detectors suggested by theories of shape perception have been found*. Just as some had supposed, it seems that neurons in the brain (at least in cats and monkeys) are capable of responding selectively to certain aspects of stimuli. These can be simple features, such as lines in particular orientations; more complex relationships, such as particular lengths *and* widths; and very complex combinations of features such as a hand shape. Small wonder that this research quickly attracted the attention of a great many psychologists.

The work of B. Julesz

One of the best-known psychological and theoretical researches to follow Hubel and Wiesel's discovery is that by Julesz (1981). Julesz has investigated the properties of visual textures to see which can and cannot be effortlessly discriminated. Following a long series of investigations, Julesz claims that the basic building blocks of visual texture are dots, elongated blobs, and terminations of lines. And in describing the role that these *textons* play in perception he makes specific reference to the work of Hubel and Wiesel—not surprisingly, for these are exactly the aspects of stimulation which their feature detectors can extract from images. Here then is clear evidence of what is known to occur in the visual system having a major influence in an important area of perceptual theory.

The emphasis so far in the two strands of research described above has been on neural *analysis* of sensory data—how information about colour and shape might be extracted from the visual image by simple neural mechanisms. We shall postpone further comment on these researches until we have given one more example of the impact of neurophysiology on perceptual theory. In this we shall attempt to explain how neural mechanisms might be capable of synthesis as well as analysis. The work to be described followed quite naturally from that above, and some of the researchers have worked in both areas.

The visual system's response to spatial frequencies

Spatial frequencies are associated with lines and edges, features which are of vital importance in visual perception. The concept of spatial frequency may be explained in terms of one of the widely used research tools in this area, the visual grating.

Visual gratings

A grating is a display comprising alternate light and dark stripes. In visual research these stripes commonly do not have sharp edges but vary smoothly from light to dark and *vice-versa* (Figure 5.9). Such *sinusoidal gratings* are used for technical reasons, in particular because they can be analysed by a powerful mathematical technique—Fourier analysis—which permits complex grating patterns to be decomposed into simpler sinusoidal components.

Any grating can be described in terms of four independent properties.

1. The *contrast* of a grating is simply the difference in brightness (or luminance or reflectance) between the light and dark areas; low contrast

gratings are more difficult to see, other things being equal. (The black–white contrast on this page is approximately 70 per cent on a 0 to 100 per cent scale.)

2. The *spatial frequency* of a grating is a function of the width of the stripes, which in turn defines the number of alternations of light and dark across unit distance. Convenient measures of spatial frequency are the number of changes per degree of visual angle or the number of stripes falling across one millimetre of the retina.

3. The *orientation* of a grating simply describes whether it is horizontal, vertical or oblique.

4. The *phase* of a grating is taken from any arbitrary starting point: is the stripe in that position light or dark?

Simple gratings are those formed from a single spatial frequency. *Complex gratings* (Figure 5.9) are formed by adding simple gratings. Conversely, complex sinusoidal gratings can be analysed into their basic components.

It is obvious that one can have gratings with stripes that cannot be seen, *either* because the stripes are too fine to be resolved, *or* because the contrast between the light and dark areas is too low. It follows that there are two distinct thresholds associated with the detection of a grating.

The Campbell and Robson experiment

In what has become a classic study of spatial frequency detection, Campbell and Robson (1968) measured these two thresholds in human observers. Using electronically generated sinusoidal gratings, Campbell and Robson selected a particular spatial frequency and set the contrast so low that the grating lines could not be seen. The contrast was then raised until the stripes were just visible. Then the spatial frequency was changed and the process repeated.

Campbell and Robson presented their threshold data in a new form of graph, the *contrast sensitivity function*, which has provided valuable insights into the process of seeing. As Figure 5.10 shows, the interrelation between threshold contrast and resolution of spatial frequency takes the form of a curve. This curve is an exceptionally useful way of describing visual performance. It predicts the fineness of detail which can be seen at particular contrast levels, it is the best way yet of comparing the vision of different observers, and it allows us to compare human vision with that in other species. Note that, in Figure 5.10, the cat is very sensitive to low spatial frequencies. This means that cats are able to see faint shadows that we cannot, which might explain the age-old association of cats with supernatural phenomena. The contrast sensitivity function has been described as 'a window of visiblity'. Interestingly, although it has long been known that other species can rival or even out-perform humans on traditional measures of acuity (the hawks have

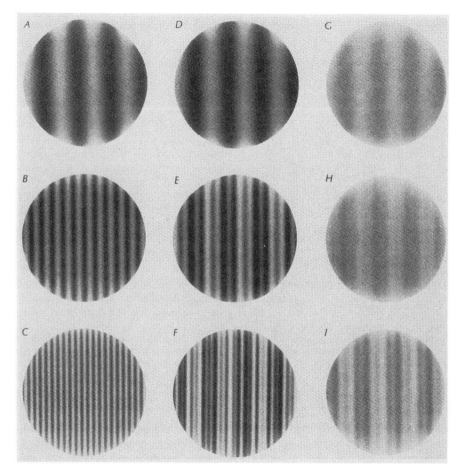

Figure 5.9 Simple and complex sinusoidal gratings. The top row of gratings differ only in contrast, those in the left column differ only in spatial frequency. The remaining gratings are formed by combining the simple row and column gratings. (From Sekuler and Blake, 1985. Reproducecd with permission of Alfred A. Knopf Inc.)

better resolving power) and on traditional measures of sensitivity (some nocturnal creatures have very high sensitivity), the human eye has the best all-round performance in terms of the contrast sensitivity function: it has the largest area under the curve, the largest window.

The use of gratings heralded a new approach to the measurement of visual performance, an approach which was to yield important new theoretical insights into the process of seeing, and which quickly led to the discovery of new and important phenomena. Three examples will illustrate the intriguing nature of these discoveries.

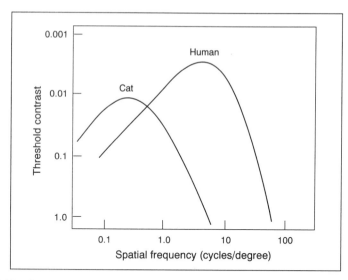

Figure 5.10 Contrast sensitivity functions. The contrast of a grating is defined as a ratio: $(I_{max} - I_{min})/(I_{max} + I_{min})$ where I_{max} and I_{min} are the intensities of the lightest and darkest regions of a grating. The contrast sensitivity functions are obtained by selecting a particular spatial frequency grating and increasing the intensity of the lighter regions until the grating is just detectable. This is continued over a range of spatial frequencies. Note that although the human function is generally superior to the cat's, the cat is more sensitive to low spatial frequencies

Spatial frequency channels

Campbell and Robson (1968) investigated the perception of complex gratings in a series of threshold determinations. Remember that a complex grating can be formed by adding a series of simple sinusoidal gratings (Figure 5.9). However, when one looks at such a grating the components are not obvious—they do not appear in consciousness—and in a sense they cannot be perceived. But when Campbell and Robson examined the contrast sensitivity functions for complex gratings they made an interesting discovery. With the display initially appearing a uniform grey, the contrast of a grating is raised until the observer becomes able to detect the spatial frequency to which he or she is most sensitive. Further increases in contrast reveal the presence, one by one, of the other spatial frequencies contained in the complex grating. And each threshold is the same as it would be if that particular spatial frequency had been presented in isolation. This is a most intriguing finding, particularly when one looks again at Figure 5.9 to remind oneself that the component frequencies are not perceptually distinguishable.

Later, Blakemore and Campbell (1969) discovered an interesting adaptation phenomenon. When a subject fixates a particular grating for a period of time and then has his or her contrast sensitivity function assessed, a drop in sensitivity is observed. Such fatigue effects are common in vision and this one was not surprising. However, the strange thing is that the effect is not general but is limited to those spatial frequencies close to that of the adapting grating. Similarly, fixating a horizontal grating reduces sensitivity to nearby frequencies, but only when these are horizontally arranged; there is no loss of sensitivity to vertical gratings. In both cases fixating has presumably fatigued some process, but the process is not general: it is orientation- and frequency-specific.

As a final example, it has been found that fatigue/bias effects are not limited to threshold stimuli. Fixate the dot at the left of Figure 5.11 and then look at the dot between the two right-hand gratings. It will be found that the apparent spacings of these two (identical) gratings will have changed, a supra-threshold effect first reported by Blakemore and Sutton (1969).

These discoveries provoked an exciting idea: *the visual system conveys information about spatial frequencies in tuned channels*. This was an insight which was to have a considerable impact upon subsequent theorizing about the visual system, as will be shown in Chapter 8.

The model of perception to emerge from the work described in this section is that vision proceeds in two distinct stages. Demonstrations such as that in Figure 5.12 prove that a scene can be physically analysed or decomposed into

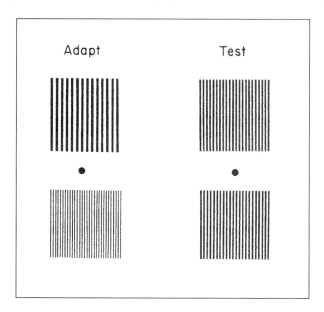

Figure 5.11 The Blakemore–Sutton after-effect. Fixate the left dot for about one minute, then look at the right dot. The upper right grating will then seem more narrowly spaced than the identical lower right grating. (This illusion was first described by Blakemore and Sutton, 1969)

a set of component spatial frequencies. But it is obvious from Figure 5.12 that this process can be reversed: the addition of spatial frequencies yields complete pictures. And if complete pictures can be formed in this manner might not the same be true of complete *percepts*? As yet, there is no strong evidence as to where the necessary syntheses take place in perception, nor do we have certain knowledge as to how this process is achieved, although we shall describe some hypotheses concerning this in a later chapter on the computational approach to visual perception. We can say, however, that the researches described above have been a rich source of ideas about vision and that the earlier work on visual analysis is beginning to be complemented by ideas as to how such analyses are later combined to form percepts.

Neural structures mediating responses to spatial frequency

An important question arises over the type of neural structures which might be capable of mediating the responses to spatial frequency described above.

Consider a hypothetical arrangement in which two gratings are moved across an aperture and that a light meter measures the energy reflected from the aperture. What will the meter reveal?

Clearly, the stripes of the high-frequency grating are very fine relative to the aperture. Therefore the meter will simply record the average luminance (or reflectance) from the light and dark stripes. Moving the grating will have no effect upon this average output.

But were the low-frequency grating to be moved across the aperture, it is clear that the larger stripes would exert changes which would be detected. Dark stripes would fill a large portion of the aperture to give a low signal on the meter; light stripes, when they appeared, would produce a sudden change in output. Thus the aperture is acting as a *filter* biased to low-frequency gratings. It is easy to see how a smaller aperture would allow the light meter to respond actively to finer (high-frequency) gratings. And it is obviously a simple matter to combine different apertures so that they could effectively *decompose* a complex grating, responding selectively to particular bands of spatial frequencies. Thus we can consider the aperture as a component in a spatial frequency detection model, with aperture size determining the frequencies to which the system is most sensitive.[4]

The question now is whether there is a known neural mechanism which could act in a manner analogous to an aperture. The reader has probably anticipated the answer to this question: *receptive fields could perform this function.*

It was for this reason that so much space was devoted earlier to the discovery of receptive fields. They are known to possess many of the properties

---

[4] The author first became aware of this way of thinking about filters, apertures and spatial frequencies in Kaufman (1974).

Figure 5.12   Computer-processed images. (a) The original photograph (of a famous psychology department). (b) An area of the original selected for processing, after conversion to pixels. (c) The result of processing the sample through a low-pass filter: the picture now contains only low spatial frequency information. (d) the result of processing (b) with a Laplacian filter. This has revealed the regions in the picture where zero-crossings occur. In this example, the 'receptive field' comprised a central excitatory region of one pixel surrounded by eight inhibitory pixels arranged in a square, with weightings of +8 for the excitatory centre and –1 for each of the 8 surrounding pixels. (e) is similar to (d) except that the receptive field or mask applied comprised a central excitatory square of 3 × 3 pixels surrounded by 72 inhibitory pixels. Thanks are due to Professor M.J. Morgan of London University College for generously providing the filtered versions in this illustration.

required for spatial frequency analysis. Remember that those receptive fields discovered to date show various forms of organization: some have on-centre/off-surround arrangements, others the reverse. Receptive fields have different shapes and sizes, and many are known to be orientation specific. As it can be shown that pairs of slit-like apertures, arranged at right angles to each other, can detect *any* grating (within their frequency range), it follows that we can now begin to understand how the visual system's responsiveness to spatial frequency may be mediated. During scanning movements of the eyes, lines and edges will move across the retina; thus large numbers of overlapping receptive fields will be stimulated by features within the visual image. There is therefore a very plausible set of mechanisms which could do the required job of spatial frequency analysis, and spatial frequency information can certainly be recombined to form percepts. Perhaps we are starting to learn something very important about the workings of the visual system. This is a very exciting state of affairs.

Of course, no one has claimed that this is a comprehensive theory, even of low-level visual perception. Nothing has been said regarding, for example, the relation between spatial frequency and colour or texture; nor have we referred to depth or motion perception. But there is now a convincing account of how one important aspect of seeing might be mediated, and a major portion of this account uses the language and concepts of neurophysiology.

SOME PROBLEMS ARISING FROM THE NEUROPHYSIOLOGICAL APPROACH

Neurophysiology and computational theory

In the sections above, we have tried to convey some of the quality of the neurophysiological approach to visual research and the explanations of phenomena which it has afforded. Readers will have noticed, however, that most of the research cited was published in the period between 1950 and the early 1970s. In a later chapter we shall describe the distinguished contribution of David Marr to visual theory. It is interesting that in the opening of his seminal (1989) book, *Vision*, Marr notes that what was promised by the great neurophysiological discoveries of the 1950s and 1960s was not being matched by comparably exciting work in the next decades: 'But somewhere underneath, something was going wrong' (Marr, 1989).

Description versus explanation

Marr's explanation for this slackening in progress was that descriptions of the behaviour of cells in the visual system do not *explain* that behaviour. Why, for example, is it adaptive to have cells in the visual cortex responding selectively to images of hands on the retina? Frisby had previously stated that:

. . . it is dangerous to assume that a property of a neuron can be directly equated with its functions; 'line detectors' have the property of responding optimally to a line of a given type but this does not mean that they are 'line detectors' in the full and proper sense of this term, that is that their function is to detect lines.

(Frisby, 1979)

Marr's solution to this difficulty lay in his development of what has been called the computational approach to vision. This is a sufficiently important development to warrant a chapter of its own later in this book. For now, we shall simply reiterate the assertion that there may be serious flaws in the type of theorizing which has formed the basis of the present chapter, and that the flaws lie in the levels of explanation adopted by theorists in the area: the difference between description and explanation. Marr's contribution was to clarify what is meant by different levels of explanation and how these can be synthesized.

Marr's doubts as to whether neurophysiological accounts of visual phenomenon are at appropriate levels of explanation deserve attention. There is, however, another problem, which goes beyond the doubts expressed over explanations in terms of the behaviour of specially functioning neurons or groups of neurons. This arises from the general model of the brain which has been widely adopted by workers in a variety of related disciplines.

A NEW TYPE OF MODEL: THE CONNECTIONIST NETWORK

Historical background

For the past 30 years or so, the most important, dominant model in experimental psychology has been the digital computer. When these machines became widely available in the 1960s and 1970s, many psychologists, and others in related disciplines, found them irresistible as metaphors for thinking organisms.

The Von Neuman machine

The classical digital computer is often defined in its abstract form as a Von Neuman machine, in honour of one of the pioneers in the area, John Von Neuman. In essence, Von Neuman machines have the following characteristics. There is an important distinction between the permanent structure of the machine—the hardware, and the set of programmed instructions—the software (it has been claimed that this might be analogous to the brain–mind distinction). The machines are rule-governed; they operate via explicit instructions. The operation of the machines is sequential. Knowledge or information within the system is stored in specific memory addresses and retrieved by means of these addresses. Von Neuman machines are controlled by special units, known typically as 'central processing units': to this extent they are essentially 'top-down' systems. Finally, it should be noted that actual digital computers need all their components to be working in order to function correctly: they can suffer catastrophic breakdowns.[5]

The listing above is a partial description both of the modern digital computer and of the human being—in the opinion of many workers in the modern discipline of artificial intelligence (AI). The achievements of such machines when performing tasks analogous to human mental functions have often been highly impressive. These range from successful object recognition to the playing of chess at Grand Master level.

Doubts about the computer metaphor

During the years when the digital computer had become the dominant model for psychology, particularly in the subdiscipline of cognitive science, a few theorists were, however, beginning to have doubts about its suitability as a metaphor of the brain and the mind. The approach described above arose from within AI research. Fundamental criticisms of AI work have been made by those who doubt whether it is in principle possible for machines to simulate human processes such as thinking and perceiving. Prominent among these critics is the philosopher Herbert Dreyfus (1972).

Dreyfus and others have marshalled a number of arguments against computer simulations, some of which will be mentioned. They are included here to show that there are those who challenge many of the assumptions underlying AI. If these are truly unsound, then the AI approach, in its basic form, could be doomed to eventual failure. We shall now summarize some of these doubts.

The first problem arises from a comparison of human performance on the one hand and the workings of neurons on the other. Once it has fired, a neuron goes into a phase when it cannot be made to fire again. This is known as the *absolute refractory period* of the neuron. There follows a period, the *relative refractory period*, when the neuron will fire, but only to increased stimulation. The durations of these periods vary, but commonly reported values for the total recovery time of neurons are of the order of tens of milliseconds. Now consider this truth concerning human perception: we can

---

[5] When starting to rewrite this chapter, the author found that his computer was behaving in a bizarre manner. Many subroutines (macros) had vanished, the computer's date functions had reverted to those of a previous year, and the screen became unreadable. After several hours, a skilled technician traced the fault to a small component which had failed and could be purchased for only £5.

do a great deal in a mere 200 milliseconds. In this small fraction of a second, our eyes can make a fixation on a scene or printed page and extract amounts of important information, before starting to move again. Using a tachisto-scope, it can be shown that the recognition of faces, words and objects, can all be achieved within 200 milliseconds. We can also make certain decisions within this period, as is shown by the study of human reaction times.

However, recognition and decision making are obviously complex ac-tivities. In visual recognition, for example, it is necessary to process the visual image and then compare it with material stored in memory, finally deciding whether or not the item is something one knows. But if such psychological processes comprised strictly sequential stages, as in a digital computer, then the refractory periods of neurons allow us to deduce that there must be a limit to the lengths of these sequences. This has been expressed by workers in AI as 'the hundred-step rule'. It seems highly implausible that the recognition of, say, a similar face could be carried out by a sequence of only 100 neurons. The obvious implication is that in the brain, in contrast to the digital computer (where speeds of processing are hundreds of thousands of times greater), neurons must commonly act *in parallel*. This is a very important deduction.

Other psychological knowledge, even everyday experience, suggests other ways in which human behaviour differs from the sequential, rule-governed, symbolic manipulation of the digital computer. Humans find it easy to work with 'fuzzy sets'. For example, we understand what is meant when someone says that a place was 'crowded'. But how to *define* 'crowded'? A crowded telephone booth differs from a crowded restaurant; both differ from a crowded stadium. Humans can see jokes and appreciate puns: it takes a novel combination of different kinds of knowledge to appreciate the wit and power of James Joyce's, 'Lawn Tennyson'. To 'see' a pun like that is to solve a problem. Can one visualize a traditional computer, with its fixed memories and sequential operations, doing such things?

Further, this elusive, 'lateral' aspect of thought is manifest not only in the ap-preciation of jokes and puns: Kekulé hit upon the ring structure of the benzene molecule after he had visualized a snake biting its tail; what could be more differ-ent than an animal and a molecule, except for this one geometrical similarity?

Humans can generalize. The author's daughter, then a little girl, once looked up at the rose window in a church and said, 'It's a telephone dial'. We see such similarities with ease: clouds can look like faces; penguins like waiters. And when we know a symbol such as the letter A, we can recognize it in any typeface, at any size, and in any orientation.

Humans can also distinguish between the essential and unessential features of patterns. In solving a problem (and perceiving frequently does require problem solving) the solver must acquire knowledge of what is and is not relevant to the solution. But it is a characteristic of many of the problems which humans can solve that the essentials are not known ahead of time.

THE CAT

Figure 5.13   Context and ambiguity: 'A' or 'H'

There are no simple rules for us, nor any for the computer. Where computers have in fact solved problems, it has been the programmers who have stipulated what is and is not relevant.

Humans can take account of context. In Wittgenstein's phrase, a mouth smiles only in a face. The expression is not *deducible* from a simple list of all the features of the face; the organization of the features *is* the expression. Similarly, humans can use context to complete percepts in ways which are often complicated and sometimes circular. Consider the middle symbol in the words CAT and THE in Figure 5.13. The resolution of the ambiguous central shape must depend in part upon the context supplied by the two familiar words; but the words themselves are formed using the ambiguous symbol. The effortless manner in which we solve this and other perceptual problems seems very mysterious and complex and not the sort of process to be easily modelled by traditional computer simulations.

Forerunners of the new type of model

Lashley's concept of equipotentiality

During the 1930s and 1940s the distinguished neuropsychologist Karl Lashley set out to discover the sites in the brain where learning and memory occurred. He failed. In a famous monograph entitled, 'In search of the engram' (1950), Lashley described a series of experiments on the rat's brain in which experimental damage was caused to different regions before and after learning. The results of these experiments showed that the precise site of an experimental lesion is less important in its effects on the rat's memory or learning ability than the amount of cortical tissue which has been damaged: the greater the damage the greater the impairment in performance, with complex skills suffering more than simple ones. Lashley elevated these results into the (self-explanatory) principles of Equipotentiality and Mass Action.

Hebb's reverberating circuits

Hebb, a contemporary of Lashley, took a discovery from neurophysiological research and developed it into a possible mechanism for perceptual learning

(Hebb, 1949). The discovery was that groups of interconnected neurons continue to show increased activity after the termination of the event which originally disturbed them. Hebb proposed that clusters of neurons displaying this *reverberating* activity acted as functional units and that modifications to such an interacting network could be the basis of both short-term and long-term learning. Hebb called these networks 'cell assemblies'.

Rosenblatt's Perceptron

As a final antecedent to the development connectionist networks, we may cite the first description of Rosenblatt's Perceptron (Rosenblatt, 1959). This was a device (in fact, like most devices to be described, it was simulated on a computer) comprising an input layer or 'retina', a decision layer, and between these a set of predicates. The retina can be interpreted as a simple array generating binary outputs when stimulated in some manner. The predicate layer comprised a set of threshold units, each connected to a subset of the retinal units and capable of computing some simple function from their outputs. The decision units were joined to the predicate layer by a number of modifiable connections. The task set for the Perceptron was whether it could adjust its outputs to match a given input: could it act as a primitive pattern recognizer?

The Perceptron was a 'one layer' computing device (it had only a single modifiable layer), and it contained vital flaws which were subsequently exposed by Minsky and Papert (1969). Nevertheless, it will become apparent that the Perceptron was an important forerunner of subsequent developments in this area.

Connectionist networks

So far we have not yet said what a connectionist network actually is, other than to sketch the Perceptron as a forerunner. In order to prepare the reader for what is to come, and to give a feel for this type of thinking, we have included Figure 5.14. This is not what is usually meant by a connectionist network. It is included simply to demonstrate that simple components, connected in certain ways, can do complicated things. In Figure 5.14 the units respond whenever they receive an input. The inputs can be excitatory or inhibitory. Consider what happens when the left-hand input unit receives an input. It stimulates the left-hand internal unit positively while inhibiting the right-hand internal unit. As a result, the left-hand internal unit will trigger a response in the output unit. However, a little thought shows that if both input units receive inputs simultaneously, the output unit will not fire. This is because of the mutual inhibition of the internal units. If we now work through the four possible input patterns (left on, right off, and so on) it becomes apparent that the output unit will respond if *either but not both* of the input units fire. What we have achieved with this simple configuration is the important logical function, *Exclusive-Or* (refer again to Figure 5.2). Now suppose (a) that the units in Figure 5.14 could be given threshold values enabling them to store inputs from more than one other unit, and (b) that the strengths of the connections between the units could be altered as a result of previous activity. The sense of excitement concerning what such a system might be able to do may be already appreciated by the reader.

After that preliminary demonstration, it is time to introduce connectionist networks. Rumelhart, Hinton and McClelland (in Rumelhart and McClelland, 1986) provide an excellent description of connectionist networks which forms the basis of the following account. Interested readers should certainly consult this invaluable exposition. One word of advice: the terminology in this area varies from writer to writer. The term *connectionism* defines the general approach to this new form of modelling. The actions of the models are

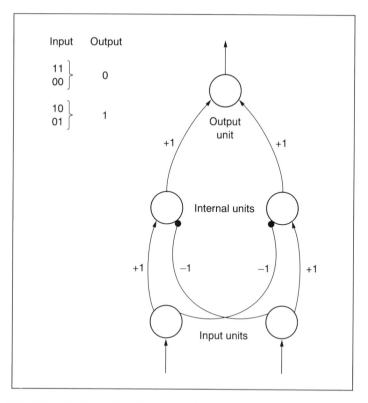

Figure 5.14 Five simple units which, when interconnected by excitatory and inhibitory links, can function as an Exclusive-Or logical gate

sometimes described as *parallel distributed processing*. Some authors use the terms *neural networks* or *neural nets*. Beware of these variants when searching the literature. In what follows, we shall use the term 'connectionist network' (or simply 'network' when the context allows).

Rumelhart *et al.* state that there are eight important characteristics of any connectionist network.

1. *A set of processing units.* The units 'represent' (in the sense to be defined later in the account of Marr's theory) some aspect of the real or hypothetical world against which the network will be tested. The representation may be *discrete*, in which case the units will represent particular parts of a display—shapes, letters, or words. Or the representation may be *distributed*, in which case each unit will represent some small feature-like entity, while the *pattern* existing among the set of units represents some more abstract aspect of the display or world. Each unit has but one function: to accept inputs from other units, compute some value, and then pass this on to neighbouring units. The computations may occur simultaneously and so this part of the network has a marked degree of *parallelism*. There are three possible types of unit: input units which we have been describing; output units, sending signals from the system; and 'hidden' units whose only interactions are with other units within the system.
2. *The state of activation of the system.* Different kinds of connectionist network use different possible values for the activation of units. These may be discrete, binary (0 to 1), or they may have a range of possible numerical values.
3. *Outputs from units.* Signals from units to neighbouring units affect the latter. The strength of these effects depends in part upon the activation level of the sending units.
4. *The pattern of connectivity.* According to the particular model under consideration, one unit may affect its neighbours in different ways. The effect may be additive or subtractive, for example. Or some inputs from units may be given weightings to increase or decrease their influence in the network. (Note the resemblance between this aspect of the model and a network of interacting neurons.) The points to remember are that units interact, and that the strengths of these interactions may be altered by various weighting functions.
5. *The propagation rule.* In simple terms, this is simply the rule governing interaction or competition between two or more inputs to a unit. If, for example, positive (excitatory) and negative (inhibitory) inputs are allowed to interact in a straightforward manner, they will cancel when their strengths (or weights) are equal. And so on.
6. *The current state of the network.* This is an addition to rule 5. To decide what will result from an interaction between units we must consider not just the interactions between inputs, as in rule 5, but how their sum or

product interacts with the current state of the unit onto which they impinge.

7. *Modification by experience.* By this Rumelhart *et al.* mean that there are different ways of changing the structure, activity, or 'knowledge' of a connectionist network. Thus, for example, new connections may form and old connections may be lost. Or the strengths of connections may be changed through experience. We are now at the core of connectionist network theory.

8. *Representation of the environment.* The environment in which a model must operate is represented across the input units. Typically, the environment is characterized as a set of labelled probabilities.

As stated earlier, the above description has been abstracted from a chapter by Rumelhart *et al.*, who are pioneers in this field. Their account is much more precise and powerful, but this precision is achieved through the use of mathematical concepts which we have tried to avoid. Nevertheless, readers who ponder over the definitions listed above will achieve an intuitive understanding of these models. To help the reader visualize networks, Figure 5.15 shows an arrangement comprising an input layer of six units, a hidden layer of four units and an output layer of six units. There are more efficient ways of representing networks which allow the weightings of the various connections to be displayed as clearly as possible, but Figure 5.15 captures the essence of a three-layer network.

Finally, it should be noted that when researchers attempt to model human processes, such as human recognition, their models may comprise two or

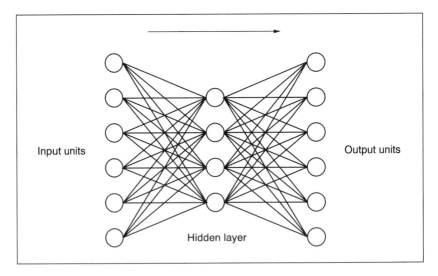

Figure 5.15 A three-layer neural net comprising 6 input, 6 output and four hidden units

more networks, each doing the job of one module within the overall model. Thus one network might function as a (primitive) retina, another might work on the output of this retina, and so on.

In essence then, a connectionist network comprises sets of simple interconnected units which interact according to weighting rules by which the strengths of their connections can change. The network can be set a problem in the form of an input pattern. A successful solution to the problem comprises a matching or otherwise acceptable output pattern. Obviously, the first 'run' through the network is unlikely to yield the required match or solution; rather, only parts of the output pattern will match the input. How does the network move towards the correct solution? The answer is that the discrepancy between input and output is fed back into the hidden layer. This is done in ways which selectively change the connections to those output units which are correct by strengthening (or reinforcing) them according to some predetermined rule. Other connections may be left unchanged or even weakened. In practice this is a more complicated process than we have outlined, and the assessment of the degree of mismatch between the desired and actual outputs may be in terms of large groups of numbers grouped as vectors. Those readers possessing the relevant mathematical knowledge can find an explanation of how vector sums and products can be made to operate on a network in the required manner in Rumelhart and McClelland (1986, see the discussion on the use of the Delta Rule.)

There is no supervisory control of the network, no central executive guiding the overall flow of information. And the common distinction between hardware and software vanishes: all units and their connections are essentially 'hard-wired', but the connections can be changed, like software. Further, knowledge is held briefly in the units and for longer terms in the connections: there is no special set of places equivalent to the memory addresses of orthodox computers. Knowledge and memory are not explicit, rather they are implicit within each pattern of connections.

It must be pointed out that very few networks exist as actual machines. Generally, they are simulated on computers. And it is the designer who typically sets the initial weightings in the connections and gives the model its initial problem (or input) and its target output. The number of trials to solution forms a measure of the performance of the model.

The achievements of connectionist networks

In a later chapter we shall describe the Marr–Poggio account of stereopsis. This very important model was tested by instantiating it in the form of a connectionist network. The model worked.

Other networks have been sufficiently successful to trigger insights of considerable theoretical importance. Networks have successfully solved problems in robotics. They have learned to complete patterns and to recognize faces. They have formed concepts from sets of features and have been able to extract meanings from letter inputs. One network can examine images from a video camera and decide whether or not a railway platform is crowded (remember the earlier remarks on 'fuzzy sets'). The network named ALVINN ('An Autonomous Land Vehicle In a Neural Network'; Pomerleau, 1989) was trained by showing it images from a road simulator. The 1200 different images included changes on a large number of parameters, such as road direction, width of road, road curvature, position of obstacles, and many others. After 40 training sessions, ALVINN drove a specially modified Chevrolet van around a university campus.

It would not be wise to describe these achievements as simulating successful behaviour; rather, they represent only pieces of behaviour. Equally, if not more significant, however, are the *emergent properties* which networks have exhibited. Here are three examples.

First, networks have shown *spontaneous generalization*. A network described by McClelland, Rumelhart and Hinton (1986) was set a classification task. It proved capable of selecting a subset of exemplars, all of which were similar but none of which had all the formal qualities required for category membership. The network had done something like a human when required to think under conditions of incomplete or imprecise information.

Second, networks exhibit *graceful degradation*. When given incomplete or slightly faulty inputs, they may not go wildly astray. They may come close to the correct solution to a problem. They get things approximately right. And when subjected to experimental damage (by removing varying proportions of units and interconnections) they do not suddenly fail to work; rather they show a general coarsening of performance, a gradual deterioration which is strikingly similar to types of brain damage. In fact, the resemblance between 'damaged' networks and neurological syndromes may be even closer than this. One 'damaged' model actually responded to word probes with words which were unlike the targets in form but similar in meaning, a behaviour which in humans is known as deep dyslexia.

Third, some networks exhibit *default assignment*. Suppose that a network finds a partial solution to a problem by locating one of the correct target items. The pattern of activity which lead to this solution will raise the strength of certain units and their connections. At the same time, however, the strengths of *similar* target items will also receive some increments. In this manner, the network can use what it knows to fill in properties of less well-known but similar target items.

> . . . generally speaking, the more similar two things are in respects that we know about, the more likely they are to be similar in respects that we do not, and the [PDP] model implements this heuristic.
>
> (McClelland, Rumelhart and Hinton, 1986, ch. 1)

This is, of course, what humans do all the time. To know that a person votes on the Right and is in favour of capital punishment gives one a fair idea of his or her views on blood sports. But how interesting that a connectionist network should show similar behaviour as an unexpected, emergent property.

It is of some interest that there are certain characteristics of connectionist networks which may eventually throw some light on the neural systems which inspired their creation. For example, the long controversy over whether perception and other forms of behaviour are innate or acquired may disappear if the parallel distributed process model, or connectionist network, becomes an accepted model of the brain. The reason is that it is not difficult to see how certain weighting functions in a network could be present at birth, with the added possibility that they could be modified by later experience. If so, there would still be an interesting set of empirical questions to ask concerning what is in fact present at birth, but the argument between two extreme theoretical positions would be expected to fade away.

The type of model we have been describing depends upon interactions between simple units. Typically, these models do not have specialized, dedicated centres located within them. Might this throw light on the fact that some areas of the brain outside the major sensory and motor centres have no easily demonstrated localized functions? Damage to the frontal lobes, for example, produces no single clear-cut deficit in performance. More commonly, what is observed is a general coarsening of behaviour, an erosion of general ability. This is very different from what happens when an orthodox computer is damaged, but very similar to the behaviour of damaged networks.

We may summarize this short introduction to this new type of model as follows. A network comprising input and output layers joined via one or more 'hidden' layers of simple interconnected units with alterable connection strengths can learn to do many highly interesting things. With their marked degree of parallelism the networks share some of the characteristics of the brain, and can mimic some of its more interesting properties. The implicit nature of the knowledge within such models—what is represented exists as patterns or relationships betweeen units, rather than as explicitly stored rules—together with the interesting emergent properties of the models in action, suggests that the connectionist network may replace the orthodox computer as a model of the brain or mind. The major insight which designers of networks have confirmed is that *systems using simple components can do very complicated things, provided these components are allowed to compete and interact.* Might this be the way the brain uses its simple components? In a sense, of course, it must be: neurons are what the brain is composed of.

Not surprisingly, such a new approach to computing and modelling has attracted its critics. Those readers who wish to follow the debate between supporters and opponents of connectionism should consult the papers by Broadbent (1985) and Fodor and Pylyshyn (1988) cited in the reference section.

GENERAL REMARKS ON THE NEUROPHYSIOLOGICAL
APPROACH TO PERCEPTUAL THEORY

An attempt was made above to describe the connectionist network approach enthusiastically, for in the opinion of many workers in perception this has been a very exciting development. It offers great promise for the continuing enterprise of combining psychological and neurophysiological knowledge. The reader should be aware, however, that these are quite early days in the development of such models. There may be limitations to this approach and flaws in its logic which we cannot yet imagine. The present author is excited by developments in this field, but his opinions should be treated with caution.

Turning to the main material of this chapter, it is clear that the gains in knowledge which we have outlined have followed a rough progression. Ingenious new techniques of measurement led to the discovery of the visual pigments suggested by psychophysical studies of colour vision. Then another major problem, the 'opponent' aspect of colour vision, was solved by the use of microelectrode probes which enabled researchers to study living neurons in the visual system. Knowledge of nerve excitation and inhibition, combined with the results of microelectrode studies, provided hard data on the characteristics of receptive fields. Finally, it was discovered that further psychophysical data on the perception of spatial frequencies could be explained by extending the concept of the receptive field.

Evaluation of this approach to theorizing involves a degree of personal choice. There have always been those who prefer to think in terms of concrete entities rather than hypothetical constructs, and this preference is not restricted to perceptionists.

One may also feel sympathy for the understandable desire to continue what is best about all this work, namely the fruitful interaction between psychology, where many of the problems of perception first become apparent, and physiology and neuroanatomy, where there are workers who are in a unique position to perform direct tests on sensory mechanisms. What have been described in this chapter are examples of the best sort of cross-fertilization between disciplines. But can the language of neurons and their physiology (or their simulations in connectionist networks) provide a full and final answer to problems in perception? Some think not.

First, to repeat a phenomenological argument made elsewhere in this book, colour is, among other things, an experience; a pain is not only activity in certain sorts of neuron, it hurts. But 'redness' and 'hurting' are part of our conscious lives. How much we hurt depends, in part, on our upbringing and upon the mores and attitudes of those around us; that is to say, upon other events and experiences which have taken place in the external world and which must be described in a language appropriate to that world. A full description of colour and pain must surely take this into account.

Then it must be recognized that to try to account for perception using the neuron as the basic explanatory device pushes one towards a reductionist point of view. It is an obvious possibility that sensory aspects of seeing—what happens in the retina, the optic nerve and the primary visual cortex—may indeed be explicable in terms of relatively simple mechanisms and systems. But the ways in which large groups of neurons interact is simply not known. Vision probably utilizes a significant proportion of the total ensemble of cortical cells, in which case the numbers involved are very large indeed: billions rather than millions. There could be interactions in such groupings too complex for the language of neurology, now or in the foreseeable future. Might it not be better to keep an open mind about the neural aspects of vision and to feel free to invoke hypothetical constructs when and where they seem appropriate? To do this would be to respect a long tradition in which supporters of Holism have long claimed that, as the brain is one vast interacting system, it is pointless to look for places where specific functions are performed or to simplify hypotheses to the level of components. Such holists will welcome the change in emphasis among those who work with connectionist networks. And indeed, connectionism may rescue the physiological approach from some of the difficulties outlined elsewhere in this chapter.

These remarks are very general in nature and the thoughtful reader will already have opinions about the issues raised.

Some readers may have found this chapter rather difficult. It has been necessary to describe some very technical researches briefly and in simple terms, and this is not easy to do. And we have had to refer on occasion to later chapters, for it is here that certain links with neurophysiological research and perceptual theory will re-emerge. After this explanation to the reader, it is time to ask what the work described in this chapter amounts to. What can be said finally about the neurophysiological approach to perceptual theory?

For a start, it is clear that this work has not generated a general theory of perception. Most of the solutions to problems described in the preceding sections have been very local. Many of these are satisfying in that they confirm the essential truth of some early perceptual theories. This is most clearly demonstrated in the research into mechanisms of colour vision, but an equally good case could have been made by describing comparable work in other modalities, particularly hearing. These solutions or explanations involve very few regions of the general model described in Chapter 1. For example, they may relate retinal outputs to the wavelength distributions of incoming light, or to brightness gradients across the retinal image. But the arc connecting the proximal stimulus and the receptor surface or structures adjacent to it is a very short one.

As we have stated earlier, there is no place in physiological accounts of vision for phenomenal experience. The contrast between, for example, the type of thinking outlined in this chapter and that which characterizes Gestalt theory could hardly be greater. Nor is it possible to see how some of the important Gestalt phenomena could be subjected to neurophysiological investigation: how to explain size constancy, figure–ground effects or Prägnanz? And it is clear that most of the work described assumes a direct causal link between events in the retinal layers and perceptual responses. But if Brunswik was correct in his insistence upon the probabilistic nature of perception, then such causal links cannot be the whole story.

What has emerged from modern neurophysiological research is something of a consensus among leading workers about the basic nature of vision. They consider that it begins with a series of analyses in which aspects of the visual image are converted to neural codes, and that these analyses must be relatively independent—for example, the mechanisms for coding colour must be different from those coding spatial frequency. But knowing *that* such coding takes place is not the same as knowing *how* the nervous system does it, which will be the theme of Chapter 8. It is also agreed that neural analysis must be followed by some sort of neural synthesis, and here there is much more uncertainty concerning possible mechanisms. This is hardly surprising, not least because such mechanisms, because of their later position in the chain of visual processing, must lie deeper within the central nervous system. They are going to be more difficult to find. But the process of synthesis may prove to be even more interesting as a research topic than anything described in this chapter. It strikes the present author as remarkable that colour and shape never drift apart. A red object never splits into its shape plus a misaligned colour; the registration is always perfect. How is the vital timing of colour and shape synchronized? It will be fascinating to try to solve problems of this calibre.

We end this chapter by asserting, once more, that reading of the discoveries which form the material of the chapter is an exciting experience. These major researches will have a permanent place in the history of perception. And even if it becomes accepted that the true explanation of perceptual phenomena cannot be arrived at using only the language of neurophysiology, then this, too, may be an important step in our understanding.

NOTES ON CHAPTER 5

Those readers to whom the main work described in this chapter is quite new should consult one or more of these excellent texts: Thompson (1967) for a lucid introduction to the early work on receptive fields, Ludel (1978) for a very clear account of neural structure and function.

The debate over three-factor *versus* opponent-process explanations of colour vision is described in most general perception textbooks, including Sekuler and Blake (1985).

Sekuler and Blake should also be consulted for their excellent descriptions of receptive field and spatial frequency research. Kaufman (1974) contains a very clear and interesting exposition of the relationship between spatial frequencies and the filtering characteristics of various sized apertures.

Frisby (1979) can be recommended as a demonstration of how knowledge of neural action can form the basis of a theory of shape perception.

Readers who enjoy polemical writing should read the criticisms by Dreyfus (1972), and Dreyfus and Dreyfus (1985) concerning the idea that the computer can serve as a model of the mind. Some of these criticisms have been incorporated into the present chapter.

Readers wishing to learn more about parallel distributed processing or connectionist networks should first read Orchard and Phillips (1991), which is a beginner's guide. The guide is supported by computer software which makes it possible to gain hands-on experience with various connectionist networks.

McClelland, Rumelhart and Hinton (1986) is an advanced, comprehensive and authoritative exposition of the general topic of neural networks.

The power of modern neurophysiological research on vision is evident throughout Blakemore (1990). Beware, however, as some of the technical work described is fiendishly complicated.

6

Empiricism: perception as a constructive process

> . . . whilst part of what we perceive comes through our senses from the object before us, another part (and it may be the larger part) always comes out of our head.
>
> (William James, 1890)

In 1959 a Canadian psychologist, Robert Sommer, described an incident leading to a trial at which he was a juror. Here is Sommer's account of the incident.

> A hunting party went out one afternoon looking for deer. While driving through a field, their car became stuck in the snow and eventually the transmission broke. Of the five men in the party, two volunteered to go to a nearby farmhouse for help. Of the remaining three, one remained in the rear seat while the other two stood at the front of the car. Meanwhile, one of the two men on the way to the farmhouse decided that there was no reason for both of them to go, and he thought he might be able to scare up a deer. Unknown to the men in the car, he circled around down a hill in front of them. At that point, one of the men standing outside the car said to the other, 'That's a deer, isn't it?' to which the other replied in the affirmative. The first then took a shot at the deer. The deer pitched forward and uttered a cry which both men heard as the cry of a wounded deer. When the deer started running again, the second man implored, 'Don't let him get away, please get him for me'. The first man fired again and the deer went down but continued its forward movement. A third shot brought the deer to the ground and both men started running towards it. By this time the third man in the car, who had been trying to find and focus his field glasses, suddenly called out, 'It's a man'.
>
> (Sommer, 1959)

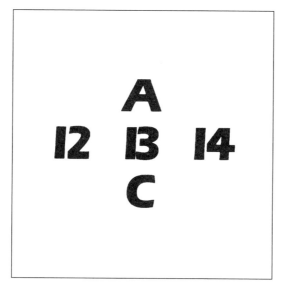

Figure 6.1   Ambiguous stimuli

The ideas in this chapter attempt to explain what happened on that tragic afternoon.

After the real-life story, consider two simple demonstrations. Look first at Figure 6.1. What do you see? Most readers will interpret the figure as a row of numbers and a column of letters. Now notice that the numeral '13' and the letter 'B' are in fact identical. Interpretation of the patterns is affected by their context.

Turn now to Figure 6.2. For many readers this will appear as a random jumble of black shapes on a white ground. If this is what you see your perception of the figure will now change.

The first hint is that the figure contains a face: can you see it? If not, then note that it is a Christ-like or Cavalier face occupying the top third of the rectangle and looking out of the page. Now can you see it? If not, note that the figure is strongly lit from one side, has two penetrating eyes, long hair and a beard. If you still cannot see the figure, look at Figure 6.3 which contains a more explicit plan of the face. If you happened to see the figure immediately, it is worth showing it to a friend and then helping him or her to see it by a series of hints. Seeing the face can occur quite dramatically and is a fascinating experience. Once seen, the face will always emerge from Figure 6.2.

It is clear that in both these demonstrations one's perceptions are not predictable simply from the parts which form the 'B', the '13' or the face. Something—the context, the hints—seems to have come between the registration of the stimuli and our final response to them. Is this an essential part of perceiving?

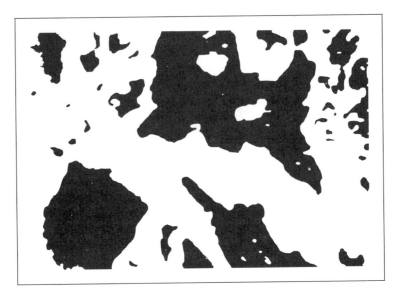

Figure 6.2 The hidden face. See the text for hints as to how to find the face. (From Porter, 1954)

Many who have worked in the field of perception, possibly the majority, have not been committed solely to one particualr theory or approach. Researchers have had their imaginations triggered in a variety of ways. They may have read about some new phenomenon and decided to set up equipment to enable them to see it for themselves. It is then a small step to make small changes and explore their effects. Soon, a research programme for the next few years has crystallized. Similarly, people can simply notice something odd about their own perceiving under unusual or unfamiliar conditions and decide to investigate what nature has tossed into their laps. And much research is still of the 'What if . . .' variety. What if chimpanzees could learn sign language? What if observers became weightless? What if an animal is prevented from using its eyes for the first three weeks of life? And so on.

In this sense it is almost possible to be a-theoretical in perceptual research. Almost, but not quite. The *framework* within which one thinks, the attitudes implied by particular experimental designs, and even the ways in which one expects observers to respond, are all subtly influenced by the current Zeitgeist. All who study perceptual phenomena have some beliefs concerning the fundamental nature of perceiving. To this extent, nobody is really a-theoretical. When such a set of beliefs and assumptions becomes widespread and strongly influential, the term 'paradigm' may be invoked. The impact of Darwinism on biology is a clear example of a paradigm shift, as is the more recent impact of quantum mechanics on theorizing in physics. (See Kuhn, 1970, for a discussion of paradigms in scientific research.)

We now assert that the dominant paradigm in perceptual research this century has been *empiricism*, which is the subject of this chapter. The thoughts which may have been suggested by the demonstrations at the start of this chapter are the same as those which led to the spread of empiricism in psychology: the idea that perception is something more than the direct registration of sensations; that somehow other events intervene between stimulation and experience. We shall attempt to show just how fruitful this idea has been.

In terms of the simple classificatory scheme outlined at the start of this book, psychological empiricism doubts whether proximal stimuli can adequately represent distal stimuli.

At this point it would be as well to warn philosophically informed readers that empiricism in psychology is not identical with the tradition which developed in the writings of Locke, Berkeley, Hume and Mill—the British empiricists. Locke, for example, was concerned with the origins of *ideas*. His writings stress that ideas can come into the mind only as the result of experience. Locke did not argue, as is sometimes claimed by psychologists, that we have to learn to see. But, as we shall show, some psychologists have claimed that this is indeed the case. Empiricism in psychology is therefore somewhat coarser and more extreme than the philosophical version. An excellent discussion of the topic will be found in Morgan (1977).

The remainder of this chapter will be organized under the following headings.

- The historical background to empiricism
- A modern version of empiricism: Gregory's theory that perceptions are hypotheses
- An evaluation of Gregory's theory
- Other modern versions of empiricism
- General remarks on empiricism

THE HISTORICAL BACKGROUND TO EMPIRICISM

Helmholtz

Hermann Helmholtz (1821–1894) had become a doctor of medicine by the age of 21. In 1847 he published a paper entitled, 'Über die Erhaltung der Kraft' ('On the conservation of energy'), which altered the direction of physics for decades to come and was the basis of the new science of

Figure 6.3   A key to the hidden face

thermodynamics. He went on to hold various prestigious academic posts, including the Chair of Physiology at Heidelberg, and the Chair of Physics in Berlin. He published more than 200 papers on mathematics, medicine, anatomy, physics, philosophy, physiology and psychology.

Helmholtz was one of the founders of perceptual research, and was probably the most gifted, original and successful perceptionist to date. The list of his discoveries and inventions is staggering: the first scientific account of hearing; the first scientific explanation of musical effects; probably the best book yet on seeing, *The Physiological Optics*; a major theory of the workings of the inner ear; a major theory of colour vision; the invention of the ophthalmoscope—Helmholtz was the first person to look into a living eye.

Helmholtz and unconscious inference

In mid-career, Helmholtz discovered an interesting problem. He had noticed that if a small piece of grey paper is laid over a red surface, it becomes tinged with green. Where does this green come from? Subsequent discoveries permit an explanation of the induced green in terms of known physiological mechanisms. But Helmholtz knew only that green is the *complement* of red. (In colour vision research, two hues are said to be complementary if their light, when mixed, yields an achromatic grey.) Helmholtz therefore offered an explanation of the induced green in terms of the viewer's *knowledge* of the fact that the grey paper, when adjacent to the contrasting red, should yield its complement.

With this explanation of a perceptual effect Helmholtz brought empiricism into experimental psychology. He argued that between sensations (when our senses first register the effects of stimulation) and our conscious perception of the real world there must be intermediate processes of a constructive nature. These processes resemble thinking, in particular inferential thinking, and because of them perception can go beyond the evidence of the senses—evidence which is often inadequate or distorted. Put another way, if distal and proximal stimulation are not identical, then intermediate processes must exist: how else can the veridicality of perception be explained? But when we introspect, we are not normally aware that we are making inferences, nor can we change our perceptions at will. Therefore the inferential processes must be unconscious.

Armed with this simple idea one can begin to explain a variety of important phenomena. For example, if the brain can calculate object distance, possibly by a process resembling triangulation, then this might be a way of compensating for the reduction of retinal image size with distance. This would provide a basis for size constancy.[1] In a similar manner, it is possible to understand why rectangular objects maintain their apparent shape when viewed obliquely. And so on.

Helmholtz did not fully explore the implications of unconscious inference. He offered some rules about the inferences—that they were inferential, that they were the result of associations and experience—but the central idea is not fully developed in his subsequent writings. However, the idea of unconscious inference did enable Helmholtz to avoid nativist solutions to the problems of perception (we see things at their proper size because we are built to see in this way, which is hardly an explanation), and this may have been his main aim.

Helmholtz's prestige, added to the basic appeal of empiricism, made this way of thinking about perception almost irresistible. The acceptance of his ideas was also reinforced by the 'inference revolution' described in Chapter 2. There was in fact some opposition to Helmholtz's views during his lifetime. For example, another great physiologist, Hering (Helmholtz's contemporary and rival), adopted a nativism which was totally opposed to empiricism. And, as we have seen, the Gestalt movement had little sympathy for the idea that

---

[1] Size constancy is interesting when it breaks down. The author's son, when a child, once asked how people could fit into a 'tiny' aircraft flying overhead. Over 100 years earlier, Helmholtz had recounted his childhood puzzlement over the doll-like appearance of people high above him in a belfry.

perception was based upon associations. But despite these important exceptions, a major paradigm had emerged: perception was to be thought of as an indirect, constructive, inferential process.

Empiricism after Helmholtz

We shall now describe a selection of discoveries made during the years between Helmholtz and the present which have reinforced the empiricist conception of perception.

Attention and set

In a classic study of human attention, Külpe (1904) used a tachistoscope to deliver brief exposures of displays of variously coloured letters. The observers in the experiment were directed to attend to some aspect of the display, say the position of certain letters. When asked subsequently to describe some other aspect of the display, for example the colours of the letters, they were unable to do so. The significance of this famous demonstration is that although all the information from the brief display must have reached the eye, at some point between the formation of the retinal image and the production of the final report, selection had taken place: what is taken in from a display depends not only upon the properties of that display but on the 'set' which the viewer has adopted. Perceptions are not simply inputs.

Drives and perception

Sanford (1936) showed ambiguous pictures to groups of school children and asked them to write down what they had seen. The experiment was run at different times of a day. It was found that twice as many food-related responses were made before compared with after meal times. Hunger can influence what is seen.

The influence of stereotypes

Early in his famous book *Remembering* (1932), F.C. Bartlett describes a demonstration which he ran during the first open day at the new psychology laboratory in Cambridge. Visitors were asked to look into a tachistoscope and report what they could see. The picture in the tachistoscope was that of a man wearing a naval officer's cap. Many viewers reported, wrongly, that the man had a beard: the current stereotype of a British naval officer. Prior expectations had influenced what they had seen. (In the subsequent researches for which he became famous, Bartlett was able to show that stereotypes and expectations exert an equally striking influence on long-term remembering.)

The New Look experiments

In the years following the Second World War, a group of American psychologists, many of whom had an interest in Freudian or other psychodynamic theories but had also received training as experimentalists, reported a series of researches which became known, collectively, as the New Look psychology (after a popular contemporary fashion in clothes).

Bruner and Goodman (1947) carried out an investigation into children's ability to judge the size of coins and found that the perception of size was influenced by the value of a coin, the effect being greater with children from poorer homes. It was then reported that it took longer to recognize 'taboo' words than control words when these were presented tachistoscopically (McGinnies, 1949). More dramatically, Lazarus and McCleary (1951) reported that after certain words had been paired with electric shock, they took longer to recognize, and that even before their recognition thresholds were reached the words induced physiological responses in observers.

The New Look experiments are now generally discredited. For example, might not the delayed responses to taboo words be a response effect: the observer wishing to make sure of being correct before uttering the taboo word? And poor children would be expected to be less familiar with high-value coins. However, publications like those referred to could only reinforce the idea that perception is a constructive process.

The Ames demonstrations

During the 1940s Adelbert Ames of the Dartmouth Eye Clinic, Connecticut, developed some of the most compelling illusions ever seen. The most famous of these are the Ames room and the Ames window (see Ames, 1949).

The Ames room is shown in plan view in Figure 6.4. It is an irregular shape with a receding rear wall. But the room is decorated in a special manner: the patterning is such that it projects an image to a viewing point in the front wall which is identical to that which would be produced by a wall at right angles to the two side walls; in other words by a normal wall.

When one looks into the Ames room, one sees it as normally proportioned. But if a person walks from one of the two far corners of the room to the other, the room stays rectangular, *but the person appears to change size*. This wonderful illusion does not disappear when one learns the true shape of the room.

The Ames window is simply a trapezoidal shape with a window design added to it in such a way that when the window is viewed obliquely from 45 degrees the outline and the details appear rectangular. When such a window is rotated one sees, not rotations, but *oscillations*, the window appearing to change its direction of rotation half way through each cycle.

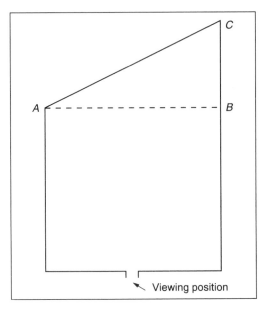

Figure 6.4 The Ames room from above. The wall *AC* is shaped and decorated so as to appear to be in position *AB* when seen from the viewing position. Viewed monocularly from the front, the room appears rectangular. However, an object moving from *A* to *C* will appear to shrink

The original explanations of these two Ames illusions was in terms of our familiarity with rectangular rooms and windows. It must be said that this explanation has been challenged (see, for example, Day and Power, 1965). But note how powerful a demonstration of the vulnerability of perception is contained in these ingenious inventions. How could one deny that perceptions are modifiable constructions, rather than direct responses to patterns of stimulation, when one has been made to doubt the evidence of one's senses in such a captivating and compelling manner?

Attention and perception

Some very famous studies of human attention were published during the 1950s and 1960s. We shall not attempt to review this large literature. It must be stated, however, that influential books by Broadbent (1958) and Neisser (1967) made a powerful case for the selective nature of much human perceiving. An observer, asked to monitor one of two aural messages delivered simultaneously, one to each ear, will subsequently be unable to say very much about the other. The observer will, however, hear his or her own name in the non-attended ear. In another widely used experimental situation, an observer who has just scanned rapidly through a visual array for a target will be able to say very little about the non-target items scanned through.

These and many other reliable effects illustrate the selective nature of perceiving and seem to show that perception can come under the control of central factors and is not determined solely by local conditions of stimulation. This is very suggestive evidence from the point of view of those who support an empiricist view of perception.

Summary

This, then, was the state of thinking concerning the indirect, constructive nature of perception 100 years after Helmholtz had formulated the doctrine of unconscious inference. To summarize: empiricism in psychology conceives of the perceiver as being not unlike the captain of a submarine. He has knowledge of the medium in which he is submerged but cannot experience it directly. So it is necessary to plan according to the knowledge which experience and training have provided. From time to time, indirect samples of the environment are taken: instruments show the distance from the ocean floor, the vessel's heading, the presence in the area of other submerged objects. The better (the more alert and experienced) the captain, the more skilful will be the evaluation of the evidence from imperfect sensors. The ship must be guided through water that can never be touched.

The sections above outline the history of empiricism in psychology and show some of the varied evidence adduced in favour of this paradigm. But the various approaches that have been guided by empiricist or constructivist assumptions have been sketched only in bare outline (except of course Brunswik's which, although written by someone calling himself a functionalist, clearly makes assumptions of a constructivist nature). It is time to give a more detailed account of a modern version of empiricism, a contemporary theory of perception which can be traced back to the work of earlier psychologists such as Bruner and beyond them to Helmholtz himself. The theory of perception developed by the British psychologist, R.L. Gregory, will demonstrate where empiricism has arrived 100 years after Helmholtz introduced the idea into the psychology of perception.

A MODERN VERSION OF EMPIRICISM: GREGORY'S THEORY THAT PERCEPTIONS ARE HYPOTHESES

R.L. Gregory

Richard Gregory, now Emeritus Professor at the University of Bristol, England, is an experimenter of unusual originality. He has also invented a

microscope, a telescope, a new type of hearing-aid, and several other ingenious devices. In Gregory's experiments, observers have been hurtled down
tunnels, swung on giant swings, and baffled by illusions. His lectures are
distinguished by the use of novel demonstrations which are so compelling that
one comes away convinced that what he says about perception must be right.
He has inspired the building of a 'hands on' science fair—The Bristol
Exploratory—and is a frequent broadcaster. The quality of his writing and his
demonstrations matches the standards set by the Gestalt psychologists and
Ames and his co-workers—which is to say, they are as good as any in the
history of perception. Gregory has enabled countless individuals to experience some of the delights which the study of perceptual phenomena affords. It
is hardly surprising that his views on perception should be so well known.

Perceptions as hypotheses

As well as being well known as a highly original experimenter, Gregory is
interested in the classical philosophical problems associated with perceiving.
In an article published as part of a debate between psychologists and philosophers (Gregory, 1974), he describes some of the properties of perceiving
which, he claims, force the conclusion that this is an activity resembling hypothesis formation and testing.

  The essence of Gregory's hypothesis theory is as follows. Signals received
by the sensory receptors trigger neural events, and appropriate knowledge
interacts with these inputs to create psychological data. On the basis of such
data, hypotheses are advanced to predict and make sense of events in the
world. This chain of events is the process we call perceiving.

  One of the merits of what Gregory calls *the hypothesis theory* is the clarity
of its presentation. Another is the care with which Gregory presents the
evidence in support of his views. Gregory's main arguments for this most
recent version of empiricism will now be summarized (see Gregory, 1980a,
1980b for the full version of these arguments).

1. *Perception allows behaviour to be generally appropriate to non-sensed object characteristics.* We respond to certain objects as though they were
   tables, having, that is, four legs and rectangular tops, even though all we
   can 'see' are three legs and the trapezoidal projection of the top. Are we
   not using more than just sensory inputs to achieve these percepts?
2. *Perception can, in familiar situations, mediate skills with zero time delay.* In
   a typical tracking experiment the observer is asked to keep a pointer
   aligned with a moving target. This would seem to be an essentially visual
   task, and visual processes are known to require a finite time. However, if
   the target position in a tracking task is made regular and predictable, then
   the observer will be able to track the target with zero time delay. How is

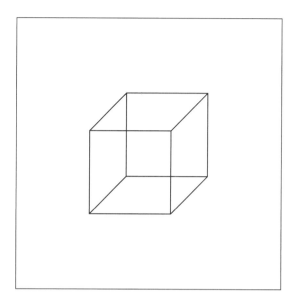

Figure 6.5 A reversible figure: the Necker cube. When fixated in the centre, the orientation of the cube may change quite suddenly

this possible without a degree of anticipation entering into the perception of the target?

3. *Perceptions can be ambiguous.* Look for a moment at Figure 6.5, the Necker cube. As one stares at this familiar figure its orientation may suddenly change: it is unstable. If a single physical pattern can induce two different percepts, perception cannot be tied to the stimulation in a one-to-one manner. In a related manner, the simple drawing in Figure 6.6 can represent two different shapes: is it a duck or a rabbit?

4. *Perception can extract familiar objects from background clutter.* Gregory uses as an example our ability to extract one person's voice from others in a crowded room. This is something which no machine has ever been able to do, although we find it relatively easy. Is this because there is a limited repertoire of acceptable speech sounds which we and the speaker share? If so, our knowledge of the language is reducing the informational demands of the task. The achievement which this form of perceiving represents is more obvious when we consider experiences in a foreign country: after a few repetitions it slowly dawns on one that, for example, the sound, 'atoo tulur', is the phrase, *à toute à l'heure*. Perceiving appears to be aided by knowledge.

5. *Highly unlikely objects tend to be mistaken for likely objects.* One of Gregory's best-known demonstrations involves a hollow mask of a face. When

Figure 6.6 Duck or rabbit?

suitably illuminated, such a mask is generally seen as normal. Interestingly, even when one knows the true orientation of the mask (and even when one has constructed it) the illusion remains, recalling Helmholtz's description of unconscious inferences as 'irresistible' and Brunswik's phrase, 'the stupidity of the senses'.

6. *Perception can be paradoxical.* Figure 6.7 is Roger Shepard's version of a famous 'impossible figure'. Note how very difficult it is to arrive at an unambiguous perception of the figure, in particular to see how the central column is supported, given the changing status of the two central vertical lines as one fixates first the bottom and then the top of the figure. Shepard names his figure, 'Doric dilemma'. This seems very appropriate.

7. *Perception can be of one thing representing another.* The perception of any picture is in a sense ambiguous: we see the lines and the surface and also the object depicted, even though the latter may in reality be many times larger than its depiction. Therefore there must be a large cognitive component in the perception of pictures.

8. *Perception is not essentially based on what is experienced.* In many experimental situations observers may be influenced by stimulus characteristics of which they are unaware. There is a very simple and reliable way to demonstrate this. If one displays two photographs of a person, both printed from the same negative but in one of which the pupils have been enlarged, this will be seen as the more attractive version. Interestingly, observers are often unable to notice any physical difference between the

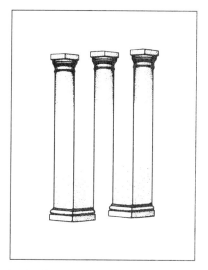

Figure 6.7 Shepard's intriguing version of an impossible figure, entitled 'Doric dilemma'. (From *Mind Sights* by R.N. Shepard. Copyright 1990 by Roger N. Shepard; used with permission of W.H. Freeman & Company)

two pictures: they have been influenced by the artificially dilated pupils, but have not noticed them.[2]

9. *People experience hallucinations.* Quite simply, we can have vivid experiences of a perceptual nature in the absence of external stimulation.

These, then, are some of the key reasons which Gregory advances in support of the idea that perception is an indirect, constructive, hypothesis-like process. His case is clearly formidable. Notice also how well supporting instances are presented: the statements above concerning empiricism and perception are some of the most explicit ever.

An application of hypothesis theory

Gregory has used hypothesis theory to develop an explanation of certain well-known illusions (Gregory, 1963). The Müller–Lyer illusion, which appeared in the present account of the Gestalt theory (see Figure 3.7), is one of the most famous of all the geometric illusions. For many years psychologists have attempted to explain the shortening and lengthening of the main parts of this figure, without, it must be said, much success. Gregory's suggestion is an interesting application of hypothesis theory to an old and hitherto intractable problem.

---

[2] In medieval Italian states, women would put a plant extract containing atropine into their eyes to dilate the pupils. The name of the plant? *Atropo belladona* ('beautiful lady').

Suppose that the feather ends of the Müller-Lyer lines are acting as cues to depth, following the rule of linear perspective that parallel lines appear to converge with distance. By this rule, the shaft with the out-turned feathers triggers the hypothesis that there is an inside corner formed by the junction of two surfaces. Look now at the ceiling of the room in which you are reading this and note how the corner formed by the two walls and the ceiling resembles the out-turned feathers. Now inspect an object which has a corner or edge pointing towards you (say a book standing vertically on a horizontal surface): the outside corners of the book can be seen to resemble the in-turned arrows of the Müller–Lyer figure. In the real three-dimensional world such inward- and outward-facing corners reveal whether an edge juts towards or away from us; that is to say, they are cues to *distance*.

In real scenes, the shrinking of the retinal image of a receding object is opposed by the mechanism of *size constancy*, which, by enabling us to see objects in their same size despite changes in distance, helps us to perceive a stable world. But if the Müller–Lyer arrows trigger this constancy mechanism, they are doing so in an inappropriate situation: the lines are actually equidistant from us on the page. So, instead of the equality of the shafts being preserved over different distances, the constancy scaling mechanism induces a perception of unequal size at a fixed distance, and this is the Müller–Lyer illusion: an adjustment of perceived size triggered when it is inappropriate. This original explanation follows quite naturally from the assumption that perceptions are hypotheses, and is a good example of Gregory's ingenious deployment of his theory.

AN EVALUATION OF GREGORY'S THEORY

Gregory's theory that perceptions are hypotheses is the most explicit and fullest development of the empiricist paradigm. We shall now offer some criticisms of the theory—some general, others more specific.

The nature of perceptual hypotheses

One possible criticism of Gregory's theory is this: if perceptions are hypotheses, what sort of hypotheses are they? In one formal approach to the philosophy of science it is held necessary to abandon a hypothesis when a single contradictory fact appears (see, for example, Popper, 1960). However, it is commonly accepted that this is not how scientists actually behave. Nor do perceivers: we do not mistrust our senses following exposure to a single illusion. Scientists modify and elaborate hypotheses according to their success, or lack of it. But how do perceivers modify their hypotheses? Is this done according to the frequency of positive and negative tests, or is the modification based upon the strikingness of confirmatory and invalidating experiences? For example, learning that a photographed face is that of a mass-murderer certainly seems to effect a permanent change in one's perception of the face. And the reader has experienced rapid perceptual learning when discovering the face in Figure 6.2. On the other hand, learning to adjust to the effects of lenses which distort the world may take hours or even weeks of exposure. What is the difference between these forms of learning? Is it a difference between learning and experience—are the two different? We are not told.

Hypotheses and language

A related general criticism concerns the relationship between hypotheses and language. What is this relationship? Hypotheses, in the normal use of the term, must be statable if they are to be tested against evidence. But we often have perceptual experiences that are difficult to describe. It can be the case that only after considerable thought by the observer can he or she describe what was seen. But the seeing came first. It would appear that perceptual hypotheses may be closer to intuitions than to formal statements. We can say that we dislike someone without being able to say why. We can walk down a flight of stairs without looking at our feet and without even noticing what the stairs look like. The hypothesis that the stairs are regular does not appear in consciousness. If hypotheses are not necessarily verbal or even conscious (remember Helmholtz and *unconscious* inference), then finding out about them is going to be difficult.

The inadequacy of sensory evidence

As has been stressed several times in this chapter, many theorists since Helmholtz have accepted his claim that sensory inputs alone are insufficient to specify the world. In support of this claim it has been pointed out that, for example, because the retinal image of an object shrinks as the object recedes, the correct perception of the unchanging size of the object implies that the sensory evidence has been supplemented from other sources. This constancy example has been used several times in this book—quite deliberately as it is a classic illustration of the empiricist argument.

But are retinal images really so impoverished? In the world (in contrast to the laboratory) retinal images will only rarely contain projections of single isolated objects. They will be much richer than this, typically including projections of other objects, the background to the objects, even the distant horizon. They will be rich in detail.

Some modern research has shown that complex images of real scenes commonly contain information which can be used to tell whether a receding object has or has not changed its size. Basically, what seems to be important is that some part of an otherwise changing image remains *invariant*. Similarly, although the shape of an object may not be uniquely specified by any single view of it, multiple views may deliver an unambiguous and correct solution to the true shape. And movement is a vital part of perceiving, a truth which has often been overlooked in laboratory research. The search for invariants, the importance of multiple views, and the difference which movement makes to seeing will be discussed at some length in Chapter 7. For now it suffices to say that empiricists may have underestimated the richness of sensory evidence when perceivers operate in the real world.

Starting to perceive

This is a problem which seems at first to be rather trivial, but on reflection can cause complete bafflement. If perception is essentially constructive, how does it ever get started? How does the naive, newborn perceiver ever establish a grasp on reality? One wonders if perception can be such an individual and chancy process. One's real-life experience suggests a great communality among the perceptions of different people. Where did this come from if all have had to construct their own idiosyncratic worlds? We shall offer a partial answer to this question later when discussing modularity. Another partial answer is contained in the work of Brunswik (described in Chapter 4). Brunswik would stress that the selection of appropriate cues is vital to survival, and that organisms which get things wrong are unlikely to survive. That is to say, the world is common to all perceivers, and it may be this single fact that regularizes the perceptions of all creatures sharing a particular ecological niche. But hypothesis theory does not engage in such functionalist explanations.

Human and non-human perceivers

This general criticism of hypothesis theory may be somewhat unfair, in that a theorist is not obliged to consider all possible ramifications of a theory; what follows should read as a statement of opinion rather than a formal criticism.

There is a trap awaiting all whose work concentrates upon the human perceiver: it is to suppose that all perceivers are like us. But all species are the product of a long evolutionary history which shaped the structures *and* the functions of the senses. It is as well to remember that, on several criteria, humans are not the most successful creatures to date. They are certainly not the most numerous, nor does their history match the duration of other groups such as dinosaurs and arthropods. All animals perceive, and must do this well enough to survive.

When we learn of the perceptual abilities of other creatures we find much that is strange:

The mayfly lives but a day as an adult. It may, for all I know, experience
that day as we live a lifetime.

(Gould, 1980)

Our (understandable) self-centredness should not blind us to the remarkably different lives of such organisms. Has the mayfly time to form and test
hypotheses? Has it the neural equipment to do the necessary statistical assessments? Probably not. But mayflies can see their world, and have been doing
so well enough for millions of years.

There are certainly major qualitative differences between our perceptual
systems and those of many other animals. The long period of post-natal
helplessness in humans may be the price paid for perceptual flexibility, and in
this they differ from many other species who can function well at birth but
who are relatively inflexible in their subsequent behaviour. But at what point
does perception cease to be reflexive and become constructive? In how many
species can we apply the theory that perceptions are hypotheses? Might it be
that our long evolutionary history enables us too to perceive the world more
directly and automatically than hypothesis theory suggests? A partial answer
may be contained in the proposal that perceptual input systems are
modular—a point to which we shall return below. There will be more to say
about this general problem in a later description of the theory of direct
perception (Chapter 7).

Hypotheses and evidence

If we accept for the moment the idea that perceptions are hypotheses, a little
thought reveals another serious problem: what is the *evidence* against which
they are tested? Gregory is not clear on this point, and it is a difficult one. One
of his own examples can be used to show the problem. He says, rightly, that
we frequently 'see' a table when its retinal image must be distorted and
incomplete. We go beyond the partial evidence of our senses via the (reasonable) hypothesis that there is a rectangular table in view.

Such a table is in view as this is being written. The top is built from parallel
rough planks (university salaries being what they are), and three legs are
visible. It would be a shock to discover that this familiar, shaky object was not
a table: the hypothesis seems to be a strong one. But what is the nature of the
supporting *evidence*? Presumably it lies in the perception of the planks and
the legs. But what guarantee is there that actual legs and planks are there? Is
it not necessary first to have hypotheses to 'acquire' these components; and
doesn't this lead to a regress of hypotheses concerning finer and finer details
of the world? But if the Gestalt psychologists were right, the parts of a table
do not simply add up to give the whole: they are seen in a manner partially
determined by this whole. This and related criticisms of Gregory's theory are

discussed more fully by the philosopher G.E.M. Anscombe (in Brown, 1974). Anscombe reminds us that a hypothesis is typically something which is answerable to data. What are the data to which Gregory's hypotheses are answerable?

There may in fact be an answer to this problem. It has been provided in the work of Fodor. In a now famous and highly influential book, *The Modularity of Mind* (Fodor, 1983), Fodor seeks to revive and develop a very old idea, namely that there are mental 'faculties'.

Fodor argues for an important distinction between the mind and perceptual input systems. The more 'central' systems, the functioning of which give rise to mental phenomena (consciousness, awareness, thought and problem solving), are essentially 'horizontally' organized. They are unencapsulated and global in nature. An example will help flesh out this idea. A striking property of human thought is the ability to reason analogically. This appears to be particularly true in the development of new art forms and in the making of dramatic scientific discoveries. Fodor shows how things get likened to other, very different things. The solar system is suddenly seen as a model of the atom; benzene as a snake-like ring. Insights are important moments in the history of discovery and invention.

In contrast there are the perceptual input systems. The essence of these, Fodor argues, is that they are *modular*. By this is meant that they are self-contained, have limited tasks to perform, are reflexive in nature, and are cognitively inpenetrable. For example, it is simply impossible to open one's eyes and *not* see a red surface as red. No amount of thought, no strongly held belief, no effort of will can alter such a basic visual response. More controversially, Fodor includes language in his list of perceptual modules. In a similar argument to that above, he claims that it is impossible for a native speaker of English to hear the spoken language as merely sounds: the module will operate, reflexively, no matter what mental set the listener adopts.

It should be stressed that Fodor's reasoning is much more detailed and thorough than this short précis might suggest. For now, though, the thing to stress is the idea that perceptual input systems are by nature *modular*. However, this does not imply that they are merely automatic transducers of stimulation. They have a very complicated job to do, which is to represent information about the world to the mind (brain) in forms which it can use. If this is true, then we can begin to understand the nature of the evidence that Gregory's hypotheses are answerable to: the automatic outputs from perceptual modules. Of course, this conclusion is not the final answer to the question of how much of perceiving is constructive in nature, but it does suggest directions for future research. A possible beginning might be a taxonomic classification of all those aspects of perception which experience, mental set and so on, can (or cannot) influence.

Addendum

In this account of Gregory's theoretical work, we have concentrated on the best-known of the writings in which he defends his proposition that perceptions are hypotheses. In fairness, it should be mentioned that Gregory's views continue to develop and that he has refined his theory in his latest work (Gregory, 1995). A short précis of his latest position will now be given as an addendum to this section.

First, Gregory acknowledges the importance of 'bottom-up processes'—most evident in reflexive behaviour, such as blinking the eyes to a looming object. No amount of knowledge allows us to modify this response. Even experienced weapons instructors blink at the sound of a gun being discharged. And much of our behaviour towards objects goes beyond their simple optical properties: we can tell how and where to grasp them, for example. In order to be able to do this, we must be using internal representations in a 'top-down' manner, which in turn allow our intelligence to do its job.

Further, using conceptual knowledge in a top-down manner may take time. But perception is commonly very fast—there may be insufficient time for conceptual knowledge to play its part. We can witness this happening when, for example, we still experience illusions which we understand and are familiar with (remember Brunswik's 'stupidity of the senses'): the percept is formed before intelligence or knowledge can be used to get things right.

Gregory therefore proposes that in addition to 'bottom-up' and 'top-down' processes there is another stage in visual perception. He calls this stage, 'sideways floppy disk operating rules'.

The importance of the sideways stage in Gregory's theory is this. There are many perceptual situations we need to deal with which are not handled adequately by reflexes (eye blinks and so on); nor can they be handled by our acquired knowledge of the world. For example, during a person's first ever exposure to a pair of stereograms in a stereoscope, it is well-nigh impossible that that person will be able to reason out what he or she 'should' see. But most people will eventually experience a sensation of depth. If this is due neither to a pure visual reflex nor to an intellectual solution to a problem, what is mediating this unfamiliar perceptual experience?

The answer to this question might be that in normal binocular viewing the visual system must in some way compare the two retinal inputs in order to use differences between them as cues to the relative depths of objects (a topic which will be dealt with at greater length in Chapter 8). To do this requires specific procedures, of which we are of course unaware—they are not part of our conceptual knowledge. If we understand Gregory's position on this issue, the stereoscope situation would be one where the specific procedures are inserted sideways, as it were: the floppy disk operating rules. Thus something is being added to raw sensory inputs—which is the essence of the constructivist position.

There will be times when the sideways disks will not be available, or when an inappropriate one has been selected. For example, it might be because we insert a disk containing procedures for dealing with objects and not pictures that we fall prey to perspective tricks induced by the latter.

Gregory raises many other interesting points concerning visual perception, particularly those associated with what he considers to be the ill-judged analogies drawn between perceivers and machines. Some of these will be included in later parts of this book.

OTHER MODERN VERSIONS OF EMPIRICISM

This chapter has concentrated upon the version of empiricism developed by R.L. Gregory and has enabled us to mention recent work within the constructivist paradigm. It is also true to say that Gregory's is probably the best-known and most thoroughly developed version of empiricism to date. The reader should be aware, however, that the broad appeal of empiricism and constructionism is such that several different general theories have emerged within this paradigm. Here is a list of some of the authors whose work should be consulted by anyone who wishes to know the various ways in which the central idea of this chapter—that perception is constructive—has been developed and refined.

Brunswik's theory

In this theory, the perceiver acts as an intuitive statistician. It is clear then that some parts of the theory are constructivist. The theory outlined in Chapter 4 should be re-examined from the more general position described in the present chapter.

Bruner's theory

This theorist's work on the role of categories has been mentioned previously (see in addition, Bruner, Goodnow and Austin, 1956), as has his work on needs and values in perceiving (Bruner and Goodman, 1947). Here is a very good example of a theory which claims that perception is active rather than passive and that the perceiver copes with the complexities of the world by meeting sensory inputs with ready formed classificatory systems.

Ames and transactional functionalism

As a result of his experimental studies of visual perception carried out at the Dartmouth Eye Institute, USA, Adelbert Ames developed transactional functionalism. His experimental findings suggested to Ames that we carry around with us knowledge of the 'typical' size and shape of familiar objects, which we usually see over a very restricted set of distances. If unusually large or small versions of familiar objects are illuminated in the dark, their apparent distance is determined partly by their actual distance and partly by the visual angle they subtend under natural conditions. Similar explanations can be advanced to explain illusions such as the Ames room and the Ames window. Thus perception is a dynamic interplay between current stimulation and expectations based upon our previous dealings with the world.

Hochberg

In the author's opinion, some of the most interesting perceptual experiments of the past 20 years are those described by Hochberg (see, for example, Hochberg, 1968). Hochberg is clearly impressed by the various Gestalt demonstrations of coherence and stability in perception, although he disagrees with Gestalt interpretations of perceptual phenomena. In some of his own researches Hochberg has studied the perception of objects when these are viewed through moving apertures. Interestingly, provided the size and speed of the moving apertures are adequate, complex percepts can be achieved even though visual information is spread over time. For example, it is quite easy to see a Necker cube when it is shown behind a moving slit: it even reverses on occasion.

From such studies Hochberg concludes that perception involves the creation and use of *schemata*; that is, in daily life we build up plans or cognitive structures which later serve to guide and control the ways in which we sample the world. This means that the partial samples of objects taken during sequences of eye movements and fixations can make sense only when they are referred to existing schemata. The fact that the perception of large complex things must inevitably be sequential (given the small angular size of clear central vision) means that successive inputs must be stored before being synthesized to whole percepts. It is during this storage that central organizing effects come into play, and this is the constructive aspect of seeing.

Niesser

One of the founders of the subdiscipline, cognitive psychology, Ulric Neisser, also made use of the concept of the schema in his account of the constructive nature of perception (for example, see Neisser, 1967). Neisser is concerned with the general nature of cognition and this leads him to an analysis of the role of attention in perception and eventually to many stimulating ideas concerning the processes of synthesis which, he claims, underlies pattern perception. Later (Neisser, 1976) he develops a model in which schemata guide the perceiver's exploratory activities while the information sampled during these explorations is used to modify schemata. It is of interest that in this later account Neisser attempts a rapprochement between the constructivist/empiricist account of perception and some of the markedly different ideas developed by J.J. Gibson, which are the subject of the next chapter.

Kelley's personal construct theory

There is a theorist whose work is seldom referred to by perceptionists: this is George Kelley, whose theory arose out of his work as a clinical psychologist. Kelley's personal construct theory is strikingly similar to some of the ideas which have been outlined in this chapter. He held, for example, that we perceive other people through, as it were, a series of filters which he calls 'constructs'. Much of Kelley's work (see, for example, Kelley, 1955) was an attempt to discover the ways in which these constructs shape perception, how they differ between individuals, how they affect behaviour, and how they relate to the emotions. Kelley's repertory grid technique for the exploration of construct systems is in use to this day. It is very odd that Gregory, for example, makes no mention of Kelley's work, for this would undoubtedly have enabled Gregory to extend the range of application of his own theory.

Computational theory and top-down processing

In Chapter 8 an account will be given of Marr's computational theory of vision. Much of this modern research, as we shall see, concentrated upon the ways in which information is extracted from the visual image on the retina. But Marr was mindful of the fact that analysis must be followed by synthesis, and he acknowledged the role which knowledge can play in contributing to such a synthesis. It is clear that empiricism is alive and well.

GENERAL REMARKS ON EMPIRICISM

The theoretical writings which have emerged within the empiricist paradigm have tended to use psychological rather than physiological concepts. Gregory's theory, for example, is closer to Brunswik's than to the Gestalt theory. We have argued earlier that this is a good thing: problems in the psychology of perception demand explanation at the appropriate level. Pain is something we feel. Although it is undoubtedly caused by neural impulses, these are not part of our awareness. Pains may be sharp or dull, neural impulses are neither.

The tradition (or paradigm) which has been outlined in this chapter has been a vigorous one. A mass of results has been obtained from highly ingenious experiments. Very little of the literature in the area can be dismissed as trivial or dull—quite the reverse, as anyone may confirm by reading, for example, Gregory's own publications. That words may affect us below the threshold of awareness is a strange fact. The effects of set and attention are fascinating, as is the fact that we can be so completely fooled by an oddly shaped room or a hollow face. It is a rewarding experience to introduce people to such phenomena, as any teacher of perception will confirm. And, as has just been stated, the empiricist or constructivist approach is still to be seen in perceptual theorizing.

Early in this chapter an account was given of some of the discoveries which inspired empiricism. Later, some criticisms were put forward concerning Gregory's hypothesis theory. At this point it seems reasonable to offer a general opinion about empiricism as a paradigm for perception.

First, it must be said that nobody is yet in a position to make a final judgement between constructivist and rival approaches to perception. The deep mysteries of perception remain and it requires an act of faith to believe that they will ever be solved. What follows is a speculation of the kind which must have occurred to many who have tried to evaluate empiricism.

The evidence adduced in favour of constructivist accounts of perception, such as hypothesis theory, comes in the main from one of two types of experimental situation: the stimuli employed are either meaningful, in an abstract sense, or they are products of the built or cultural environment. Consider: the perception of patterns under conditions of brief exposure, drawings which could represent the corners of buildings, oddly shaped rooms, hollow masks, twin-track tape recordings, glowing objects in darkened corridors. These are the sorts of situation faced by observers in many of the classic experiments which have sustained empiricism. But none of these existed in the African grasslands where human perceptual systems reached their present state of evolutionary development. The evolution of the modern human being obviously antedated human civilization. Has this research been appropriate?

This general point may be reinforced by another example. Consider the problem of flying. Most people could be taught within minutes to keep a light aircraft straight and level under conditions of good visibility. In fact, people have stolen aircraft and taken off successfully without ever having handled the controls before (most of them died when attempting to land, however). But nobody can fly for long in cloud without special instrument training—a claim which is borne out by a long list of fatalities. Why is this? The reason is that when an aircraft starts to deviate from its heading, for whatever reason, detectors in the inner ear correctly signal the initiation of the turn. But as the turn continues, the lack of change of radial acceleration causes these same detectors to signal that the body is now travelling straight ahead. At this point any attempt to straighten the aircraft will feel like *a turn in the opposite direction*. The situation is now out of control and can only worsen. The pilot, who cannot get back into step with the manoeuvres of the aircraft, is about to become an accident statistic.

For a trained pilot the situation is completely different, and quite safe. He or she has practised ignoring sensations from the inner ear in order to concentrate upon the readings from the flight instruments. In time, these seem to become the 'natural' source of information about the behaviour of the aircraft. But this takes much learning. And it is of course highly artificial and almost completely cognitive, at least in the initial stages of training.

It is difficult to resist the conclusion that perception under blind flying conditions is learned, interpretative and constructive. And this may be true of perception *whenever the situation is in any way artificial or unnatural*. This must happen whenever meaning must be extracted from a symbolic display. Meaning clearly implies knowledge, but a word does not signal directly what it stands for: 'fin' is part of a fish in English but means 'end' in French. One could not possibly perceive the meaning of a word without learning.

Hence it is possible that we can perceive constructively only at certain times and in certain situations. Whenever we move under our own power on the surface of the natural world, and in good light, the necessary perceptions of size, texture, distance, continuity, motion and so on, may all occur directly and reflexively. The claim that this is in fact the case is a tenet of the theory to be discussed in the next chapter.

The relative brevity of this chapter should not be taken as indirect evaluation of the importance of empiricist explanations of visual perception. On the contrary, it would be quite possible to write an entire volume on this topic alone. This account has been kept as short as possible for two reasons. First, the empiricist approach dominates modern thinking. The reader has only to consult any standard general perception text to find all the main empiricist demonstrations and interpretations stated with clarity and conviction. It can be claimed that this paradigm has been so dominant during the past 40 years that, until recently, it *was* the general theory of perception. Second, when describing a radically different approach to perception in the next chapter it will be necessary to describe again many of the claims made by modern empiricists. So we have not yet finished with the general topic of empiricism or the specific version of it represented by Gregory's hypothesis theory.

NOTES ON CHAPTER 6

See Boring (1950) for an account of empiricism in psychology and a good description of Helmholtz's speculations about the inferential nature of visual perception.

Helmholtz's position relative to the 'inference revolution' is clearly described in Gigerenzer and Murray (1987).

Many of Gregory's publications are collected in Gregory (1974). Consult Gregory (1980a, 1980b) for detailed arguments in support of the idea that perceptions are hypotheses.

Gregory's position regarding the brain/computer analogy is described in Thorpe and Zangwill (1961). See his paper entitled 'The brain as an engineering device'.

For a philosopher's reaction to the claim that perceptions are hypotheses, see the comment by G.E. Anscombe published in Brown (1974).

Constraints of space precluded any discussion of the work of Rock (1983, 1995), another modern worker who has incorporated aspects of empiricism into his theory.

7

Direct perception and ecological optics: the work of J.J. Gibson

> . . . perceiving is an act, not a response, an act of attention, not a triggered impression, an achievement not a reflex.
>
> (Gibson, 1979)

The theoretical position to be described in this chapter owes a great deal to the work of one man, the American psychologist, J.J. Gibson. His claim that perception is in an important sense direct, and his development of what has been called 'ecological optics', are among the most interesting theoretical developments in modern perceptual research. Since his death, Gibson's ideas have been refined and developed and he himself changed his views during the course of his career. In what follows we shall give a general account of what seem to be the most important aspects of this approach to perception; for the sake of clarity and economy we shall not always indicate whether a particular idea or argument belongs to Gibson or to a follower of his, although major theoretical differences will be pointed out. The general term, direct perception, will be adopted. This has been given to the body of theory developed by Gibson and his followers which, it has been claimed, represents a new paradigm. The reader will note that, once again, visual examples dominate the account of a theory. In terms of the informal classification of regions of concern to theorists outlined in Chapter 1, we shall see that the concern of Gibson and his followers is very much with the relationship between distal and proximal stimuli (about which some startling claims are made) and the brain's response to patterns in proximal stimuli. In addition, the theory stresses the contribution of motor activity to perception.

The remainder of this chapter will be organized under the following headings.

- J.J. Gibson
- An outline of the theory of direct perception

- An evaluation of the theory of direct perception
- More recent research
- General remarks on direct perception

J.J. GIBSON

Gibson was born in 1904 and died in 1979. He was educated at Princeton and later took a teaching post at Smith College. He became known for his experiments and his theoretical writings after moving to Cornell, where he stayed for the remainder of his career.

Gibson's education gave him, initially, a behaviourist approach to his subject, although by the 1960s Gibson had come to disagree fundamentally with the assumptions of behaviourism. In fact, as his friend and colleague R.B. MacLeod has pointed out (MacLeod and Pick, 1974), in one sense Gibson was a functionalist of the old pre-behaviourist school. It must also be pointed out that Gibson came into contact with the distinguished Gestalt psychologist, Kurt Koffka, towards the end of the latter's career, and came to hold his work in high esteem.

As a young experimental psychologist Gibson worked on a variety of problems. He was interested in the effects of mental set on performance, he studied human conditioning, and he did orthodox psychophysics. He was then an empiricist—a theoretical position which he gradually abandoned after studying adaptation effects in perception.

It was known that if an observer wears spectacles which distort the visual world, prolonged exposure to the distortion leads to a degree of recovery. For example, if the spectacles cause vertical lines to appear curved, the lines seem to straighten after a period of practice. Removal of the spectacles then causes the world to bend in the opposite direction for a time. The usual explanation of this ability to adapt to distortion was that the brain gradually reduces the discrepancy between the distorted visual input and normal tactile inputs: in Berkeley's original sense, touch teaches vision.

However, Gibson found (to his surpirse) that adaptation occurred if the observer simply sat and stared at vertical lines. Further, simply staring at curved lines, without using spectacles, caused their curvature gradually to lessen. Such effects convinced Gibson that perception could not be merely a compound of simple sensations and that empiricist interpretations must be flawed. Much of the remainder of Gibson's career was devoted to attacking what he considered to be the misleading and harmful notion of sensation.

During the Second World War Gibson worked on the applied problems of pilot selection and testing. Flying clearly demanded accurate perception of space, but:

... as I came to realise, nothing of any practical value was known by
psychologists about the perception of motion, or of locomotion in space,
or of space itself. The classical cues for depth referred to paintings or
parlour stereoscopes, whereas the practical problems of military avia-
tion had to do with takeoff and landing.

(Gibson, 1967b)

Gibson became convinced that perception from aircraft made important use
of information from the ground and the sky (particularly when there was a
covering of cloud), and that this information was in the form of patterns of
movement, the flowing textures which arise as a result of motion relative to the
ground. Gibson's preliminary analysis of this situation is shown in Figure 7.1.

In 1950 Gibson expressed these views in detail in his book, *The Perception
of the Visual World*. This became a classic and its main findings are now
included as standard in most textbooks on the perception of space. The importance of movement in perception and the usefulness of considering perception under real-life conditions, as opposed to simple laboratory
experiments, were beliefs which remained with Gibson for the remainder of

Figure 7.1 Optic flow during a landing approach. This is the sort of visual phenomenon which was brought to Gibson's attention during his involvement with flying
training. (From Gibson, 1950)

his professional career. Gibson's theoretical position evolved over the years and the following account will tend to emphasize his later ideas.

With the possible exception of his work on perception and art, all Gibson's writings are original and interesting. He wrote superbly and is still well worth reading.

AN OUTLINE OF THE THEORY OF DIRECT PERCEPTION

Objections to empiricism

A good way to appreciate the arguments for direct perception is to understand what Gibson and his followers objected to in the most popular contemporary paradigm for perception, namely empiricism. We have given an example of this approach in the earlier description of perceptions as hypotheses (pp. 164–168). Here, as a reminder, is a summary (some would say a parody) of this position.

In any momentary visual fixation of the world, the relationship between distal and proximal stimuli is likely to be imperfect: retinal images shrink as objects of fixed size move away from us; a table shows only three legs; tilted rectangles yield trapezoidal retinal images. We see things that are not physically present when we complete gaps in patterns or see illusory contours. Colour resides not in objects but in our heads. The sensation of tickle does not resemble the objects which induce it. In other words, sensory inputs are commonly too impoverished or too degraded to specify aspects of the world.

Because sensory inputs (or sensations) are not rich enough to mediate perception, the perceiver must add to them. The elaboration of sensory data involves inferential processes utilizing memory, habit, set, and so on. Survival pressures require that inferential processes deliver 'correct' solutions most of the time—we successfully go beyond the sensory evidence—but sometimes inferences fail and we experience illusions or other 'errors' of perception.

The essence of the constructivist paradigm therefore is that perception of the world is essentially indirect: something must be added to the incoming stimulus information before the final perceptual response is attained; sensory inputs must be represented as images, schemata, models.

Gibson and his followers argued that this assumption leads inevitably to a particular research strategy: if the visual image is the starting point for elaboration, study visual images; if successive samples of the world are important, present such samples under controlled conditions using brief exposures; in order to present brief exposures in a controlled manner, keep the viewer's head still; the use of brief exposures will eliminate errors due to eye movements. And so on.

Data from such studies must then be fitted into some sort of model. As events take place 'in' time (the time of Newtonian physics—even, unbroken, unidirectional) the perception of these events includes the perception of their sequence and of time itself. Thus the model chosen for perception will inevitably involve stages: successive samples must be stored before being elaborated. This in turn requires the involvement of different types of memory, iconic, short term, long term, and so on. And as the model now includes stages it is natural to think in terms of information flowing between them. Inevitably there will be the conceptual leap into believing that perceptual processes resemble the workings of the *digital computer*.[1]

As we attempted to show in the previous chapter, the constructivist or empiricist approach has been a fruitful way of thinking about perception. It has generated numerous ingenious experiments yielding important data. But the question remains: is awareness only indirect? Is our perceiving really mediated by internal representations? Direct perception theorists think not.

Gibson and his followers (see, for example, Costall, 1981, and Reed, 1987, for valuable discussions of what follows) argue that the constructivist, indirect paradigm has a very long history (which explains in part why it is so pervasive). The Galilean doctrine that nature is composed of matter residing in physical space and time led to the Cartesian doctrine of the essential separation between the mental and the physical. This raised, inevitably, the major philosophical and psychological question of how the realms of the physical and the mental meet: if our minds are essentially different from the world, then we cannot know it directly; all we can know are images of the world—sensations arising from it which are used to represent it.

Reed (1987) points out that, to this day, psychologists tend to view space and time as the 'receptacles' of objects. There is thus an automatic tendency to separate psychological activity from the biological and physical aspects of the perceiver. Seen from this perspective, the physical world is meaningless and neutral. Gibson's aim was to find out how organisms become aware of this world, how they come to behave as though the world is sensible and meaningful. Hence, although he was against cognitivism (the postulation of mental representations formed from sensations and so on), what Gibson attempted was a cognitive theory: he wanted to explain how organisms come to know the world. But in seeking this explanation Gibson was determined to avoid the dualism, inherent in the traditional view of the perceiver, which separates perceptual experience from the objective world. His work thus represents a radical challenge to the existing philosophical framework within which most theories of perception have arisen.

To achieve his aim Gibson was led to reconsider the nature of stimuli and the ecologies, and their relationships with perceiving organisms. We shall see that by the end of his career Gibson had arrived at a new way of describing

---

[1] This was true when Gibson was first developing his theory. Gibson died before connectionist networks began to make an impact in psychology (see Chapter 6).

stimulation, he had rejected sensations as useful explanatory concepts, he had abandoned the distinction between sensory and motor aspects of behaviour, and he had given a new impetus to the study of the environment and its inhabitants. More fundamentally, Gibson was able to claim that when the appropriate ways of describing perception had been found, many of the problems which had engaged earlier theorists evaporated.

In terms of our organizing classification, we can assert that a major part of Gibson's work was an attempt to show that distal objects and events can in fact be specified by patterns of proximal stimulation, and that perceptual systems resonate directly with the information contained in these patterns. Thus the regions emphasized in Gibson's approach are (1) the world, (2) incoming stimulation and (3) the brain. Gibson was not interested in events at receptor surfaces or in the peripheral transmission of sensations.

As a starting point for an attack on the idea of indirect perception, Gibson and his followers would begin with a discussion of the nature of light.

Light and the environment

In any textbook discussion of, say, the problem of size constancy (to use our familiar example), the starting point is usually a simple optical diagram. Single lines, representing rays of light, are drawn from an object to the eye (see Figure 7.2). When the object is drawn as further from the eye, the ray diagram shows how the visual angle at the eye is diminished, as is the (inverted) visual image on the retina. Why then doesn't the object appear smaller to the viewer?

The problem changes, however, when we consider a real scene. The viewer is in, say, the centre of a room, with a light source overhead. The light source (a window, a lamp) is emitting light in many different directions. This emission may comprise several million rays, in contrast with the one or two in a classical ray diagram. Further, not all the light from the source comes directly to the eye: some rays (a few million) may reflect from a wall to the object and then to the eye; others may strike the floor and then the object before entering the eye. Other rays may come to the eye not from the object but from the surface on which the object is standing. The eye is bathed in a sea of radiant energy, of complex interactions between light rays moving in different directions, many of which have been reflected by surfaces. The visual world comprises *surfaces under illumination*.

The next point is so obvious that it is in danger of being overlooked: it is *because* light travels in straight lines that it can carry *information* about the environment through which it has travelled and from which it has been reflected. In a mad universe in which the rays swerved erratically, light could not be informative.

It is a happy chance that since Gibson started writing about the richness of light in this way, the development of the laser hologram has provided a

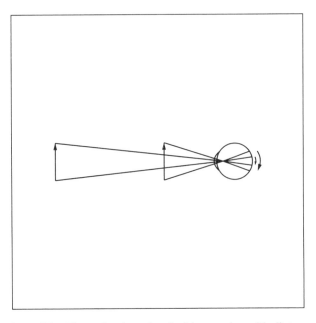

Figure 7.2   The reduction of retinal image size with distance

powerful confirmation of his claim. When laser (that is, very coherent) light is shone onto a real scene, reflected rays can be captured on a photographic plate. If a reference beam is now shone directly onto the plate, the two beams form a complex interference pattern. When the plate is developed photographically and illuminated with laser light, the original scene is recreated in an extraordinary manner: it is in the form of a three-dimensional image which can be studied as though it were the original (see Figure 7.3). If one object is in front of another, one can move one's head and look behind it; one can focus a camera on different objects at different distances in the three-dimensional space. But when the photographic plate used to generate the hologram is scrutinized in order to find an image or picture of the original scene, none is to be found. What is on the plate is simply the interference pattern. Moreover, the information necessary to create the hologram is contained all over the plate: one can break the plate into small pieces and each piece can then be used to generate a three-dimensional image of the original scene. Light (and interactions between light rays) can be a rich source of information.

To summarize: if we examine light arriving at the eye in real situations we find that it is *structured*. It is highly complex and potentially rich in information. A single momentary retinal image may be impoverished, but this is not true of the arrays of nested solid visual angles through which the head and the

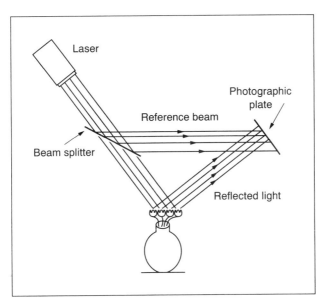

Figure 7.3 The construction of a hologram. The reference and reflected beams from the laser form an interference pattern on the photographic plate. When this plate is developed and illuminated with coherent light from the laser, a three-dimensional image of the original scene is created

eyes sweep during normal perceiving. As we come to understand more and more about these arrays and the potential information contained in their structure, the less frequently shall we need to invoke supplementary, indirect processes in explanations of seeing.

Perception and evolution

Gibson was undoubtedly influenced in his thinking by an important book by Walls (1942). In *The Vertebrate Eye and its Adaptive Radiation*, Walls presents a mass of evidence to show how the astonishing variety of vertebrate eyes can be explained by considering the range of habitats or ecological niches which their owners occupy. Any extant animal is by definition successful and embodies the results of millions of years of evolution. To understand what an animal's perceptual systems can do we must consider the environment in which they evolved, for it is this environment which shaped the systems. We should consider the animal and its environment as two interacting systems:

> The words 'animal' and 'environment' make an inseparable pair. Each term implies the other. No animal could exist without an environment

surrounding it. Equally, though not so obvious, an environment implies an animal (or at least an organism) to be surrounded.

(Gibson, 1979)

An animal is what it is given that its niche is what it is; an animal's wings, gills, snout, or hands describe that animal's environment. Likewise, a complete description of a niche describes the animal that occupies it.

(Michaels and Carello, 1981)

These statements are worth elaborating (as Gibson and Michaels and Carello do in their books), for they describe an idea which can be a powerful stimulus to the imagination. Consider this very unusual environment: boiling sulphurous mud. This environment can be analysed in detail—its lack of oxygen, its acidity, the ferocious temperature. When these factors are combined we have effectively defined the only creature which could inhabit such a strange niche: it is in fact a rare bacterium. When, on the other hand, the structure of a relatively 'simple' multicellular organism, *Taenia saginatta* (a tapeworm), is examined, it can be seen to lack musculature, thus it cannot move far in its daily existence. It possesses none of the usual major sense organs. *Taenia's* body comprises a long chain of segments, each quite flat in form and sheathed in a membrane which is not destroyed by weak acids but which permits absorption by osmosis. We are close to defining the only environment which could support such a creature: the large intestine of a warm-blooded vertebrate.

The case for ecological optics

The environmental niche determines the structure of an animal and its senses. To understand the animal's perceptual systems it is necessary to consider the environment in which these systems evolved. But what exactly do we need to know? Gibson's advice (in the case of vision) would be unhesitating: find out about the patterns of light which arrive at the eye from the environment and ask what potential information about the environment is contained in these patterns. This is a first step. Later we can discover whether particular aspects of this information are or are not utilized in perception. But we must begin by examining the lit environment, and to do this we need a new science: ecological optics.

When we draw simple ray diagrams (such as Figure 7.2 for example) we are using classical optics. This is a science which is neutral with respect to the viewer, and extraction of principal rays is a legitimate simplifying exercise. But, as we have shown, pondering over simple ray diagrams makes the problem of size constancy seem formidable. Similarly, simple physical measurement leads to puzzlement over the phenomenon of brightness constancy: why, for example, does coal look black on a summer's day when it can be shown that the light which it reflects is many times more intense than that from snow on a winter's evening? How do we continue to perceive the 'true' properties of these stimuli when simple measurement suggests that this should be impossible?

One answer, using an ecological approach, is that classical optical science largely ignores the complexity of the real environment. When an object moves further away from the eye its visual image does indeed get smaller. But this is not the only change which occurs in the complex pattern of light arriving at the eye. Most objects consist of textured surfaces and the grain of this texture gets finer as the objects recede. Objects obscure a portion of the textured ground against which they are seen. The further away an object is the closer it will be to the horizon, and so on. And although the light reflected from a dark object under strong illumination may be quite intense, it will be less intense than light from more reflective objects present in the same scene. The important point is that objects are not usually seen in complete isolation. The optical array commonly contains far more information than that associated with a single stimulus object. The use of classical optics and an over-concentration upon laboratory experiments may cause us to overlook this important truth. (See Gibson, 1961, for a much fuller discussion of this point.)

The role of invariants in perception

One of the most important concepts in direct perception theory is the invariant. The emphasis on invariants may prove to be Gibson's single most important contribution to psychology, and understanding invariants is the key to understanding direct perception.

Gibson frequently stressed the importance of movement in perceiving (see, for example, Gibson, 1966). Indeed, he insisted that the distinction commonly drawn between sensory and motor aspects of behaviour is artificial and leads to false problems, such as the question 'Why doesn't the world move when we move our eyes?' For Gibson, the changes brought about as a result of our motor behaviour should be thought of as an integral part of the process of perceiving. We rarely receive a static, unvarying view of any object or scene. We move our head and eyes, we walk around the environment, things come into and out of view: perception is an active process.

Imagine that one was reduced in size to the point where one could get inside an eye. What would it be like, down among the rods and cones of the retina? What one would *not* see would be part of an image, the edge of a static picture. Instead, one would see shimmering patches of light flickering across the retinal cells. At any moment the textures in the environment would project countless points of light into the eye. As the eye moved, fresh patterns would sweep across one's position. The scene would appear kaleidoscopically complex, even chaotic. But this jumble of coloured patches of light is not in fact random. Among the pattern of change are lawful regularities—the movement of adjacent parts are correlated.

An example will serve to illustrate this claim. One is approaching a textured surface. At each moment the patterns of stimulation from the envriontment are changing. But this change, although complex, is non-random. Photographic analysis of the scene (and even informal introspection) reveals that the changes in the textures seen (and thus the changes at the retina) follow patterns of *flow*. That part of the vertical surface with which one will eventually make contact remains stationary, although growing in apparent size. All around that point one can notice a radial expansion of textures flowing around one's head (see Figure 7.4). The textures expand as one approaches them and contract as they pass beyond the head. And the situation we have described will be the case *whenever we move towards something*. In other words, over and above the behaviour of each texture element is a higher-order pattern or structure, and this is available as a source of information about the environment. In this case the flow of the texture is described as *invariant*.

Here is another example of the lawfulness which can be exposed when familiar situations are examined thoughtfully. How do we know that an object which has gone out of sight has not gone out of existence?

> Any movement of a point of observation that hides previously unhidden surfaces has an opposite movement that reveals them. This is the law of reversible occlusion, which states that the hidden and unhidden real things in a locale can be interchanged by moving around. Going out of sight is not the same as going out of existence. The perception of persistence does not rely on the persistence of perception, but on tests using reversible occlusion.
>
> (Reed, 1987)

The essence of invariants is that they are associated with change. They can be thought of as higher-order properties of patterns of stimulation which remain constant during changes associated with the observer, the environment, or both. Modern theorists distinguish between two types or styles of invariant: transformational and structural.

Transformational invariants

These are patterns of change which can reveal what is happening to an object or objects. For example, when an object moves away from us at constant speed, its apparent area (the size of the angle subtended at the eye) diminishes lawfully. In fact, the decrease in area is proportional to the square of the

Figure 7.4   Optic flow surrounding the point of eventual collision

distance. Whenever this relationship is present it must mean that the distance between us and the object is changing in a regular manner. Departures from this invariant rule can mean only that (1) the rate of movement has slowed or accelerated, or (2) the object is actually changing size. Here it is the *style* of change which is a source of information.

Structural invariants

These are higher-order patterns or relationships which remain constant despite changes in stimulation. As an example of a structural invariant, consider a situation in which two objects having the same physical size are at different distances from an observer. Clearly, the visual angles subtended by the objects (and hence the sizes of their retinal images) will be different. How can we know that the objects are in fact the same size? This is of course yet another way of introducing the problem of size constancy.

Analysis of the situation described above reveals that there is indeed an invariant property of the stimulus array that could serve as information specifying that the objects are the same size. The invariant is a subtle one: if the objects are in a natural environment, then they will usually be viewed in a scene containing a visible horizon; it can be shown that the *ratio of an object's height to the distance between its base and the horizon is invariant across all distances from the viewer* (ss Figure 7.5). Analysis of light with reference to the environment has yieldéd a possible solution to the problem of size constancy.

There is a similar regularity in the relationship between size, distance and an observer's eye-height, which interested readers can check for themselves.

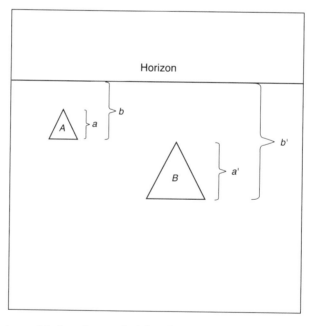

Figure 7.5   A possible invariant underlying size constancy. If $a : b = a' : b'$ than A and B are the same size

Suppose your eye-height when standing is 150 cm. You are looking across a level view in which there are two trees, one near, one far. How can you tell whether they are the same height? The answer is that the horizon (because it is at optical infinity) will intersect each tree at a point 150 cm above the ground: your eye-height. If this is, say, a quarter of the way up each tree, *then the tree heights are identical*: $150 \times 4 = 600$ cm (6 metres). What an encouraging demonstration of the richness of information that light can convey under natural conditions.[2]

Affordances, invariants and meanings

In Gibson's later writings (for example Gibson, 1971a, 1977, 1979) increased emphasis is placed on the *affordance*—a concept which has been refined by several of his followers. It is at this point in the theory that the relationship between perceiver and environment assumes great importance. The environment contains invariant information, the detection of which has survival value for a perceiver.

> Roughly, the affordances of things are what they furnish, for good or ill, that is, what they *afford* the observer.
>
> (Gibson, 1971a)

Gibson goes on to list a series of possible affordances. These include, for humans, surfaces that are stand-on-able or sit-on-able, objects that are graspable or throwable, objects that afford hitting, surfaces that afford supporting, substances that afford pouring. A single object may give rise to more than one affordance: an apple, for example, affords eating and grasping and throwing.

It is clear that affordances are the *meanings* which an environment has for an animal. As meanings, the affordances guide behaviour: they tell the observer what is or is not possible. The range of possible behaviours in response to affordances has been described as the set of *effectivities* available to the organism, although some theorists believe that the term 'actions' is all that is required. It is clear that this part of his theory reveals the influence of the functionalist tradition on Gibson's thinking.

The originality of Gibson's approach to invariants and affordances, these seemingly abstract properties of things and events, lies in his remarkable assertion that they can be perceived *directly*, without prior synthesis or analysis. Thus the properties of an object which reveal that it is graspable (just consider the vast array of different objects to which this description could be

---

[2] Interestingly, it looks as though the horizon plays a similar role in the perception of distance, size and depth in pictures. (see Sedgwick, 1980; Rogers and Costall, 1983.)

applied) are there to be perceived directly from the pattern of stimulation arising from the object. This is a very bold idea.

Two further aspects of the theory of invariants and affordances should be stressed.

First, we must remember that understanding perception requires the joint study of an organism and its environment. This essential relationship must always be borne in mind. To start with a familiar human experience: when a piece of music is transposed to a new key, the new set of notes may be completely different; but something is preserved in this change, namely certain important relationships between successive notes. This identity (or near identity, for the situation is a little more complicated than this) of musical intervals provides a basis for the equivalence of tunes across keys. But this equivalence will be experienced only by a perceiver sensitive to interval information: it will be of little use to the tone-deaf. Similarly, when a rectangle is tilted away from us its projected shape becomes trapezoidal (see Figure 7.6), but it continues to look rectangular. How?

There is a geometry which can treat a trapezoid as a *transformation* of a rectangle. That is to say, the rectangular shape can be 'recovered' from a trapezoidal projection. It follows that there is something invariant in the property of the shape which might allow an observer to decide that he or she is seeing a tilted rectangle. But whether or not sensitivity to this

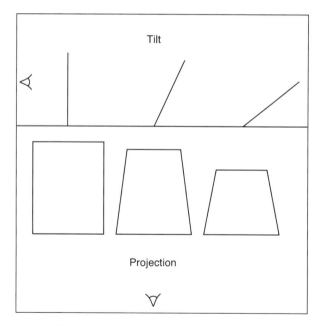

Figure 7.6   The projected shape of a tilted rectangle is trapezoidal

transformational invariant is the basis of shape constancy is an empirical question which is not solved simply by isolating the *potential* invariant: we need to know whether a particular perceiver can use such information. Gibson's important term here is *attunement*: organisms need to be attuned to affordances before they can exert their power to shape actions.

Second, it is important to remember that an invariant or affordance for one species may not be an invariant or affordance for another. Sensitivity to certain odours, to ultraviolet light, or to the earth's magnetic field, provides some species with information which is quite outside our own direct experience, and which we could never use. Failure to recognize this important fact may be the reason for many misunderstandings of the apparent oddities of animal behaviour: our pets are not miniature humans.

The question now arises: *How* does the perceiver come to perceive invariants and affordances? Is it necessary to learn which invariant properties of an array are useful? Are we born with the abilty to detect affordances? How do we extract the higher-order information contained in optical arrays? Direct perceptionists have addressed these questions, and we shall now attempt to summarize their main conclusions.

On the question of whether or not perception is learned, Gibson and his followers would remind us that we and other successful organisms are the products of millions of years of evolution. The environmental niches in which our sense organs operate have been responsible for the evolution of the organs; as they have shaped their structure, so also must they have shaped their performance. Thus learning has indeed occurred in the development of perception, but this has been during the history of the species rather than the lifetime of the individual. The same sort of evolutionary pressures which have 'taught' our kidneys to respond correctly from birth could have shaped our visual systems to respond in certain ways to contours or gradients of texture.

There is, however, a role for learning during the history of the individual perceiver: humans (and many other 'higher' animals) must surely learn which affordances can be relied upon to satisfy certain goals. That is to say, although the invariant stimulus properties comprising the affordance of, say, 'graspableness' may be perceived immediately, knowing when graspableness is an appropriate property to search for is situationally determined and must presumably be learned. The role of learning in perception is to educate attention.

Resonance

If the perception of the real world involves detecting appropriate invariances in the rich and ever-changing sea of stimulus energy, it is natural to ask how these invariants are detected. Is there, for example, a moment in the visual process when the relative motions of different texture elements are extracted, possibly by correlating their directions and speeds in order to detect texture flow? Gibson's reply to this question would be that it is the wrong way to begin to consider the problem. Such a way of conceptualizing perceptual processes leads to the reductionism, the reliance on hypothetical stages within processes, which disfigures the empiricist approach to perception.

A direct perception theorist knows that there are identifiable peripheral processes to be observed in receptor systems (such as the contour sharpening brought about by lateral inhibition in the retina), but the conclusion would still be that the reductionist approach is wrong. Gibson and his supporters argue that the response to stimulation is a response involving the whole organism, and the nature of this response is described by Gibson as follows:

> I suggest that the nervous system operates in circular loops and that information is never conveyed but extracted by the picking up of invariants over time . . . a perceptual system does not respond to stimuli (although a receptor does) but extracts invariants.
>
> (Gibson, 1976)

Once again, the active role of the perceiver in extracting informative, invariant patterns is being stressed. Later, Gibson extended his notion of information pickup by likening perception to a process of *resonance*, which he explains by analogy with a radio set. To elaborate: the space in any room in a modern city is filled with electromagnetic radiation broadcast from large numbers of transmitters, some close at hand, some many miles away. This radiation is non-random: it can convey information. On switching on a radio, all we may hear is the hissing noise arising from its own circuits. But on tuning the ratio, we may suddenly hear speech or music: it is now set to resonate with the information available in the electromagnetic radiation. We are witnessing a process of *information pickup*.

The direct perception theorist can now challenge us with this question: 'In which part of the radio is that particular sound being processed?' The answer must be that it is everywhere, for all parts of the radio's circuit are active during the transduction of the radio waves into audible music. Remove any one part of the circuit and the set will fail. But that part cannot then be said to 'compute' music or speech—these are rendered audible by the behaviour of the whole radio, with its components acting together as a single system. The radio is not a perfect analogy, of course, for it is a passive device—we do the tuning; but during perception information is obtained, rather than imposed.

Thinking along such lines suggests that the nervous system may be better modelled by analogue, rather than digital, devices. To reinforce this point, consider an old-fashioned slide rule. This is a means of multiplying and dividing pairs of numbers without engaging in common arithmetic; one simply adjusts two scales (adding or subtracting two quantities) and reads off the answer. The trick, of course, is that the markings on the rule are drawn to represent logarithmic quantities. *The necessary mathematics has been built into the structure of the device.* Is this the role of evolution in the shaping of the senses?

Realism

It should be clear from this brief introduction to direct perception and ecological optics that Gibson and his followers assume a philosophical position, that of *direct realism*. Stated very simply, direct realism is the assumption that there is an external world of objects and that we can become aware of these as a result of our perceptions: proximal stimuli can specify distal ones. This doctrine is contrasted by Gibson with the position that, as our senses must intervene between external objects and our experience of them, all that we can be directly aware of must be sensations or sense-data. That is to say, we cannot experience a hot object directly, but must construct this percept from sensations of heat, touch and pain.

Gibson accepted that sensations do exist and that we can be made aware of them by training or by adopting certain mental sets. We can be aware of our own physiological states; and no other person can experience that vague presence in our visual field created by our nose.

> Physical acoustics tells the man-in-the-street that sensations of loudness, pitch, and pitch mixture are in his head, and only arise because they correspond to the variables of sound waves in the air. He could not possibly hear a mechanical event; he can only infer it from the data. But nevertheless he goes on hearing natural events like rubbing, scraping, rolling, and brushing, or vocal events like growling, barking, singing and croaking, or carpenter's events like sawing, pounding, filing and chopping. Ecological acoustics would tell him that the vibratory event, the source of the waves, is specified in certain invariant properties of the wave train. . . . Information about the event is physically present in the air surrounding the event. If the man is within earshot, he hears the event.'
>
> (Gibson 1967a)

This is as clear a statement of his position as we can find in Gibson's writings. Naturally, the philosophical differences between direct realists and their rivals are debated at greater length than this. The arguments can be quite complicated, as may be seen by consulting some of the references to be given later.

AN EVALUATION OF THE THEORY OF DIRECT PERCEPTION

We come now to a general assessment of the direct perception tradition which Gibson founded during his career. We shall list what seem to be the most pertinent criticisms to have been levelled against direct perception, and shall then describe some of the achievements of this new approach.

The meaning of 'direct'

A valuable debate on direct perception (Ullman, 1980) begins with an interesting question. What does it mean, asks Ullman, to say that any process is direct? We shall offer a slightly modified version of Ullman's illuminating analogy. Consider arithemetical multiplication. The input to the 'process' of multiplication is a pair of numbers, the output is their product. Now there is a way of making such a process direct. This would be to create a lookup table. A range of numbers run across the top and down the side of a matrix. Each row/column intersection contains a product of two numbers. Multiplication done this way could be described as direct. And by this we mean that the process of multiplication *cannot be decomposed*.

In practice, however, such a lookup table would quickly become cumbersome and even unusable—imagine looking for the product of column 257 and row 9367. Over the centuries it has been found that a more powerful and flexible way to multiply is to treat each number as composed of units, tens, hundreds, and so on. We then take the digits in a certain order, multiply, record, and carry over when necessary. But this method of doing multiplication cannot be described as 'direct'—it requires the application of different rules at different stages. This in turn means that, as a process, multiplication of large numbers the traditional way is decomposable—it is therefore indirect.

When supporters of the theory of direct perception use the term 'direct', are they using it in the sense defined by Ullman? If so, some evidence can be brought against them. Arithmetical calculation may seem far removed from perceiving. Here is a more psychological example which can be used against direct perception (it was suggested by an article in the Ullman debate, cited above).

It is quite easy to make an outline wire model of Necker's reversible cube. The simple device shown in Figure 7.7 should be painted matt black for the best effect, then viewed at arm's length with one eye closed. Very soon the viewer will experience a reversal of perspective, such that the far sides of the figure suddenly appear closer than the near ones. If now one slowly twists the cube, it will appear to move the wrong way, that is, against the motion of the hand. Then, when the figure reverses back to its correct orientation, twisting results in normal movement.

The point of this simple demonstration is that although the stimulus array does not change physically, two distinct motions may result from the rotation of the cube. But in order to predict which motion a viewer will experience, it is necessary to know which of the two possible orientations of the cube is being seen. It is quite clear that in this case the perception of orientation (correct or

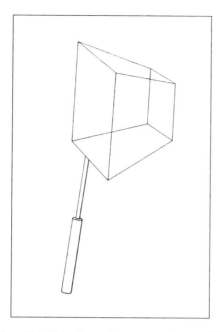

Figure 7.7 A reversible solid. This shape (a truncated pyramid) comprises a large rectangle at the front joined to a smaller rectangle at the rear. When constructed from blackened wire and viewed monocularly, the perspective will occasionally reverse. If the handle is then twisted, the parts of the shape will appear to move in the wrong direction. (A miniature version of this apparatus is easily assembled from the wire surrounding a champagne cork)

reversed) comes prior to the perception of motion (correct or reversed). Does this not mean that the perception of the cube's motion is decomposable into stages and hence cannot be direct? How would a direct perception theorist respond to this suggestion?

The direct perceptionist might reply as follows. The hollow cube has been *designed* to be difficult to perceive; it has been carefully shaped in such a manner that information in light reflected from it specifies an ambiguous object. After all, it might be added, Necker's discovery in 1832 of the illusion named after him came not from an examination of crystals (his main interest) but of *drawings* of them. Crystals aren't ambiguous, but two- or three-dimensional sketches of them can be, although only rarely—which is why Necker's illusion was a novelty.

Results from a famous experiment by Shepard and Metzler (1971) can also be used to support Ullman's criticism of the term 'direct'. This was a reaction-time study in which observers had to report, as quickly as possible, whether two shapes flashed onto a screen were or were not identical. The second shape of each pair could in fact be identical to the first, or could be a mirror image of it. The main independent variable in this experiment was the rotational difference between the shapes: for example both could be identically oriented with respect to the top of the screen, or one shape could be rotated away from the other. The fascinating result was that the times taken to make the key decision—were the shapes identical, or mirror images?—increased linearly with the extent of the rotational difference between them. That is to say, it was as if observers had to engage in a process akin to rotating the representations of shapes before they could make decisions. The greater the necessary rotation, the longer the reaction time.

The role of mental imagery in conscious life has long been argued about by psychologists, some of whom deny that there can be pictures in the head which we can use to solve problems: the problem of representation is a complex one. Nevertheless, the Shepard and Metzler finding does suggest that some process was intervening between the perception of the shapes and the ability to arrive at correct decisions. If it is accepted that this is a reasonable interpretation of Shepard and Metzler's results, then it is likely that this aspect of perception is decomposable and therefore indirect.

A possible answer to Ullman's general question concerning directness and decomposition might be that he has confounded different levels of analysis. Gibson held that perception is direct in the sense that information is extracted directly from optic arrays and that our awareness of the world is not itself mediated by schemata or representations. He did not deny that mediating processes exist (and he accepted that awareness of the world via words and symbols must be indirect in this sense). But it is the direct relation with *information* which is important—the fact that it is not necessary to decompose it to sensory elements and sensations. However, direct perception theorists have never been very clear about the nature of the processes which mediate their relationship, apart from suggesting that the nervous system somehow 'resonates' with information. Perhaps they should be more explicit about resonance and the sense in which it is a direct process.

The detection of invariants

The detection of invariants is of central importance in the theory of direct perception. Attunement to higher-order patterns within a mass of stimulation forms the basis of awareness. However:

> Although one can criticize certain shortcomings in the quality of Gibson's analysis, its major and, in my view, fatal shortcoming lies at a deeper level and results from a failure to realize two things. First, the detection of physical invariants, like image surfaces, is exactly and

precisely an information-processing problem, in modern terminology. And second, he vastly underrated the sheer difficulty of such detection.

(Marr, 1982)

These are important criticisms. Gibson and others believe that there are invariant properties in physical events which afford the perception of those events. But workers in the field of artificial intelligence, such as Marr, have set themselves explicit goals, one of which is to devise systems that will simulate the process of seeing. When these workers try to create some model which will actually extract invariants, they commonly find that it is a very difficult thing to do. It can be argued, of course, that Marr and his colleagues have adopted a faulty model of the perceiver: certainly, the motor activity which Gibson holds to be vital to perception, plays a very small part in Marr's theory. But Marr's comments, coming as they do from someone who has tried to simulate seeing, must be taken seriously. This is not to say, of course, that theorists such as Gibson are wrong; rather that asserting that something must be the case may delude one into thinking that one understands how it is the case. The danger is that a theory may be leading one away from those very problems which it might be fruitful to pursue.

The nature of affordances

The most subtle forms of invariance are affordances. Reading Gibson and others on affordances is rather like reading Freud on dreams: one is convinced at the time, but reflection brings doubt.

It is clear that to know and describe the relatively straightforward invariances used in, say, the perception of space is a formidable task. But if certain objects in the world directly afford eating, just what is it in the nature of the optic array which can make explicit this affordance? In Gibson's terms the answer (in the visual modality) must be some nested array of solid visual angles; but, as he admitted, we do not really have any idea of the characteristics of such a complex array, and the answer must be many times more complicated than that to the already formidable problem of the spatial invariants. The situation is even worse than this: even if we could define some affordances for a perceiver, it would still be difficult to predict behaviour. This is because, in terms of the theory, organisms may have to learn to attend to particular affordances. Before we can predict behaviour we must know not only the affordance available but the perceiver's current attentional state. This is a formidable requirement.

On the general question of affordances, however, there are reasons for optimism. We shall attempt to justify this claim in a later section on more modern research. For now, we shall simply remind the reader that the essence of affordances is that they are always *relationships* between organisms and their environments. It follows that to insist upon predictive power is to fall into the animal–environmental dualism which direct perception wishes to avoid.

Can affordances ever mislead? Gibson changed his position on this aspect of affordances. Initially, Gibson held that a surface afforded walking, and that was that. But as Costall (1981) points out, '. . . surfaces are not where all the action is'. They may or may not afford walking—ground covered with a dusting of snow does, but a thinly frozen lake does not. Later Gibson modified his statements on affordances to recognize their probabilistic nature, thus moving much closer to Brunswik's earlier statements (see Chapter 2) concerning the ecological validity of cues.

Resonance

The idea that a nervous system mediating some form of perception behaves in a wholistic manner, resonating to invariant properties among stimuli, is initially attractive, particularly to anyone who has waded through innumerable 'stage' models of perception. On reflection, however, we are forced to conclude that resonance is barely more than an interesting and novel speculation. With stage models of perception we can at least be sure, most of the time, of what we could expect to observe in the nervous system, had we the necessary techniques. More importantly, for the psychologist, we have hypotheses about the temporal and logical ordering of processes. We should expect, for example, retinal sharpening or filtering to occur before binocular fusion processes; that the recognition of familiar forms would come even later, when meaning has been 'added' to the input; and so on. But how are we to observe resonance? If the answer is, *whenever an organism is functioning as though properly in touch with the real world*, then this amounts to a tautology. If behaviour was not appropriate or adaptive then we would not wish to invoke resonance.

We can ask whether the process of resonance could, *in principle* be observed using new techniques of anatomical observation. Does the nervous system resonate to different modalities simultaneously (it surely must in bimodal perception), and if so, is there a cost to be paid in terms of capacity? Do all nervous systems resonate in their own particular ways, or has evolution produced only one form of resonance?

The truth is that we are told very little about resonance. The metaphors used (the radio, the slide rule) are intriguing and stimulating, but they are only metaphors. It could be said that a demand for neurological plausibility is unreasonable at this stage of our knowledge of perception, and is to site the problem at the wrong level of discourse. But then we should be given some guidance as to a possible operational definition of the term resonance, or the type of evidence which would convince its proponents that they were wrong.

In response to such objections a direct perceptionist might reply as follows. A criticism which focuses on the nervous system, asking where resonance occurs, misses the point: resonance is a relationship between the perceiver and the environment. Until there is much more knowledge about the nature of such relationships, and until we can learn to stop thinking about organisms in isolation, it is pointless to look for a place where resonance occurs: resonance is not that sort of concept.

There may now be, however, a better answer to criticisms concerning resonance. As we attempted to show in an earlier chapter, parallel distributed processing models (or connectionist networks) have some striking features which distinguish them from von Neuman machines. Of great relevance here is the fact that what is represented in network is, in a very important sense, represented all over the network, not in any one special place. Thus when a network learns to discriminate, say a male from a female face, the learning is a property of *the entire network*: the knowledge is everywhere. Is it too fanciful to conclude that such a network is *resonating* and, in this manner, is arriving at the 'answer' to the question implied by the input? The present author feels very optimistic concerning the relevance of such a mechanism for the interesting concept of resonance. Readers may choose to be more sceptical and interpret the above remarks as merely an analogy combined with another analogy.

Direct perception and traditional, laboratory-based research

To end this section we shall simply assert that Gibson and his followers, when writing about the importance of invariants and affordances and the types of research that psychologists should do, have a tendency to underestimate the achievements of the single-variable type of experiment to which they are opposed. This may be for polemical reasons of course.

But is this attitude fair? For example, much of what we know about human perception has come from what were, originally, causal or accidental observations. Any careful observer, at any time in the past, could have noticed the patterning of optical flow and its relationship to our movements and position in space. Of course it took an intelligent researcher to explore this phenomenon to the point when it could be imbedded in a convincing theory of perception; nevertheless, the phenomenon was there to see, easily controlled and easily manipulated.

In contrast, how do we know that infrared radiation affords prey detection by snakes? Simply observing snakes in a natural environment won't do: when the prey moves in the dark there are changes in sound and smell, as well as in the direction and strength of infrared radiation. Only careful experimental studies, in which all variables save infrared are controlled, can convince us that we have isolated the correct invariant.

Here is another powerful counter-example to criticisms of traditional, laboratory research. It is a fact, long recognized, that when the perception of an object is difficult and its shape and identity elusive, movement of the object (or movement around it) commonly resolves any ambiguity. We have all had numerous experiences of this kind of thing: the brown patch against the tree becomes an owl as we approach; the two-headed monster in the field, we discover, is a pair of cows. And of course, the importance of the observer's movement is repeatedly stressed in Gibson's writings.

An interesting question now arises: How many views, how much movement do we need, in order to see the uniqueness of any shape? The answer is contained in a new theorem, unknown until recently even among mathematicians: a shape is uniquely specified by *three views of four non-coplanar points* (Ullman, 1979). This is a very important gain in our understanding of the perception of three-dimensional objects. However, the research leading to this discovery consisted of experiments employing highly simplified stimuli, often displayed under very artificial conditions, such as brief exposures, or the casting of shadows onto screens. The result, however, has been an undoubted success.

Finally, we may comment on a tendency in writings on direct perception to define problems out of existence. Evidence of this has been given when discussing the extraction of invariants and Marr's appraisal of Gibson's work. We can only repeat our earlier point that to say that something simply is the case, may be to loose one's grip on a real problem. In an interesting and provocative section on learning, Michaels and Carello challenge the concept of memory:

> And just as we do not need a vessel in which *ancient* history is brought to bear on the present, we do not need a vessel (memory) in which *recent* history is brought to bear. Plainly and simply, experience changes the animal.
>
> (Michaels and Carello, 1981; italics in original)

If it *is* so plain and simple, why has it been so difficult to discover the laws of learning and forgetting after a century of research?

MORE RECENT RESEARCH

Philosophical issues raised by Gibson's theory

There have been attempts to make philosophical refinements to Gibson's theory since his death. For example, contemporary direct perceptionists have been rightly concerned over the implications of Gibson's use of the term 'realism'. Noble (1981), Reed (1982, 1987) and Katz (1987) have all contributed towards a better understanding of the issues involved.

Katz (1987) has examined Gibson's interpretation of the term 'realism'. Had Gibson really adhered to a basic form of realism, Katz argues, then his theory could not have taken the form that it did. To assume the existence of an objective world, independent of perceivers, and also perceivers who are in but separate from that world, leads to some serious problems: 'How could one conceive an ultimate structure that applies in all conceivable circumstances, from every imaginable point of view?' Perception, says Katz, is a matter of circumstances '. . . determined jointly by subject and by object'. If there is only one world to be perceived, how can perception in one species differ from that in another? And how can we explain errors in perceiving? But Gibson constantly stresses the need to consider (for example) affordances in terms both of the world and the perceiver. For this reason, Katz suggests that Gibson's is really a *relativist* rather than a naive realist.

Costall (1981) is concerned with the same issue. As organisms play an active role in the creation of environments we must abandon Gibson's distinction between the objective world and perceivers which is implied by statements on realism. In other words, when Gibson discusses realism, he tends, like others, to treat the organism as nothing but a perceiver—a view which his general work was aimed at denying.

Costall cites modern biologists who also reject the idea of the environment as a 'pre-existing slot' within which the organism must fit. Costall makes a strong case for what he describes as *mutualism*. And if we acknowledge that the world has changed since the beginning of life and that organisms indirectly influence their environment, we must concede that '. . . in an important sense, the world is other organisms'. Costall hopes that a stress on mutualism will provide a much sounder underpinning for the framework of direct perception.

Noble (1981) has made a detailed study of the origins of the indirect approach to awareness. He traces it back to Descartes's corporeal ideas hypothesis. In essence, Descartes argued that, as sensations do not resemble the objects which cause them (as in tickling, for example), there must be two distinct worlds: the world of objects, and the world of thinking creatures. What follows from this is the concept of mental processes operating on the 'deliverances' of the senses. This is, as we have shown, the basic form of an argument for indirect awareness and perception. Noble's contribution is to show what a long history this idea has had, and how it has been refined over the years until it has become interwoven into the fabric of psychological thought. What was originally a scientific hypothesis has become dogma, and this in turn is the source of some of the resistance to the new paradigm represented by direct perception.

The papers cited in this section should be consulted by anyone who wishes to learn more about the effort which has been put into the philosophical refinement of the theory of direct perception.

We turn next to an outline of a small sample of the ingenious experiments to have been inspired by Gibson's ideas. At the very least, they may demonstrate how fruitful his ideas continue to be.

Empirical researches

Affordances

Accounts of research on affordances by post-Gibsonian psychologists tend to use certain special terms and concepts. It may help readers who wish to pursue this topic further, and read the experimental literature, to begin with a short exposition of some relevant terms before describing some of this newer research.

Extrinsic measures are objective measures of some aspect of an object or situation expressed in standard units such as grams, metres and seconds. *Intrinsic measures* are extrinsic measures that have been rescaled in terms of some dimension of the observer or actor in a situation. Some intrinsic measures are defined as *pi numbers*, which are dimensionless, body-scaled ratios, useful when describing the *fit* between an organism and its environment.

As the fit between an organism and its environment is altered, so is the nature of the affordance (and the value of pi). The *optimum point* of such a fit corresponds to a 'best' match between the organism and the environment; it will be the preferred value of the affordance and will be associated with stable, maximally efficient behaviour. Further changes in the fit will produce a *critical point* corresponding to a phase transition or *critical boundary* in behaviour. Thus, for any human there will be a walking speed which is most efficient and most comfortable. As readers will be aware, speeding up one's walking becomes increasingly uncomfortable until, abruptly, one breaks into a run. That is to say, slow running is more comfortable (and more efficient physiologically) than very fast walking. The change from walking (where part of the body is always in contact with the ground) to running (where the body leaves the ground between steps) can be described as a change of *gait*.[3]

We shall now give a detailed account of one of the most interesting attempts to find and measure an affordance.

A study of stair climbing (Warren, 1984)

Gibson recommended the study of the environment in which organisms evolved. it may seem a strange leap from this to the study of people's perception of staircases. However, we can think of stairs as simplified versions of

---

[3] Some animals have a variety of gaits. Horses walk, trot, canter and gallop. Cats have gaits, but the present author cannot decide how many.

uneven terrain and hope that it will become possible in the near future to extend the techniques developed in the study to be described to more natural surfaces.

The Warren experiment has been selected for two reasons: first, its thoroughness, as it is difficult to see how it could have been better designed and carried out; second, the surprisingly clear-cut and fascinating findings which emerged.

The stair-climbing variables selected by Warren were riser height (R), the height of each vertical step, which combines with tread depth (T) to give the stair diagonal (D). The person climbing the stairs has mass, climbs at some favoured rate, and is limited in the size of vertical step he or she can take by the overall leg length (L), thigh length (L_1) and lower leg length (L_2).

As Warren points out in his introduction, the search for a formula for ideal staircases has a long history. Clearly very shallow staircases (low riser height, deep tread) are inefficient: it takes too long to get high. On the other hand, one can easily think of staircases with riser heights so great that few could climb them. What architects have sought is some compromise which fits the average person and allows most efficient climbing. The French architect Blondel (1675–1683) suggested that as a comfortable pace length was 24 (French royal) inches, two inches should be subtracted from tread depth (T) for every inch of riser height (R):

$$2R + T = 24 \text{ in.} \tag{1}$$

A similar formula was still in use as late as 1978.

Given that an affordance is a *relationship* between an organism and the environment, Warren's aim was to investigate the relationships between staircases and climbers of the staircases, and then to express these as dimensionless pi numbers. If pi numbers can successfully predict behaviour and changes in behaviour (critical points) then a new affordance would have been discovered. Warren began by focusing on the relationship between riser height and leg length. The expression linking these two can be expressed as a pi number:

$$\text{pi} = R/L, \tag{2}$$

where R is the riser height and L is the leg length.

Figure 7.8 shows a mechanical model of a climber. Clearly, the maximum riser height which a person can use will demand maximum leg flexion; any greater height will require the person to jump or make use of the hands.

The lengths of the legs (L = total leg length) and lower legs of groups of tall and short observers were measured. From the model shown in Figure 7.8 it was calculated that critical riser height must be:

$$R_c = L + L_1 - L_2 \tag{3}$$

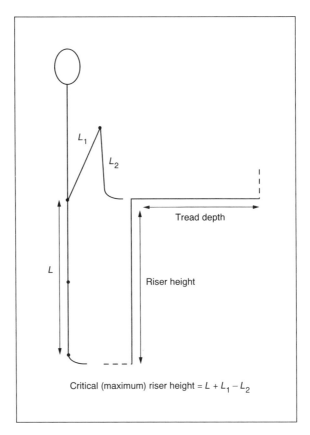

Figure 7.8 The anatomical limits in stair climbing. Note that although the thigh adds to the height of the raised foot, the lower leg subtracts from it. This sets a limit on the height of step that can be mounted using the legs alone

where L is the total leg length, L_1 is the length of the thigh and L_2 is the length of the lower leg. That is, total leg length *plus* the length of the flexed thigh (which is adding to the height the foot can attain), *minus* the length of the lower leg (which hangs downward, therefore subtracting from the maximum height the foot can attain). When anatomical data from the tall and short groups of observers were substituted into the above formula, the result was a pi value of $0.88L$ (total leg length) for both. Note that as the ratio of lower and upper leg segments tends to be constant, this value of pi tends to be constant across people of different heights.

The two groups of observers were then shown a series of projected life-size pictures of an experimental staircase. This was built in such a manner that the riser heights could be changed. The various versions of the staircase had been photographed from two different vertical positions corresponding to the mean eye-heights of the tall and short observers, respectively. The observers then rated each staircase on a seven-point scale, indicating whether they considered it to be climbable or not.

An analysis of these ratings showed that the percentage of 'climbable' judgements dropped from 100 per cent to 0 as riser height was increased. The riser height at which mean ratings of each group crossed the chance or 50 per cent value was taken as a perceptual boundary for that group. The outcome was that the *perceived* critical riser height for the tall group was 0.88L; that for the short group 0.89L. Compare these with the value of pi calculated from anthropometric data (0.88). This is an impressive result, but there is better to come.

Three short and three tall male volunteer observers climbed an adjustable moving staircase. As they did so, gas samples of their breathing were collected and oxygen and carbon dioxide analyses performed. From these it was possible to calculate the rate of energy expenditure required to mount different riser heights at various climbing rates.

The search now was for *optimum* rather than critical values of pi. Multiple regression analyses, followed by a set of curve-fitting exercises, permitted the calculation, for tall and short groups of observers, of that riser height associated with maximum ascent at minimum energy cost. The optimum value of pi was found to be the same for both groups of observers. With optimum riser height = R_o, and total leg length = L, it was found that for both groups of observers:

$$Pi = R_o/L = 0.26. \qquad (4)$$

Following this finding it is possible to ask whether observers are capable of visually detecting the optimum riser height to suit them?

Once again, tall and short groups of observers were asked to judge a series of black and white pictures of stairways having six different riser heights. However, on this occasion they were asked to judge the relative ease of use of the staircases. The rest of the experiment was essentially the same as the first one. The results were striking. For both groups of observers (using the same terms as above), pi = R_o/L = 0.25.

There is thus an extraordinarily close match between an optimally efficient riser height and an observer's visual perception of that height: the affordance is detectable.

In summary, Warren's results tell us that the *critical* riser height for an individual (the point at which his or her behaviour must change from climbing to jumping or using hands and knees) is equal to 0.88 of his or her total leg length. To find that riser height which affords *optimum* stair climbing, multiply the climber's leg length by approximately 0.25.

There is one very interesting aspect of the result for the visually preferred riser height (the optimal affordance). The bodily dimensions of Americans are well-known as a result of large-scale anthropometric surveys. Using Warren's pi number in combination with data on the distribution of leg lengths in the American population yields a value for optimum riser height which is considerably higher than the riser heights commonly used in stairways. Thus Warren's observers *did not simply express preferences for the familiar.* His results do not therefore seem to reflect learning processes. This experiment could serve as a model for others wishing to find quantifiable data concerning affordances.

Infant perception studies

Eleanor Gibson, Gibson's partner until his death, is a distinguished experimental psychologist. She has reviewed the concept of the affordance from a developmental point of view (Gibson, 1982). In a convincing argument for the importance of the affordance for theories of development, Gibson takes as a starting point the claim that:

> Perceiving an affordance implies perception that is meaningful, unitary, utilitarian, and continuous over time to the extent that environmental events that pertain to the observer may require. To what extent must young creatures (human or otherwise) learn to perceive them? And if they must learn, how is it done?
>
> (Gibson, 1982)

Gibson then reviews some of the research which is relevant to these questions. Work on 'graspability', for example, appears to show that objects of graspable size are responded to differently from non-graspable objects by the age of three months. This discrimination is revealed by patterns of hand and arm movements towards the objects. Other studies have shown that when infants aged about 14 weeks put their hands out to grasp moving objects they move them to positions *where the objects will be*: they seem able to extract the relevant affordance for prediction.

When three-month old infants are habituated to the sight of objects which have been subjected to certain rigid transformations (rotations around horizontal and vertical axes for example), a non-rigid deformation (squeezing) causes the object to be attended to once more. Infants thus appear capable of distinguishing between these two fundamental ways in which objects can change.

It has been found that by six weeks infants will blink when faced with a looming object, that they are sensitive to optical information concerning impending collision. (Parents reading this should sit down again—these infants never actually get bumped.)

Another reviewer, von Hofsten (Hofsten, 1983), describes experiments which have shown that infants can fuse information across modalities by an early age. For example, when viewing two moving films (shown simultaneously, side-by-side) of an object rising and falling, they prefer (they spend a longer time looking at) that film which is synchronized with the appropriate sound of a contact with the ground.

Von Hofsten reasons that the stability of our perceived world is vitally dependent upon our ability to perceive the permanence of objects during changes across space and time. Studies have shown that infants at eight months will attempt to retrieve hidden objects, and that when an object goes behind an occluding surface and a different one emerges on the other side, the infants show signs of surprise.

Butterworth's detailed reviews (1983, 1988) include many infant studies which are directly relevant to the theory of direct perception and should be consulted in full by interested readers. It has been shown, for example, that infants placed in an experimental room which can be moved towards or away from a stationary viewer will fall over in just the same way that adults do when faced with this sudden change in optic flow—which has not been caused by their own movements. This happens to infants who are still too young to stand—they topple from a sitting position. Similarly, when infants are lowered towards the ground they raise their heads just before what would be the moment of impact; this response to information in the expanding optic flow is present by three months.

In another study reviewed by Butterworth (Granrud *et al.*, 1984), infants watched computer-generated displays of randomly moving dots. An impression of discontinuity at an edge was created by having part of the texture on the screen continuously deleted by the remaining texture. To adult observers this looked like one moving surface sliding behind another. (Such occluding effects are referred to frequently by Gibson in his later writings.) It is known that infants, faced with a choice, will attempt to grasp the nearer of two objects. In this study, infants aged five months reached and attempted to touch the television screen at a position where one surface appeared to be above the other. It seems, therefore, as though infants can use dynamic properties of stimulation to acquire knowledge of depth.

His study of published research in this area leads Butterworth to suggest that the vital distinction which each of us must acquire—that between ourselves and the world—is imposed very early in life by the structure of the optic array, which is what Gibson would have predicted.

Summary   The above was not a review of contemporary infant research—there is too much of it to fit into a single chapter—rather, it was an attempt to show the originality of the problems being posed to infants. For the theorist this area of psychology is potentially very important. It may well be that results from infant studies will eventually help us to decide upon the correctness (or otherwise) of key parts of the theory of direct perception. It can be said here that the ability of infants to respond to higher-order, invariant properties of stimulation is looking more and more impressive. Gibson may have been correct in believing that such abilities have been acquired through the course of evolution and do not have to be learned during the development of the individual. At the very least it can be claimed that the perception of some invariants comes very easily and naturally to the human infant: a fact which supports direct perception but which will have to be accounted for by any general theory.

A new invariant: the cardioidal strain transformation

When we see a familiar person who has aged, our perception of the face tells us two things: first, that the face has changed; second, that it is, however, the same face. This is a complex situation involving simultaneous perception of identity and change. What is the basis of this physiognomic perception? How can we see the continuing identity of a face? A partial answer is that some of the important changes which occur during ageing can be described by a mathematical function, the cardioidal strain transformation (see Figure 7.9). The outline of a skull can be fitted by a cardioid. As the skull ages, small changes in the parameters of the cardioid can match the changing shape. And it is changes in the shape of the skull which are partially responsible for changes in our faces as we grow up. Now when a sketch of a face is subjected to controlled distortion by cardioidal strain, it appears to age (Todd *et al.*, 1980; Pittenger and Shaw, 1975; Pittenger, Shaw and Mark, 1979). It seems clear that there is something which persists during the ageing of a face, an invariant which can be recovered from the cardioidal function, and which we seem to be able to perceive. What seemed like a very difficult problem has begun to yield to the application of the concept of the invariant.

Studies of optic flow

The first study to be described under this heading is that by Lee and Reddish (1981). Researchers such as these are beginning to understand optic flow, the importance of which Gibson stressed repeatedly in his writings.

When the gannet (*Sula bassana*) sights fish it dives at the surface of the water, often from heights of up to 30 m. During the dive the gannet adopts an increasingly swept-back wing posture. During the dive the wings, although swept back, are not fully so: the partial closure leaves enough wing for steering. However, the terminal velocity attained during a dive may reach 50 mph: if the gannet entered the water at this speed with its wings partially deployed it would damage itself. Immediately prior to hitting the surface, the bird stretches its wings straight back to enter the water in the most streamlined posture it can adopt (see Figure 7.10). What information is available to the gannet to allow it to time its motor behaviour so precisely?

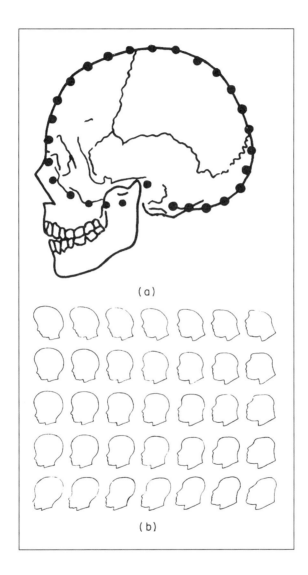

(a)

(b)

Figure 7.9   (a) A cardioid fitted to the profile of a skull; (b) outline drawings of a face made to age in appearance by subjecting the original outline to a cardioidal strain transformation. ((a) is from Shaw, McIntyre and Mace, 1974. Copyright 1974, Cornell University; used with permission of Cornell University Press. (b) is from Pittenger and Shaw, 1975. Copyright 1975, American Psychological Association; reprinted with permission of the publisher)

Figure 7.10 Changing wing positions of a diving gannet, *Sula bassana*. How does the gannet time these changes? (From B. Nelson, *The Gannet*, 1979. Published by permission of Academic Press Ltd)

Lee and Reddish have proved that there is a regularity in the changing visual image of the textured surface of the sea. This constant is *the inverse of the rate of dilation of the visual image of texture elements.* Lee and Reddish named this constant *tau.* They constructed a model, which includes tau, to show how information specifying time-to-contact can be extracted during a dive. They then tested data from films of actual diving behaviour against their model. The fit to a curve based on their equation is a good one.

The second study to be described, Dienes and McCleod (1993), is not directly about optic flow phenomena as such, but is so close in spirit to the Lee and Reddish research described above that it can be included in this section.

How does one catch a ball? Dienes and McCleod actually refer to a cricket ball, but their answer is general (and is quite fascinating).

The ball is hit and flies upwards and towards the boundary. If a fielder is to catch the ball, it is clearly necessary to be in the right place as the ball nears the ground. But how far and how fast should he or she run? The answer (arrived at by geometric reasoning and empirical research) is wonderfully simple. The ball rises and then falls in a parabola. Let us assume that the catcher makes a decision to go for the catch when the ball first starts to descend.

If a = the angle of the catcher's gaze to the ball, then he or she must run at a speed such that:

$$\frac{d^2(\tan a)}{dt^2} = 0, \tag{5}$$

this is to say that the catcher must keep the acceleration of the tangent of the angle of gaze with respect to the horizontal at zero. The acceleration of the tangent is equivalent to the acceleration of the vertical projection of the ball. When this value is negative, the catcher is running too slowly and the ball will drop to the ground in front of him or her; when positive, the catcher will overshoot the point where the ball will land. So catching may require changes in running speed. When running speed is correct, and equation (5) is satisfied, the catcher's gaze (and head position) will also be changing at the correct rate.[4] Readers should now go out and attempt to catch some high balls in order to appreciate this very convincing account of the perceptual basis of a familiar skill.

To end this section, we must stress that the study of optic flow becomes much more complicated when the movement of an observer towards a surface or object is not straight on. For example, in walking and driving, we commonly need to estimate the chances of collision with an object or surface towards which we are moving *obliquely*. Similarly, we don't always look straight ahead when moving. The resulting oblique relationships between angle of gaze, direction of movement, and converging paths are much more difficult to analyse. Interested readers should read Cutting (Cutting, 1982, 1986; Cutting, Vishton and Braren, 1995) who has made major contributions to the study of perception during motion.

Affordances and the psychology of design

Data and theories arising from within experimental psychology have often been used in applied fields. An obvious example is in engineering psychology (ergonomics) where, for example, experiments on displays and controls have led to greatly improved visual displays in industrial equipment, cars and aircraft. However, much of this work has not been strongly theoretical; problems arose and were solved using psychological knowledge. For example, psychophysical research has provided data on visual acuity under different conditions of stimulus intensity. From the data it is not difficult to recommend the optimum size and shape of lettering on, say, motorway signs. To stay in this area, readers will have noticed the increasing use of green-yellow clothing by maintenance workers, police and fire fighters when working on motorways. This colour is a compromise based on the peak wavelength sensitivities of the rod and cone cells of the retina—one of the earliest discoveries by psychophysicists researching visual performance.

---

[4] Dienes and McCleod state that changes in head position could be monitored by the vestibular system of the inner ear, or could be based on unconscious calculations using the perceived distance and height of the ball.

Thus, applied psychology has often concentrated on work and workers: people having to do special things, often with special machinery. But what about more everyday situations?

We turn now to a brief description of work which has attempted to use general psychological principles in order to create better designs of objects and systems. The relevance for this chapter is the fact that the work to be described takes as its starting point Gibson's concept of the affordance.

D.A. Norman

Donald Norman is well known for his distinguished contribution to the study of human memory and cognition. He is also someone who became increasingly irritated by aspects of modern design, whether of objects or of systems. His more popular writings (Norman, 1988, 1992, 1993) contain wonderfully entertaining accounts of his personal battles with doors, refrigerators and airline schedules. A more technical account of his work is included in Norman and Draper (1986).

> I have studied people making errors—sometimes serious ones—with mechanical devices, light switches and fuses, even airplanes and nuclear power plants. Invariably people feel guilty and either try to hide the error or blame themselves for 'stupidity' or 'clumsiness'. I often have difficulty getting permission to watch: nobody likes to be observed performing badly. I point out that the design is faulty and that others make the same errors. Still, if the task *appears* simple or trivial, then people blame themselves.
>
> (Norman, 1988)

Norman decided to do something about this.

The essence of Norman's position is that humans naturally do some things well, others badly. Bad design fails to recognize this fact. Here are a few examples, drawn from Norman's own writings.

If each key on a telephone has one and only one function, people will quickly learn to use it effortlessly and without error; it will be a pleasure to use. Where the telephone has more functions than keys, its use will require thought and recourse to memory (or the instruction book)—phoning will be less natural, and hence less pleasant. Similarly, we have all struggled to use a strange gas cooker in which the burners are arranged in a square but the controls are in line: which control is linked to which burner? When mappings are natural (the controls could also be arranged in a square), we can control such appliances almost without thinking. Poor mapping leads to errors.

We know more than this about errors. Humans profit from feedback to confirm that their actions have been appropriate, and yet in many computer networks one can wait for minutes on end before the (busy) system responds. Having given a computer an erroneous command, the outcome should not be fatal—we should be offered a chance to retrieve the situation.

Basing his analyses on what is known about humans, and using the concept of the affordance, Norman is able to describe many examples of good and bad design.

> Affordances provide strong clues to the operations of things. Plates [on doors] are for pushing. Knobs are for turning. Slots are for inserting things into. Balls are for throwing or bouncing. When affordances are taken advantage of, the user knows what to do just by looking: no picture, label, or instruction is required. Complex things may require explanation, but simple things should not.
>
> (Norman, 1988)

Norman's writings constitute an argument for 'user-centred' design. They urge us to oppose the worst that modern technology can do to us, and to insist that this technology enhances rather than diminishes our lives. Norman's writings suggest ways in which this goal could be achieved.

N. Moray

We shall end this section by describing some challenging opinions advanced in a 1994 keynote address to the International Ergonomics Association Meeting in Toronto by the psychologist, Neville Moray.

Readers who consult the publications by Norman cited in the previous section will quickly realize that their guiding philosophy is liberal and humane. Nevertheless, it is worth remembering Chomsky's remark that most people in the world have never made a telephone call. Norman works in the wealthiest country the world has known. But what of the third world? As Moray remarks,

> . . . the world of ergonomics is effectively the world of western liberal capitalism, in which the quality of life is directly dependent on industrial and commercial development and a steady growth in the economy.
>
> (Moray, 1994)

For the Third World, the concerns are not about the ease of use of computers and telephones. Rather they have to do with population explosions, inadequate and polluted water supplies, illiteracy, poor communications, lack of energy resources, and the devastating effects of mass epidemics.

Moray recognizes that it is unlikely that these formidable problems will be solved simply by exporting Western technology to the Third World. And he is too realistic to believe that the answer to all problems lies in the application of psychology. But it would be an act of bad faith to turn our backs on the problems. Can anything be done?

Moray says that, at the least, we should be able to apply our knowledge to help in the *design* of systems for conserving water and energy. We should be able to suggest how to make cities more liveable. By helping design tasks and methods and the tools for carrying out the tasks, a contribution is possible.

All this will strike the reader as laudable, but possibly far removed from the theme of this chapter. Here is a single example from Moray's address which would have beneficial effects immediately.

Typhoid is a major killer in the Third World. The illness is caused by contaminated water; more specifically, water that contains human faeces. Put crudely, an important source of infection is the hand—indirectly connecting the rectum and the mouth. Can the link be broken by encouraging people to wash their hands after evacuation? Propaganda may not work in a country with poor communications. Poverty may have resulted in low educational standards—rates of illiteracy may be high.

What *affords* hand-washing? One answer is, the sight of water. A lavatory has been designed such that, when flushed, the water to refill the tank is delivered first to a bowl above the tank. The user is prompted to wash the hands by this affordance, and the now contaminated water is used in the next flush. This is an affordance-based design that could save lives. It is a long step from Gibson's pioneering work to this clever design. But how encouraging.

GENERAL REMARKS ON DIRECT PERCEPTION

There is more material in the theoretical writings of Gibson and others than can possibly be summarized in a single chapter. Readers are urged to read some of the references given below for a more detailed account of a major theory. However, it is our opinion that statements of the theory (once the major points have been grasped) are less interesting in the abstract than when they are coupled to experimental researches and demonstrations. In a sense, this theory of perception is under-specified. Things become more exciting when parts of the theory are tested. This is the reason why this chapter has included so many accounts of experiments. The work on cardioidal strain and ageing faces is more compelling than simple assertions about invariants; the richness (and complexity) of optic flow phenomena became obvious only when researchers attempted to measure them. Solid horizontal surfaces afford walking on—it is difficult to disagree with that statement—but it is very interesting that infants quickly come to perceive that affordance. And now we have a new way of thinking about the things and systems we must deal with in our daily lives: Do they offer good affordances?

At the core of the empiricist or constructivist theory of perception is the belief that proximal stimuli cannot fully represent distal objects, and therefore something must be added to incoming information in order to achieve valid perception of the world. The essence of the theory oulined in this chapter is that under 'natural' conditions—that is, in the unbuilt environment—there is a richness and structure in the countless stimuli available to an observer at each moment such that the world can in fact be specified. Although we must acknowledge the criticisms of Ullman (1980) and others concerning the decomposable (and therefore indirect) nature of perception under some conditions, we should remember that Gibson did not believe that his theory applied to the perception of cultural artefacts.

As Gibson and others have reminded us, the human is just one of a vast range of perceiving animals. If the theory of direct perception stimulates more research into the perceptual abilities of non-human species, it will have rendered an important service. Phrases such as 'perceptions are hypotheses', convincing at the human level, do not seem to carry as much weight when we look at the behaviour of dragonflies or tapeworms.

This ends our discussion of the work inspired by Gibson's ecological optics and the theory of direct perception. Although we have pointed to what seem to be weaknesses in this work, we have also tried to convey something of the excitement of this way of thinking about perception. It is likely that the debate over the correctness or otherwise of Gibson's approach will continue for some time to come. It should be an interesting debate.

NOTES ON CHAPTER 7

MacLeod and Pick (1974) is a collection of essays written in honour of Gibson.

The Ullman reference (above) is the start of a debate for and against direct perception. Ullman's critical analysis of direct perception is followed by a series of comments by various researchers arguing for and against the theory. This is an invaluable debate.

Fodor and Pylyshyn (1981) is a rigorous analysis of the implications of Gibson's theory.

The Michaels and Carello reference cited is an excellent introduction to direct perception. It conveys an enthusiasm for the Gibsonian approach which is highly infectious. Its existence has made it difficult to write parts of the present chapter; having read Michaels and Carello, unconscious plagiarism is an ever-present risk. Their book is highly recommended.

Since the first edition of this book appeared, the author has experienced growing doubts over Gibson's writings on art. A section on this topic has been removed from this edition. Readers who wish to judge for themselves should read Gibson (1971b).

Readers wishing to follow current work on direct perception should read some of the references cited under the heading 'More recent research' above, and then look in the latest editions of the same journals.

The Psychology of Everyday Things (1988) is an interesting and entertaining introduction to D.A. Norman's work on design and his use of the concept of affordance.

8

Marr's computational approach to visual perception

This chapter will attempt to outline what many consider to be the most important development in perceptual theory in recent years. To date the emphasis has been on visual perception, although there are good reasons to believe that successful applications will be made in other sensory modalities. We shall illustrate the approach by describing the work of one man, David Marr, whose contribution can be placed within the context of the new discipline of artificial intelligence (AI).

In terms of the informal classification of areas of concern to theorists, described in Chapter 1, we shall see that Marr and others in his discipline concentrate heavily upon processes in the peripheral visual system and show how these extract information from proximal stimuli.[1] At the same time, however, knowledge of the external world is used in a highly original way to impose constraints upon models.

This chapter will be organized under the following headings:

- David Marr
- The background to the artificial intelligence approach
- Marr's theory of vision and his programme for research
- Applying the theory
- Further aspects of Marr's work
- An appraisal of the computational approach to vision
- General remarks on Marr's approach to visual perception

---

[1] Once again, we remind readers that some of the material in this chapter will be easier to understand if they can acquire some outline knowledge of the general organization of the visual pathway, from retinal cells to the visual cortex.

DAVID MARR

David Marr's first interest was in mathematics which he studied at Cambridge, becoming a Wrangler. After this distinguished start to his career he did graduate work in the department of physiology at Cambridge, where he developed a model of the functioning of the cerebellum. He then learned the techniques of computer modelling at the Massachusetts Institute of Technology, where he spent the last years of his life. Marr had specialized knowledge of mathematics, physiology, computer science and experimental psychology. His work on artificial intelligence led to numerous papers on perception and, finally, to his book, *Vision: A Computational Investigation into the Human Representation and Processing of Visual Information*, which was published posthumously (Marr, 1982). David Marr died of leukaemia in 1980 at the age of 35.

THE BACKGROUND TO THE ARTIFICIAL INTELLIGENCE APPROACH

Forerunners of artificial intelligence

Artificial intelligence research in general, and the computational approach to vision in particular are part of an important scientific movement. The historical background to this movement can be outlined by describing three important developments: information theory, cybernetics, and the construction of large digital computers. These developments may seem somewhat irrelevant to the study of visual perception, but in fact they comprise the theoretical tradition out of which the computational approach crystallized.

Information theory, as developed by Shannon (1948), made it possible to quantify the information flowing through any system, whether that system was a telephone cable, a television channel, or a person reading a page of text: the measure was essentially neutral with regard to the content of a message. One obvious application of the new calculus was in neurophysiology: a nerve fibre fires according to an all-or-none principle and at certain rates. This transmission of discrete impulses can be viewed as a code, and the rate at which information can be transmitted by one or many neurons may be assessed. Similarly, when a person reacts at maximum speed to one of several possible signals, information theory can be used to assess that person's information-handling capacity. To be able to compare such apparently different situations using an objective measure of information seemed to many to be a very useful development.

Cybernetics, which was developed initially by the mathematician Norbert Wiener, is the application of mathematics to various systems, particularly those which show self-regulation. Initially applied to self-regulating machines, certain concepts from cybernetics quickly proved useful in psychology and physiology. A notable example is 'feedback', which describes how part of the output from a machine can be used to regulate and control the input. 'Negative feedback' typically promotes stability by using the difference between a desired level of output and the actual output level to reduce the input to the system; this damping effect is used to maintain homeostasis in living organisms. 'Positive feedback' tends to have the opposite effect, using output to increase gain and drive the system into instability. Thus an after-image (which will form if one stares at a bright light) which is off-centre in the visual field will induce reflex pursuit movements of the eyes which try, vainly, to centre the image. The movements cause the image to appear to move even further to one side and so the pursuit continues, the apparent speed of the after-image getting faster and faster.

We remind the reader of an earlier discussion of the impact of digital computers on modern thought in Chapter 5. By the 1950s there were large numbers of these remarkable machines. For many psychologists they became irresistible as a metaphor for the human brain. This led to some extravagant claims:

> Intuition, insight, and learning are no longer exclusive possessions of humans: any large high-speed computer can be programmed to exhibit them also.
>
> (Simon and Newell, 1958)

> . . . the task of a psychologist trying to understand human cognition is analogous to that of a man trying to discover how a computer has been programmed.
>
> (Neisser, 1967)

The developments listed above created a new discipline: artificial intelligence (AI). This engineering approach treats organisms as machines controlled by processes. And some of these processes are perceptual. Perception thus offered an obvious challenge to workers in the new discipline.

The research to be described did not arise solely from theoretical considerations. The period when Artificial Intelligence was forming as a discipline was also a time when important empirical discoveries were occurring in the study of perception and related areas. We shall summarize some of the most important of these to show the sort of knowledge that was available to Marr when he started to build his theory of vision. Four examples will convey the quality of this empirical work.

Receptive fields in the visual cortex

In Chapter 5 reference was made to work by Hubel and Wiesel (1962, 1968), who succeeded in recording the electrical responses of living cells in the visual cortex of the cat and the monkey to various patterns of stimulation. One of the most striking and thought-provoking discoveries was that the visual cortex contains cells responding differentially to lines and edges according to the orientation of these stimuli. This was a remarkable finding, for it suggested that the visual system analyses visual inputs into specific components, and that the mechanisms which do this are 'wired into' the nervous system. It is therefore possible that the perception of certain basic features of the world is unlearned (although subsequent research showed that the activity of the cortical cells can be modified by prolonged experience).

The Julesz random-dot stereograms

Julesz (1960) discovered random-dot stereograms. When these are fused in a stereoscope a powerful illusion of depth is seen. The depth arises because the paired stereograms contain central portions which differ slightly, thus capturing the cue which normally triggers stereopsis: disparity of left and right views. The strange and wonderful thing about the Julesz demonstration is that the disparity is not visible when one scrutinizes the individual stereograms: one appears to be looking at random textures—arrays which contain no hint of form (see Figure 8.1). This proves that the visual system can extract disparity information in the absence of pattern recognition, a remarkable discovery.

Spatial frequency channels in the visual system

Pantle and Sekuler (1968), Campbell and Robson (1968) and other workers studied various visual systems to see how they respond to changes in the spatial frequencies of test gratings. The *spatial frequency* of a grating is simply the number of changes (commonly the number of black and white stripes) it contains per degree of visual angle. It was found that if an observer stares for a time at a particular grating, sensitivity to that grating is temporarily reduced. That this is not a general loss of visual acuity is shown by the fact that sensitivity to other spatial frequencies remains unchanged. A related discovery was that recordings from the visual cortex of the cat reveal the presence of cells which are differentially sensitive to particular spatial frequencies. It began to look as though one could consider the acuity of vertebrate visual systems in terms of tuned channels. Thinking about vision in terms of spatial frequencies led in turn to the use of powerful new techniques of analysis, the most successful of which has been Fourier analysis. These have been very fruitful developments.

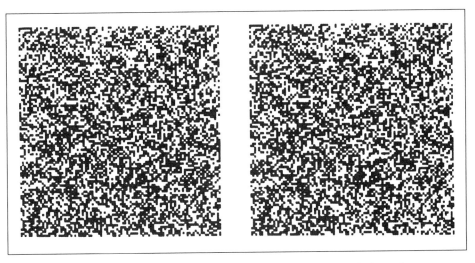

Figure 8.1 Two random-dot stereograms. These are best viewed through a stereo-scope; however, if they are fixated either with the eyes crossed, or by staring 'through' the page to infinity, the stereograms should fuse. Following fusion a small central diamond will be seen to emerge in depth from the apparently random textures. (From Julesz, 1971. Copyright 1971, Bell Telephone Laboratories, Inc.; reprinted with permission)

Early examples of the computational approach

Land and McCann (1971) and Horn (1974) offered a solution to a classic problem in perception: How does the visual system 'know' that the varied appearance of a coloured surface is a property of the surface rather than its illumination? Their suggestion was that while the effects of changes in illumination are usually gradual, changes due to a surface's geometry—its edges, boundaries between facets, and so on—are usually abrupt. If a visual system could somehow ignore or filter out the gradual changes, what remained would be information about the characteristics of the surface rather than its illumination; perception could then be veridical. A solution of the problem was as follows: sample the lightness values of a surface by paired, closely contiguous detectors and record differences in their outputs. Placed on a homogeneous surface under an illumination gradient, the differences in outputs will be very small and can be ignored. However, when the two detectors straddle a boundary between two surfaces of different lightness, there will be a large difference in their outputs. In this manner the true surface lightness (or reflectance) properties will be detected and changes due to illumination will not.[2] This was not, of course, an *empirical* contribution, although it was inspired by some striking new colour phenomena which Land had discovered and which caused him to challenge the traditional theories of colour vision.

Describing the genesis of his own ideas, Marr says of the Land and McCann work:

> I do not now believe that this is at all a correct analysis of colour vision or of the retina, but it showed the possible style of a correct analysis . . . gone is any explanation *in terms of neurons*—except as a way of implementing a method. And present is a clear understanding of what is to be computed, how it is to be done, the physical assumptions on which the method is based, and some kind of analysis of the algorithms that are capable of carrying it out.
>
> (Marr, 1982)

As we shall show, the *style* of explanations in perceptual research was something which Marr attempted to change. Marr's contribution to the study of visual perception will now be described.

MARR'S THEORY OF VISION AND HIS PROGRAMME FOR RESEARCH

One of Marr's acknowledged contributions lies in his attempt to clarify our thinking about information-processing systems. In what follows the reader should keep the following points in mind: (1) the term 'information' is used here more loosely than in the technical sense (where it is related to reduction of uncertainty), and (2) 'information-processing' is not mere transduction of energy. For example, a telescope changes light by magnification, but magnification is not an informational process—the image is simply a linear transformation of the object. As nothing else is really changed by the magnification we cannot apply informational measures to this effect. Note, however, that we can see things through a telescope which are invisible to the naked eye. This is because the eye itself is a non-linear device. So when we consider the eye and the telescope *as a single system*, it becomes appropriate to use informational concepts and measures.

---

[2] The actual algorithm needed to achieve this result is in fact slightly more complicated than this: it requires the cumulative storage of ratios of successive output differences, together with rules for deciding which surface in an array can be designated as a standard white.

Representations and descriptions

Marr's definitions of these terms are as follows:

> A representation is a formal system for making explicit certain entities or types of information, together with a specification of how the system does this. And I shall call the result of using a representation to describe a given entity a description of the entity in that representation.
>
> (Marr, 1982)

These definitions, which appear quite abstruse at first glance, may be clarified by a simple example. From a satellite photograph of a country we draw an outline map. Suppose that the satellite's optics have great resolving power and that they can assess the maximum height in each 10 square kilometre area of the terrain, allocating a numerical height value to each. We can now select and add to the map all points with heights of 200 metres, 400 metres, and so on, each represented by a coloured dot. Joining dots of a particular colour (representing a particular height) with straight lines will generate a crude contour map of the country.

Next, data are obtained concerning the distribution of people in the country and a single dot is printed to represent each thousand of the population. Lines can be added to represent roads and rivers. Finally, we add some markings to represent, say, birth rates in various regions.

A map of the country has been created from which certain interesting conclusions might be drawn; for example, that more people live in valleys, roads wind round hilly areas, and people living on high ground are more fecund. Now although we have described a single map, it is obvious that five distinct *representations* (outline, height, population density, rivers, roads) have been used to arrive at five *descriptions*: the map can be thought of as formed from five superimposed transparencies.

That was an imperfect explication of Marr's definitions, for the procedures we imagined were not ones which can be done by machines; they would normally be carried out by geographers. However, the important point stands: we have used *symbols* to represent things or events.

Three levels of understanding information systems

Marr's own example of an information-processing task is one that is definitely performed by a machine. (From now on all quotations are from Marr, 1982, unless stated otherwise.) Marr describes a cash register. It is at this point that he introduces the distinction between the three levels of explanation which he insists must be kept separate in our thinking about any informational process. This distinction pervades the whole of *Vision* and may well be one of Marr's enduring contributions. The three levels which Marr distinguishes are: (1) the computational theory, (2) the algorithm and (3) the hardware implementation.

The computational theory

Marr asserts that at this level of enquiry we must ask, 'What is the goal of the computation, why is it appropriate, and what is the strategy by which it can be carried out?' In the example of the cash register, the function of the machine is clearly to add sums of money. And it is this procedure of addition which brings the machine within the class which we define as information-processing devices: several subtotals may be 'compressed' into a final sum from which they cannot be recovered, so the process is not a linear translation or transduction.

In this example, the computational theory is simply *the rules of arithmetic*— that is to say, it should not matter in what order we enter data into the cash register; if we enter a zero sum, then the total should be unaffected, and so on. We are describing what the machine achieves and also the *constraints* upon it. These constraints allow the processes within the machine to be defined. At this stage we may be completely ignorant as to *how* the machine does its arithmetic.

The algorithm

'How can the computational theory be implemented? In particular, what is the representation for the input and output, and what is the algorithm for the transformation?'

The input to the machine is known (key entries which represent sums of money in decimal notation), as is the output (total sums of money displayed in decimal notation), but what has the machine actually *done*? The machine could have translated keyed entries into electronic or mechanical equivalents of decimal quantities. Or entries might have been translated into binary form (which would be very likely if the cash register was linked to a large computer network). So there is something to discover about the *representation* of the data which the machine will process.

Knowledge of the representation may prompt guesses about the algorithm or formula used within the machine. Clearly, the *algorithm* chosen will depend in part on the nature of the representation. For example, if the machine is operating according to binary arithmetic, then the algorithm must include some procedure which will change entries from decimal form prior to adding, and then reconvert before displaying totals.

The hardware implementation

'How can the representation and algorithm be realized physically?'

A machine such as a cash register is not fully understood until the implementation is known. We know the computational theory of the machine (the rules of arithmetic) and can form hypotheses as to how input and output are represented and how the correct answer is attained. But there is still an area of ignorance: how does the machine actually work? It might contain interlocking cogs like an old-fashioned mechanical calculator. Or it might assign voltages to particular numbers using thermionic valves. Or (and most probably) the machine might function by the operation of a series of electronic switches—devices which can represent one of two possible states. The question concerns the hardware of the machine, the nature of its component parts and how they operate.

A brief recapitulation

Many readers, including those with some previous knowledge of perceptual theories, may find these ideas rather strange. As they are central to Marr's approach, it might be useful to pause at this stage and offer a short summary and another example before proceeding to describe more of his work.

The starting point for seeing is the image on the retina; the end point is our awareness of the world. We seem to have a picture of the world available to us whenever our eyes are open, and we call this seeing. But the truth is that light stops at the retina. There can be no actual picture in our heads, only neural activity. It follows that this neural activity is representing the world *symbolically*, and we must therefore strive to understand this symbolic process or processes. Marr argues that symbolic representations of various aspects of the world, initially obtained from the retinal image, are combined into the descriptions which we call seeing.

Marr suggests that the most rigorous way in which to conduct research is to ask a series of systematic questions arising from the computational approach.

Let us consider, as an example, the perception of contours. In this case the appropriate sequence of questions would be:

(1) Why is it important to be able to perceive contours? If the visual system can extract them from the visual image, what use is this to the perceiver? In other words, what of importance in the real world correlates with contours in the visual image? Why should the visual system work to make them explicit? How might contours be represented symbolically in our heads? If we can see a contour is it likely that this has arisen from an edge—a feature which reveals discontinuities between the surfaces of different objects? It is clear that this last question matches Brunswik's concern over the ecological validity of cues. It is equally clear that to answer the questions requires knowledge about (a) the visual system, (b) the purposive aspects of the perceiver's behaviour, and (c) the nature of the real world, which sets constraints upon our theory. This last point is very important. We need to know, for example, how many types

of edges there are in the world. When edges form junctions, in how many ways can this be done? What is the relationship between the inside and outside angles of, say, a transparent object? It is necessary to think about topology.

(2) When the preceding questions have been answered, it is possible to think about the algorithm. In the present example, we start with the retinal image which is a set of light intensities spread across part of the retina, this is the input. The output must be a symbolic representation of lines or edges appearing in conscious experience. Now the question arises as to *how* a process operating on the retinal image could deliver contour information.

The example we have chosen is a relatively easy one, for quite a lot is known about contour perception. A successful algorithm would utilize a well-known property of retinal cells, namely the ability of some cells to inhibit the action of others. Developing this idea suggests that it would be useful if contour perception involved processes which did not pass on information to later stages in the visual pathway from areas in which retinal illumination was homogeneous, or even graded in intensity, but which produced outputs in response to *rates of change within gradients* (the second differential of intensity). This would 'extract' the relevant contour information. We would now start to think about possible excitatory and inhibitory fields in the retina to see whether they could respond to entire edges, and it would be necessary to suggest plausible rules by which these fields could interact.

It is possible to test hypotheses concerning algorithms of the sort described above using electronic circuits designed so that the components simulate mutual excitation and inhibition. This can reveal whether the circuits can respond in the hoped-for manner to, say, the second differential of a brightness gradient. This can be done in two ways: (a) by actually building assemblies of photodetectors and electronic components, or (b) by computer simulation. Many ideas in artificial intelligence have been tested in this way.

(3) Having designed a plausible algorithm it is now necessary to consider how it could be put into practice. In the present case, independent evidence strongly suggests that it is the retinal ganglion cells which initiate the process of contour extraction. In fact, inhibitory relationships have actually been demonstrated among these cells. It would be of obvious interest to observe the activities of large groups of such cells, but technical problems make this impossible at present.

A challenge to the reader

This, then, is the way in which Marr believes we should approach the task of understanding vision. Lack of progress in the past has often stemmed from failure to ask the right questions about perceptual systems, or from confusion between the three levels to which research attention can be directed. As a test of the reader's understanding of Marr's point, we offer the following challenge (first put to me by my colleague Dave Earle): *Apply the computational approach to an ordinary lock*. What is the computational theory of locking? What would be an appropriate algorithm for the lock? In what way(s) might the algorithm be implemented? Those who find it easy to answer these questions have certainly grasped Marr's argument.

The stages of visual perception

Early in his book Marr describes how his thoughts on vision developed until he reached his most important insight. What was required, he realized, was 'a theory in which the main job of vision was to derive a representation of shape'. Vision can do much more than this, but informing the perceiver about brightness, colour, texture and so on is secondary to deriving a representation of shape. The problem then is to discover how vision derives reliable information concerning the shapes of objects in the real world from information contained in the retinal image.

Marr's theory is that perception proceeds as an information-processing system and that this system is organized into successive *stages*: it is unlikely that reliable or stable conclusions about objective shape could be derived in a single step. Marr also uses his knowledge of computer science to formulate a guiding principle, *Modular design*. This principle simply states that when developing computational systems, it is wise to break down the computation into component parts which should proceed as independently as possible. The reason for this is that if part of a system goes wrong and this part interacts strongly with others, debugging the complete system becomes a formidable problem. Marr's hunch is that many of the processes of vision are modular, and for this important reason.

We shall now outline Marr's views on the stages of visual perception.

1. *The image.* The 'function' of the retinal image can be defined as representing intensity. The image is a spatial distribution of intensity values across the retina and is the starting point in the process of seeing.
2. *The primal sketch.* The function of this stage of vision is to take the raw intensity values of the visual image and make explicit certain forms of information contained therein. The most important information concerns the spatial or geometrical distribution of intensity changes and the manner in which they are organized. The types of information which are becoming explicit at this stage are such as to afford the possibility of detecting surfaces.
3. The 2½-D sketch. At this stage of the visual process the orientation and rough depth of visible surfaces are made explicit: it is as if a 'picture' of the world is beginning to emerge. Note, however, that at this level what is

emerging is organized with reference only to the viewer; it is not yet linked to a stable, external environment.

4. *The 3-D model representation.* Here shapes and their orientation become explicit as tokens of three-dimensional objects organized in an object-centred framework; that is to say, in a manner that is independent of particular positions and orientations on the retina. By this final stage of vision the perceiver has attained a model of the real external world.

APPLYING THE THEORY

The reader who can see the potential rigour and clarity afforded by Marr's ideas may yet wonder how the approach actually works, how Marr moves from verbal description to a scientific attack on the problem of vision. Selections of Marr's work will now be examined in more detail to convey the style of the computational approach. The first topic is the primal sketch.

Work on the primal sketch

The starting point for this early stage of vision is the array of intensities represented in the retinal image. Marr's theory holds that certain *primitives* or *place tokens* are derived from the image. These are: zero-crossings (which will be explained below), edges, bars (which can be thought of as pairs of parallel edges), blobs (the ends of bars or small clusters of dots), terminations (of edges or bars), edge segments, virtual lines, groups, curvilinear organization, and boundaries.

The development of the primal sketch begins with the derivation from the spatial retinal array of primitives which can be thought of as *tokens*. The idea of tokens is very important in this approach. To explain this a little more fully consider a recent trend in television commercials, the reverse zoom. A typical advert starts with a shot of a group of individuals. Because we see these as individuals, each must have been assigned a visual token. Now the camera zooms out and we start to see that the people form various groupings. Finally, we see, from a great height, that the people are arranged as letters in a word (the advertised product etc.). Seeing each letter as a coherent whole implies that it too must be represented in the visual system, and thus, in Marr's terms, another token has been created. Of course, the tokens formed in the visual system are 'really' neural events. When Marr or other theorists in artificial intelligence use actual visual tokens to illustrate the successive processing of images, this is argument by analogy.

During the development of the primal sketch groups of adjacent tokens that have a common orientation are replaced by 'level-one' tokens representing this orientation. Then, if there are whole groups of similarly oriented level-one tokens, these are used to construct boundaries between parts of the full primal sketch. There is nothing mysterious about these notions. Remembering our illustrative example of a map, it is obvious that when a sufficient number of concentric contours occupy a given region, they could all be replaced by a single purple patch to indicate a mountainous area (cartographers do this routinely); the patch would form a token, like those formed for the letters and words in our television commercial example.

A question arises as to *how* the initial primitives of the primal sketch are actually extracted. The attempt to answer this question leads Marr to a most impressive piece of work and demonstrates the advantages of his background in artificial intelligence. We shall concentrate upon the primitive known as the *zero-crossing*.

When a photograph or an actual image (such as that on a television screen) is scrutinized, it is obvious that important information about the shape and orientation of objects comes from edges, contours and boundaries: that is, from areas in the image where intensity values are changing rapidly. Clearly then it should be important to represent these portions of the image in the primal sketch. But what sort of process can take intensity values as inputs and deliver tokens representing lines, edges and so on as outputs?

The first step in the required processing is to smooth the image. Light is 'noisy' and it is important to minimize this noise before doing further processing. A process which will do this is *convolution*. One way of convolving an image is to choose a particular position (often defined as a *pixel*) and then apply weighting functions so that, following convolution, the intensity value at the position is replaced by the weighted sum of itself and adjacent pixels. The process is then repeated at all positions on the image. In starting to think about this problem, it occurred to researchers that one method of weighting would be to apply a Gaussian distribution to successive portions of the image such that regions under the centre of the Gaussian were weighted strongly, those in the periphery less so. The width of the Gaussian can be controlled by adjusting its standard deviation: the wider the distribution the greater the degree of smoothing of the image and the smaller the range of spatial frequencies transmitted. A narrow Gaussian will pass more high spatial frequencies. (As we shall see later, combining a positive Gaussian filter with a negative one—in which the weights are subtractive rather than additive—yields valuable results in this method of processing.) The type of technique we have described is in fact widely used in applied situations such as computer image-enhancement.

Now examine the graphs drawn in Figure 8.2 (adapted from Marr, 1982). In this figure (a) represents a change in intensity in part of an image; this is the input to our hypothetical process. Part (b) is a representation of *the first derivative* of the intensity change; by this is meant simply that the intensity curve in (a) has been replotted in (b) to show the rate of change of intensity:

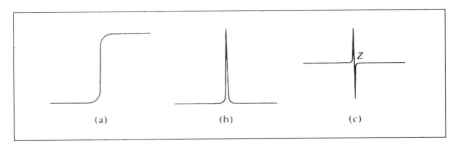

Figure 8.2 The extraction of a zero-crossing. See text for full explanation. (From *Visions* by David Marr. Copyright 1982, W.H. Freeman & Company; reprinted with permission)

this is clearly zero at the start, then rises rapidly before falling to zero again. Part (c) is *the second derivative* of (a) and represents the rate of change of (b). This amounts to saying that if we examine curve (b) we can find points when it too is changing rapidly; plotting these changes in (c) reveals that the curve is initially at zero, then rises positively (upwards) quite rapidly to a peak before diminishing (in a negative direction) with equal rapidity. In moving from its positive to its negative peak the graph crosses the horizontal zero axis. This, in Marr's theory, is the primitive we require: the *zero-crossing*. We have moved from an image (or part of one) to a representation. (In a later part of his theory Marr guesses that the *sign* of the zero-crossing may be represented; this would give additional power to the extraction processes.)

The computational theory has suggested the zero-crossing as a primitive. The next stage is to construct an algorithm—a set of rules by means of which zero-crossings may be extracted from images. Marr's suggestion takes the form of an *operator* or mathematical function: $\nabla^2 G$, where ∇^2 is the Laplacian operator

$$\nabla^2 = \frac{\delta^2}{\delta x^2} + \frac{\delta^2}{\delta y^2}$$

and G is the two-dimensional Gaussian distribution,

$$G(x, y) = \exp\left(-\frac{x^2 + y^2}{2\pi\sigma^2}\right).$$

The reader for whom this sort of formula is very unfamiliar should not feel discouraged: Marr is simply describing a mathematical process which will convert intensity changes in a two-dimensional image into zero-crossings, rather as in the one-dimensional case illustrated in Figure 8.2. What happens is this: ∇^2, the Laplacian operator, extracts the second differential information which we require. G, the two-dimensional Gaussian distribution, will blur the image by controlled amounts. The result of using these two formulae simultaneously is that zero-crossings can be extracted over a range of spatial frequencies. Put another way, $\nabla^2 G$ is a band-pass filter.[3] As we shall show, this is very important.

It is mathematically certain that the above operations will do the required extraction, but, of course, these are ideal, abstract formulae. There is, however, a filter which closely approximates the $\nabla^2 G$ operator: this is known as a difference of two Gaussians (DOG). The performance of DOG filters is known and they have certain advantages for the present purpose, one of which is that, like the $\nabla^2 G$ operator, they too can be tuned to different scales. The importance of tuning can be demonstrated very easily. The reader should stare at this page with partially closed eyes. Then the page will be seen as an area of brightness which differs from the surface on which it is lying. Similarly, the paragraphs on the page can be seen as blocks of dark grey against the white page. But on opening the eyes again it can be seen that there are discontinuities in brightness operating at a much finer scale: one is aware of lines of black print and spaces between words and letters. This shows why a successful filtering process attempting to capture zero-crossings should be capable of operating at more than one scale. More importantly, by using spatial frequency filters tuned to different scales and comparing their outputs, the chance of detecting an actual edge—one that is present in the external world—is greatly increased. In fact, Marr and Hildreth (1980) have proved that if several different spatial filters over a contiguous range of sizes indicate the existence of a zero-crossing in the same position in the image, *then this must arise from a single physical cause, for example, an edge in the world*. This is a most important finding. Knowledge of the physics of the real world is confirming major theoretical assumptions.

It is, however, possible that the reader is experiencing some puzzlement at this point. Why, when $\nabla^2 G$ will do the required extraction of zero-crossings, should emphasis suddenly switch to DOG filters? The answer is that when considering a suitable algorithm in this attempt to solve a problem, Marr is remaining aware of the next stage he must deal with: the implementation. Now the formulae summarized by the symbols $\nabla^2 G$ are, as we have shown, highly complicated. It is unlikely that there are neural mechanisms in the early stages of the visual system which can perform directly the advanced mathematics required. However, from what is known about the ganglion cells of the retina and their receptive fields, it is entirely reasonable to suppose that these receptive fields could yield outputs, one type of which resembles positive Gaussian weighting functions, another negative ones. Thus the DOG has the advantage over $\nabla^2 G$ in that one can begin to see how its job could be done by neurons.

---

[3] Low-pass and high-pass filters transmit low and high spatial frequencies, respectively. A band-pass filter transmits a particular range of frequencies. Used alone, G would act as a low-pass spatial frequency filter.

An important advantage of the AI/engineering approach to vision is that it is possible at this stage to make a powerful indirect test of the theory so far. It is possible to substitute photographs of real scenes for retinal images and process them through actual filters. Then, by examining the outputs of these filters, one can see to what extent lines, edges and so on, have been made explicit and whether the shapes in the photographs have been separated. It is also a simple matter to assess filters other than DOGs to compare their performances (if the reader will look back to the computer-processed photographs in Figure 5.12, it will be seen that a DOG filter can be approximated by superimposing a mask containing positive and negative weighted regions over a pixel array).

Marr's publications contain numerous illustrations of such filtering procedures. We must point out, however, that it is not yet *proved* that zero-crossings are computed by the visual system, but this is not Marr's main concern at this stage.

After finding an appropriate computational theory and related algorithms it becomes necessary to consider the hardware implementation; to look for neural devices which will extract zero-crossings and other primitives. From what is known about the neurophysiology of the retina and visual pathways, it is obvious (as was stated above) that this search should concentrate upon systems or cells having inhibitory capabilities, such as retinal ganglion cells and others in the lateral geniculate nucleus which show receptive field properties.

Receptive fields can be organized in various ways and have various shapes. Marr's guess concerning the cells delivering information about zero-crossings is that they are the retinal ganglion and lateral geniculate cells known as X-cells: in particualr those having on-centre/off-surround organization (firing when the centre of the receptive field is stimulated, inhibited when the surrounding portion of the field is stimulated), and the off-centre/on-surround cells (having the opposite type of organization). In a striking demonstration of the probable truth of this part of the theory, Marr displays, simultaneously the outputs of DOG filters to lines and edges and the outputs of actual X-cells responding to the same stimuli. The similarity between these outputs is remarkably close.

An application to problems of stereopsis

Following that description of work on the early stages of vision, we shall show more of the rigour and power of the computational approach by describing an attack on a second problem. We shall now give an outline of a possible solution to the problem of stereopsis.

The reader who wishes to experience at first hand the high quality of Marr's work should consult the relevant chapters of *Vision*, or the original research paper by Marr and his collaborator, T. Poggio (Marr and Poggio, 1979). Beware, however; this is very difficult material and it can take several readings before one feels confident that the arguments have been mastered. It is nevertheless well worth the effort.

Stereopsis is a term having two meanings. First, it refers to that extra sense of solidity and depth which is experienced when using two eyes rather than one, an experience which is confirmed by the superiority of binocular depth discriminations. It is a cue to the relative rather than absolute distances of objects. Second, stereopsis is triggered when two slightly different views of a scene are viewed in a stereoscope. In this case the two flat patterns are inducing an illusion of depth which can be manipulated in attempts to gain an understanding of normal stereopsis.

Classical work showed that the basis of stereopsis must lie in the difference between the left- and right-eye images. When these fall onto corresponding areas of the two retinae, disparate images will induce an illusion of depth. That this *disparity* is a necessary and sufficient cue for stereopsis is demonstrated by the ability of random-dot textures to induce depth when the actual disparity is hidden, as it is in Figure 8.1. This figure shows that the problem of stereopsis is a formidable one. How is depth assigned to such stimuli? And how is this possible in the absence of all the familiar monocular cues to depth such as size, perspective, and shading, and also the absence of recognizable form (one cannot, for example, match a detail such as a branch of a tree in the image of one eye with the same detail in the other eye's image)?

The value of the computational approach becomes evident at the start. Simply to state, as many have, that disparity is the basis of stereopsis, is insufficient as an explanation. Marr goes deeper, and begins by asking two questions: How is disparity *measured* by the visual system? and, How is it *used*?

We shall outline Marr's attempt to deal with the first of these questions, the measurement of disparity.

Marr's analysis of the situation at the two eyes during binocular viewing leads him to recognize two major related problems (he was by no means the first person to describe them). Although the problems are easy to describe, it has taken over a hundred years to find plausible solutions.

Figure 8.3 is a diagram of the situation when a person looks at a row of, say, lights at a fixed distance from the two eyes. The eyes have been drawn symbolically in order to display the patterns of stimulation at the two retinae. As the process of vision starts at the retinae, stereopsis must take the inputs there as the vital information concerning the locations of the lights. Thus the solution as to where the lights are must be found in the relationships (or matches) between the two retinal patterns. But examine the situation closely: by drawing rays from each light to the two eyes we create the crossover pattern shown in Figure 8.3. This figure is important because it reveals that *the patterns*

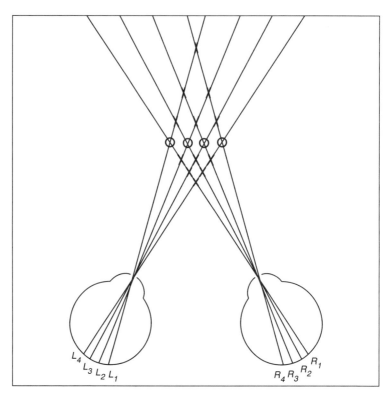

Figure 8.3 The false location problem in stereopsis. The circles represent four coplanar objects viewed by the two eyes. L_1–L_4 and R_1–R_4 are corresponding positions on the left and right retinae. Crossings represent false locations: positions from which patterns of stimulation at the eyes could arise which are identical with those arising from the four objects. The problem is to account for the fact that the visual system can solve this problem and avoid false locations

falling upon the left and right retinae are not uniquely determined by the configuration of the lights, but could have been caused by any of a number of alternative configurations: those represented at the various crossover positions in the diagram. We have used a small number of stimuli in this illustration; the number of *false locations*, as they are known, grows exponentially with the number of stimuli and would be huge in many real-life situations.

The two problems then are: (1) How are parts of one image correctly matched with parts of the other, while (2) avoiding those matches arising from false locations? In other words, how is the truth obtained from the ambiguous information in the two visual inputs?

Marr realized that if he could account for the stereoscopic depth induced by random-dot displays, which are meaningless and contain no other depth information, then an account of 'normal' stereopsis would follow quite easily. The dot displays contain, in a sense, 'pure' disparity. A world sprayed with dots is also simpler to consider.

As would be expected, the computational approach to stereopsis involves three levels of discourse, the first of which is the computational theory.

The computational theory of stereopsis proceeds as follows. We are considering the perception of a three-dimensional world containing only textured surfaces, and have discovered a fundamental problem: How is a dot seen by one eye correctly matched in the other while avoiding false matches?

Marr starts by adopting two constraints set by the nature of the world in which the visual system evolved.

1. A given point has a fixed position at any moment in time.
2. Matter is cohesive. Surfaces are not arranged in ways that can trick us. They cannot, for instance, suddenly bend or change their curvatures without yielding some clue to such changes.

The formal computational theory begins with three matching rules applied to a textured surface which is in binocular view.

1. Black dots can match only black dots. We are considering surfaces which contain only black dots and white spaces, and the rule is simply stating that a point on a surface seen by one eye stays the same when seen by the other.
2. A black dot in one image can (truly) match only one dot in the other.
3. Disparity, the magnitude of the difference between the left and right eye matches, varies smoothly. Once again it is being assumed that the world does not (cannot) play tricks.

We now have the beginnings of a computational theory. Can a combination of the matching rules and the constraints suggest a solution to the problem of stereopsis?

Marr now presents an interesting analysis of the situation at the eyes when both are looking at the same scene. This analysis is illustrated in Figure 8.4. In this figure the positions of 'descriptive elements' in the left and right images are plotted along the two axes. Horizontal and vertical lines represent lines of sight from the left and right eyes respectively. Where these lines intersect are possible disparities, that is, positions of matches and false locations, as shown in Figure 8.3. The dotted diagonal lines are lines of constant disparity, or positions along which the differences in left- and right-eye views of a surface have the same magnitude.

This deceptively simple diagram is an important part of Marr's proposed solution of the problem of stereopsis. The aspect of the diagram to note is that *the distribution of matches and false locations is not chaotic: both are spatially*

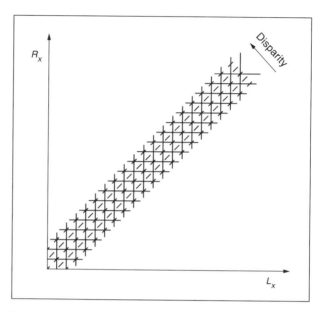

Figure 8.4 The Marr–Poggio analysis of stereopsis. The vertical and horizontal axes plot the distribution of stimuli to the two eyes: where these meet are possible positions giving rise to disparities of view of the same object. The dotted diagonal lines are lines of constant disparity. Rule 3 of the Marr–Poggio algorithm requires correct matches across the eyes to cluster along the diagonal lines. This limits the set of possible solutions and thus a potentially chaotic situation becomes a manageable problem: there are noticeable regularities that could be the basis of the true matching of left and right stimuli during stereopsis. See the text for a fuller account of the stereo-matching algorithm. (From Marr and Poggio, 1976. Copyright American Association for the Advancement of Science; reprinted with permission from *Science*)

distributed among the two images in an orderly manner. A regularity such as this, existing in the physical world, suggests that here is a source of information. This in turn implies that there should be a solution to the problem of correct matching.

Support for this optimistic conclusion comes when the simple matching rules described above are combined with an equally simple logical analysis of the situation. Remember that by implication there can only be one match on any single line of sight. Now assume that, for example, the density of dots in each image is 20 per cent. In other words, there is a one in five chance that a dot will be present at any location. Now consider the correct plane in Figure 8.4. What can be said about the density of possible matches—of dots which can signify by their disparity that a particular surface is present? Clearly this too must equal 20 per cent. But what of the density of possible matches on the *incorrect* planes in the figure? A little reflection shows that as these planes are the wrong ones, dots will match only by chance. This gives us the same probability of matching which would occur if two transparent sheets, each with a (random) dot density of 20 per cent, were superimposed. This probability is calculable and is simply the product of the two individual densities (more simply, their probabilities, which are the inverse of the densities): $p = 0.2$ squared equals 0.04. Hence, provided that the difference between the density (or probability) value in the 'true' situation is detectably different from those in all remaining situations, the matching rules will yield a unique solution.

The question now is whether the visual system (or a mathematical algorithm) can profit from the orderliness which has been demonstrated. With this in mind, Marr continues by asking what could be the input to the stereo-matching process required by the computational theory. He suggests that it must take the form of zero-crossings from filtered images. Evidence outlined earlier suggests that the visual system has various tuned spatial frequency channels. If the first attempt to find stereo-matches uses inputs from the larger (lower spatial frequency) channels, this will have two benefits. First, the number of possible matches (and false matches) is reduced because the search through the arrays is coarser. Second, finding some evidence of corresponding matches in an array can direct eye movements so that finer and finer channels can be used for further searches.

The algorithm

Marr now considers various ways of designing an objective procedure which will lead to a solution of the problem. His proposal is that the $\nabla^2 G$ operator is applied to each image and the zero-crossings (mentioned earlier in this chapter) are extracted. The operator will act as a band-pass filter.

As the algorithm is developed a surprising result emerges. It is of the nature of bandpass filters that the zero-crossings which are output cannot occur at less than known spatial separations. Thus the probability of finding a match between zero-crossings in each eye can be calculated, as can the probability of finding false correspondences. Marr shows, in a plausibility argument, that in a variety of situations, the desired matches will far outnumber false matches when a particular disparity value close to the truth is being evaluated. If a new disparity value is assessed (and, let us say, is false) then the ratio of correct to incorrect matches will fall dramatically. All that one needs to add to the algorithm is the ability to know a good situation, in terms of successful matches, from a poorer one.

Although we have managed to avoid the let-out phrase, 'It can be shown . . .', the reader may feel a sense of unease at this point. Does this technical claim that something will work dodge a real explanation as to *how* it might work? Two additional points may help convince the sceptical reader.

First, it is important to remember the *constraints* which the computational theory made explicit. Think about the two eyes looking at a flat surface. The two views must be slightly different. The size of this difference (the disparity between the two images) contains the information as to where the surface is in depth, and this is what the visual system is trying to calculate. But remember that in normal viewing there really is a surface before us. An element of the surface seen by one eye is actually present to the other—it cannot suddenly move or disappear. And if the selected disparity value is correct, it will be correct over a major portion of the display, for a physical surface does not move away or change in an instant (this is one of the constraints adopted above). If the visual system makes a wrong calculation as to the disparity value for part of the surface, then not only are the matches at that point wrong, they will be generally wrong all over the image. In other words, it is because of plausible assumptions which can be made concerning the real world that certain procedures can be guaranteed to have a high rate of success.

There is a second reason for thinking that Marr's algorithm might be correct: it works.

A connectionist network designed according to the algorithm which we have outlined can solve the Julesz stereogram displayed in Figure 8.1. We do not need to take this part of Marr's work on trust; we can see it work in practice. The algorithm is sufficiently explicit and powerful to allow the computer to find the hidden disparity in random-dot displays and represent the depth difference associated with it. Put very crudely, the network functions by comparing portions of each of the stereograms. Only if a particular unit receives inputs from two identical features (two white dots or two black ones) will it become active. If then units representing the same lines of sight from the two 'eyes' receive inputs from parts of the display which would represent different disparities, inhibition passes between them to check this incorrect state of affairs (which would violate the uniqueness constraint described above). After a number of iterations the network settles upon the correct answer: the part of the displays seen in depth by human observers has been delineated. This is an impressive and convincing demonstration.

The neural implementation

The final stage of what Marr considers to be a satisfactory explanation (or model) of stereopsis is the implementation. What sort of neural hardware could carry out the operations contained in the algorithm? Marr admits that the search for a plausible neural implementation of his theory may be premature, given our rather hazy knowledge of the neurology of some parts of the visual system. He does, however, offer some hypotheses as to how his model could be implemented.

The ways in which cells in the visual system could mimic the operations of the $\nabla^2 G$ filter have been dealt with earlier. The detection of zero-crossings can be achieved by simple logical gates which neural cells can mimic by suitable interactions between excitatory and inhibitory processes. In stereopsis it is necessary to combine binocular information about zero-crossings and their signs (positive-going/negative-going) in order to match, say, black dots to black dots. Once again logical devices (in this case AND gates, which fire when both possible inputs are active) are capable of doing the required work, with each gate having as one of its inputs the difference between the left- and right-eye inputs at the position of whichever zero-crossing (left eye or right eye) is chosen as the starting point for the comparison; the zero-crossing forms the other input to the gate.

Exactly where in the visual system these AND gates will be found is uncertain. Marr guesses, on the basis of published microelectrode studies, that the proposed disparity detectors may lie in Area 18 of the visual cortex. The fine resolution of depth which is possible at the limit of stereo acuity may be based, at least in part, on the activities of granular cells in layer ivcβ in Area 17 of the visual cortex. These would use inputs from the high resolution spatial outputs from the filtered images.

FURTHER ASPECTS OF MARR'S WORK

The understanding gained from the attack on the problem of stereopsis allows Marr to extend the computational approach to other areas of perception. Further chapters in *Vision* contain interesting discussions of directional sensitivity, the perception of motion, shape and contour, lightness and brightness, shape from shading, and, finally, the perception of three-dimensional objects when perception moves from viewer-centred to object-centred frames of reference. In terms of the model of vision, the processes have finally arrived at a description of the objective world.

Many of the later parts of *Vision* are very interesting. In a discussion of the recovery of shape from silhouettes, for example, Marr's careful analysis of the stimulus situation allows him to predict when a silhouette is a reliable guide to shape and when not: it is reliable when the portions of a surface generating the silhouette are in the same plane, not otherwise. Reading these sections one feels that few can ever have thought so analytically and deeply about the nature of the three-dimensional world and the ways in which it gives rise to visual images.

Towards the end of his book Marr attempts to outline how we perceive three-dimensional shapes. An important part of this work concerns the ways in which the visual system uses *canonical forms* in a *modular* organization (that is, split into different parts). As an example, consider the attainment of the three-dimensional representation of a human being. One possible canonical form which would be useful here is the cylinder. Following the principle of modular organization, an initial cylinder could be constructed to represent a person, provided the visual system could first decide upon the direction of the principle axis: in this case, from head to feet. This would be a self-contained unit in the shape description. It is possible to enrich the description, using the same canonical form to represent the head, the torso, the arms and legs by small cylinders. Next the arm could be represented by a set of cylinders, one of which is the hand. Finally, the hand cylinder could be elaborated into a set of cylinders representing the wrist and the fingers. The same canonical form— the cylinder—has been used throughout, but successive applications at different scales yield descriptions which are increasingly 'lifelike'. In terms of the computational approach, a three-dimensional model of a human being has been attained.

It is clearly inappropriate to attempt a detailed description of the whole of Marr's work. We shall, however, state an opinion, which is that, despite the ingenuity of his reasoning, Marr's ideas on the perception of objects are less impressive and convincing than the earlier chapters of *Vision*. This is hardly surprising: the problems are much more formidable. Thus, for example, the account just given of Marr's approach to the perception of three-dimensional shape gives one the impression (and this is not true in other parts of Marr's work) that while his ideas seem quite plausible in terms of machine recognition of objects, the evidence that this is how a living visual system might function is less than compelling.

AN APPRAISAL OF THE COMPUTATIONAL APPROACH TO VISION

It would be unwise to offer too confident an evaluation of the computational approach to perception. The work of Marr and his colleagues was carried out in laboratories specializing in artificial intelligence research. It has taken some time for the ideas of these workers to become widespread in psychology and physiology. As we have been able to demonstrate, many of the concepts and mechanisms invoked to explain perceptual phenomena are complicated. The language is not one which is familiar to many who work in other disciplines. The mathematics is occasionally difficult, and lacking the facilities to use the various operators and filters described by Marr means that some readers have to take his findings on trust. This state of affairs is changing, but it will be some time before every worker in perception will be able to demonstrate computer-filtered images as easily as they can generate, for example, Mach bands, random-dot stereograms or rotating shadows.

Particular problems

There are, however, two studies which are worth reporting here as they throw some doubts upon the adequacy of one important part of Marr's computational model.

Mayhew and Frisby (1981), who work within the computational framework, present psychophysical evidence from experiments using stereograms. It will be remembered that in Marr's model the raw primal sketch makes intensity changes in the image explicit by using primitives such as bars, blobs, terminators, etc. These in turn are replaced by more abstract tokens which lead to the achievement of the full primal sketch. In the full primal sketch only two-dimensional projections of objects are represented. The system is not concerned with the extraction of three-dimensional disparity information until the later stage of the 2½-D sketch.

Mayhew and Frisby used sawtooth patterns as stereograms. In these cases the depth which resulted is not predictable from knowledge of zero-crossings—the primitive which Marr adopts as the input to a stereo-matching process. Mayhew and Frisby have published examples in which the positions of zero-crossings are identical in two stereograms (and hence cannot signal disparity) and yet these can induce stereopsis. Thus in Marr's model one would have to include other sources of information—for example, the peaks obtained from the convolutions—in order for stereopsis to be achieved. More importantly, Mayhew and Frisby present convincing arguments in favour of a model of stereopsis in which disparity is computed much earlier than the 2½-D sketch: probably at the level of the raw primal sketch.

Watt (1988) and Watt and Morgan (1985) have also pointed to weaknesses in Marr's and Hildreth's work on zero-crossings. They have developed an improved algorithm of greater complexity than Marr and Hildreth's and one which more closely matches human discrimination. The two references cited above should be consulted for a detailed account of these highly interesting developments.

The author's colleague, Dave Earle, has published evidence which suggests that another part of Marr's thinking may be wrong. Earle used Glass patterns (Glass, 1969; Stevens, 1978) which Marr cites as important evidence in favour of part of his model. A Glass pattern forms when two patterns of dots or other simple shapes are superimposed. The first pattern is typically a random array, the second is some transformation of the first—an expansion or a rotation, for example. Depending upon the transformation, merging the two displays gives rise to an organized pattern having a strong radial or circular appearance. A typical pattern is shown in Figure 8.5.

To account for the organization of Glass patterns, Stevens (1978) proposed that local pairings between adjacent elements are represented by the visual system as virtual lines. Marr adopted this suggestion and made virtual lines

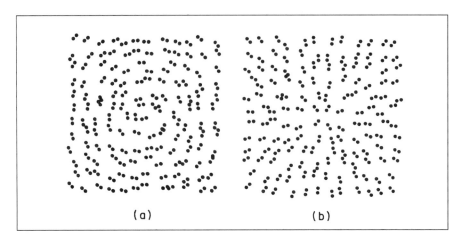

Figure 8.5   Glass patterns: (a) is formed by superimposition of a random array and its rotation; (b) is formed by superimposition of an array and an expanded version of the same array. (Prepared for the author by his colleague, Dr D.C. Earle)

one of the primitives of the primal sketch. Thus Glass patterns must be revealing some of the workings of this stage of vision.

Remember that in Marr's model the primal sketch is not concerned with the three-dimensional information in the image. Glass patterns should not occur if the two component patterns are presented stereoscopically, one to each eye. In an elegant series of demonstrations, Earle (1985) has created stereograms in which Glass pattern structure is in fact destroyed by apparent depth; more importantly, he has also designed stereograms in which novel *three dimensional* Glass patterns arise when no structure is visible in the two-dimensional components. This important finding suggests that if virtual lines are constructed by the visual system at some stage in image processing, the stage must be one in which depth is made explicit. Combining Earle's findings with those of Mayhew and Frisby cited above we are forced to the conclusion that a detailed but important part of Marr's model has been tested and found wanting.

We have gone into considerable detail in the above paragraphs. This was a deliberate tactic. It is hoped that it will illustrate the high degree of precision of thought and experiment demanded of those who wish to test parts of Marr's theory.

General criticisms

We shall now offer some general comments on the computational approach to visual perception as exemplified by Marr's writings.

Workers in artificial intelligence distinguish between bottom-up and top-down processes. Bottom-up processes involve lower-level, more peripheral systems which are relatively autonomous. Their outputs can be fed into higher levels of the system. Top-down processes are well described by their name. To use one of Marr's own examples, it might have been the case that the visual system solves the problem of stereopsis in a top-down manner. A major portion of the image in the left eye (say, the representation of a tree) would be chosen and compared with the right-eye view of the object. Then the branches could be scanned, then the twigs, and finally the leaves, comparisons being made at all these scales. This process would profit from, and be guided by, the perceiver's knowledge of trees. It would be a top-down process. (In this case, however, our ability to see depth in meaningless random-dot stereograms tells us that stereopsis must in fact make considerable use of bottom-up processes.)

When this distinction is applied to Marr's model it is clear that he was guided by certain top-down considerations. The basic idea that the *goal* sought by a perceptual process should feature large in any explanation of that process obviously involves a degree of top-down modelling. However, much of Marr's detailed work concentrates upon what are clearly bottom-up processes, such as, for example, those involved in contour extraction and texture discrimination.

Marr is generally most convincing when he speculates about bottom-up processes. We are told what is required to achieve some desired result, what the inputs and outputs to the necessary computations must be, and which neural mechanisms could do the necessary work. It is always satisfying to work through expositions of this kind. They contribute importantly to the high quality of *Vision*.

It is when Marr speculates about processes involving knowledge of the world acting in a top-down manner that his work becomes less convincing. For example, do we carry in our heads those canonical shapes such as generalized cones and cylinders which he postulates as the primitives for three-dimensional shape perception? How could we test this possibility?

The computational approach arose from within artificial intelligence research. Fundamental criticisms of AI have been made by those who doubt whether it is in principle possible for machines to simulate human processes such as thinking and perceiving. Some doubts concerning the machine as an analogue of the mind have been reviewed in Chapter 5. There are a few others to which the reader's attention should be drawn.

As an example, consider some of the arguments advanced by Gregory (1995). Gregory makes the point that although digital computers work by carrying out computations, analogue computers do not. If in fact the brain works as an analogue device, then it does not compute and is therefore not a computer. Thus the fact that Marr can *describe* certain visual processes in terms of algorithms does not prove that they work by algorithms. We know that perception is rarely entirely accurate but that it is fast, even though its hardware is relatively slow. Facts such as these reinforce Gregory's belief that analogue models will more accurately capture the ways in which the visual system operates. If he is correct, then Marr's assumptions concerning the ways in which the visual system computes solutions to problems, may be ill-founded.

GENERAL REMARKS ON MARR'S APPROACH TO VISUAL PERCEPTION

This chapter on Marr's work must end on a note of appreciation. There seems little doubt that whatever the eventual fate of the computational approach generally, or of Marr's contributions in particular, readers of *Vision* have been in contact with an interesting and original mind. The quality of Marr's work should exert a permanent influence upon theorizing in perception. The idea of different levels of explanation of processes is a powerful one. Realizing that a newly discovered neural mechanism can never provide a sufficient explanation of any aspect of perceiving until one has asked the computational question— what *function* does the mechanism subserve?—is a definite gain in theoretical sophistication. So, too, is the idea that the real world exerts constraints upon possible solutions to perceptual problems. This discipline could help theorists to avoid adopting algorithms simply because they work. If Marr's rigorous approach to perception is widely adopted, then some of the mistakes of the past will be avoided. *Vision* is a landmark in the history of perceptual theory.

NOTES ON CHAPTER 8

The reader should now acquire a copy of Marr's book, *Vision*. This is quite hard going in places but it is hoped that this chapter will have given the reader confidence to tackle Marr in the original: there really is no substitute.

Frisby (1979) is an enjoyable, clear, and extremely well-illustrated exposition of some of the themes within the computational approach. Written by an obvious admirer of Marr, it conveys much of the enthusiasm of workers in this field.

Bruce and Green (1990) is an exceptionally good textbook on visual perception. Although the sections on the computational approach to vision are much more detailed (and difficult) than those in the present chapter, they are well worth working through.

For a critical but balanced evaluation of *Vision* read Morgan's excellent review (1984).

Marr's obituary appeared in *The Times* in December 1980.

9

Overview and conclusions

REVIEW

Seven very different approaches to theorizing in perception have been discussed. At this point a brief evaluative summary will be given of each approach. This will be followed by a general discussion of the problems facing theorists in the general area of visual perception.

Psychophysics (Chapter 2) gave a rigour to the study of perception. It is what first brought perceptual research and theory under the general heading of Science. The merits of psychophysics are obvious: this is the source of much existing knowledge of perception. Psychophysics showed that experimentation is an appropriate way in which to study perception, and that the use of calibrated stimuli, presented under controlled laboratory conditions, can yield important insights into the workings of the visual system. Theories in this area have been based on impressively reliable data, and there has been a steady development in theoretical sophistication and power over the years. How interesting and encouraging that a century after Fechner's pioneering work, the controlled presentation of precisely calibrated stimuli, to which observers are required to make the simplest of responses, should continue to provide new insights into the workings of perception.

There are, however, drawbacks to the experimental method in general and psychophysics in particular. First, the approach assumes a mechanistic model of the perceiver: stimuli cause responses, even when responses are described in terms of statistical models of the observer. The approach has typically ignored those aspects of perception in which perceivers seek out stimulation, in which they actively sample the world. The stimuli used in psychophysics have tended to be artificially simple, so that the situation facing the observer is unlikely to match that in which he or she operates most of the time, where stimulation is rich and changing and in which stimuli commonly interact in complex ways.

The Gestalt theory (Chapter 3) was based upon the numerous discoveries made by proponents of this approach. A powerful case was made for the dynamic nature of perceiving, the tendency for perception to tend towards coherent, meaningful, simple solutions. The Gestalt demonstrations of the emergent properties of stimulus interactions present an important challenge to all future theories of visual perception. The decision of the Gestalt theorists to concentrate upon strong, reliable effects may provide a lesson for others who wish to make discoveries about perceptual systems. Finally, the emphasis upon the phenomenological aspects of perception, which was such an important part of the Gestalt approach, is something which is still worthy of debate among contemporary theorists: what is it that theories of perception are trying to explain?

The weaknesses of the Gestalt movement lie mainly in its naive approach to theory and explanation. As was shown in Chapter 3, the Gestaltists sometimes fell into the trap of mistaking description for explanation. Gestalt theory was, for the most part, not predictive. And when the Gestalt theorists attempted some sort of explanation of the effects they had discovered, they made an unfortunate decision in their choice of a brain model and an equally serious mistake over the selected level of explanation. We attempted to show in Chapters 3 and 8 how modern developments might be able to remedy these deficiencies.

Brunswik's probabilistic functionalism (Chapter 4) properly drew attention to a number of hitherto neglected aspects of visual perception: that the cues upon which organisms depend are not certain but only probabilistic; that much of behaviour reveals vicarious functioning; that a careful analysis of the environment from a functionalist viewpoint can sometimes suggest answers to apparently intractable problems. Brunswik's arguments against the classical reductionist approach to experimentation are still relevant, and while his own suggestions concerning the correlational analysis of representatively designed experiments have not been widely adopted, this too seems to be a fruitful idea: one which modern researchers, armed with better methods of statistical analysis, might well attempt. Tribute must also be paid to Brunswik for his pioneering role in what has been described as 'the inference revolution'.

The weaknesses of Brunswik's approach are, first, that he did not give due recognition to the gains which have been made using the orthodox classical methods which he attacked, methods which uncovered phenomena quite as important and interesting as those which he described. Second, the disappointing outcome to some of Brunswik's own experiments suggest that the superior approach he claimed to have designed may not be as easy to apply as he believed: Brunswik did not appear to learn from his own failures. Finally, Brunswik's many stimulating ideas were not communicated in a manner guaranteed to cause others to give them serious consideration.

The neurophysiological approach (Chapter 5) has demonstrated the benefits of combining disciplines. Discovering the neural mechanisms underlying certain perceptual phenomena has been an impressive achievement, one which has confirmed the essential correctness of a number of psychological theories. Knowledge of actual mechanisms has helped some theorists in their work; this knowledge has also provided a useful constraint upon subsequent speculation. Generally, the work described in Chapter 5 was of the highest scientific and intellectual calibre. As we attempted to show, the development of connectionist networks and their early successes may eventually tell us how complex groupings of the basically simple building blocks of the visual system—neurons—are able to mediate the complex processes of vision.

In the past, an important weakness of the neurophysiological approach to vision has been its tendency towards reductionism. Another weakness is that the language used inevitably remains 'within' the organism. Connectionist network models may overcome the first of these drawbacks. The second is more serious as it means that the neurophysiological approach cannot, of itself, pay proper consideration to the nature of the environment from which stimuli arise—it would be difficult for it to deal with the probabilistic nature of stimuli, for example. Further, explanations at the level of neurophysiology cannot deal with the subjective nature of seeing, with the phenomenological experiences which reveal the existence of perceptual problems in the first place. Finally, knowing that neural systems have certain properties, revealed during experimental research, does not mean that the usual functions of these systems have been discovered. As Marr and others have argued eloquently, knowing *that* a neural system does something does not tell us *why* it does it.

Empiricism (Chapter 6). A good case can be made for the claim that this has been the most successful approach to forming a general theory of perception to date. The contents of almost any general text on perception, or any lecture course, comprise in large part the data, the explanations and the problems unearthed by workers in the empiricist tradition. Empiricism has dominated experimental psychology for a century. A large part of its success lies in the number of powerful demonstrations which are available to shake one's confidence in the veracity of one's perceptions: illusions, distorted rooms, context and learning effects, and impossible figures. In fact, we used this technique in Chapter 6 in order to show the reader just how convincing this approach to perception can be.

The doubts about the empiricist approach were described in Chapters 6 and 7. Is perception always a constructive process? Are stimuli (or sensations) really so impoverished that the information associated with them needs to be supplemented by memory, reasoning and so on? Do the problems studied under simplified laboratory conditions adequately reflect the situation facing perceivers in the real world? Does perception proceed essentially in stages? Can the dualism between the organism and the objective world be defended?

At this point, we remind the reader that human perception occurs in two distinguishable environments. The natural environment in which perception evolved comprises surfaces and textures, solid objects, rich patterns of mutlisensory stimulation, movement and change, horizons, and so on. But another environment has formed, the age of which is but a moment in evolutionary terms: that of human culture. Here, we have language and symbols, two-dimensional patterns representing three-dimensional things, machines that move us passively through space It is not surprising that human perceivers can usually cope with this artificial environment: they created it. But the ways in which perception engages with the artefacts of our culture may differ importantly from the ways in which it deals with the natural world.

The theory of direct perception (Chapter 7) arose in part as a reaction against empiricism. One of the chief merits of this relatively new approach is the emphasis it places upon the study of the natural environment and the richness of stimulation available to active perceivers. Another merit has been the attempt to counter the distinction between the organism and its ecology, between what happens 'inside' and 'outside' the perceiver. There is a freshness about the direct perception approach which will sharpen conventional thinking and may ultimately force some major revisions upon constructivist theories. As we attempted to show towards the end of Chapter 7, results from research into the ways in which perceivers achieve 'fits' between themselves and the environment (pi number, gaits, intrinsic scaling, and so on) are confirming that the theory of direct perception can generate fruitful and testable ideas. Optic flow is also being subjected to very precise quantitative analysis in recent research.

The theory of direct perception has its weaknesses. It shows a tendency to understimate the challenge posed to the visual system by, for example, the need to extract invariants. Some problems have been simply defined out of existence. The resonance model has not yet achieved plausibility, although connectionist networks may eventually suggest solutions to this problem. Finally, the marked differences between this approach and more traditional theories of perception are becoming blurred as direct perceptionists turn their attention to the various indirect modes of perceiving, which, they accept, are part of human experience.

The computational approach to visual perception (Chapter 8) has produced theories which are at present quite narrow (for example, the theory of stereopsis outlined in Chapter 8). These are among the most rigorous theories to have emerged in the study of vision. However, where theories arising from within the artificial intelligence paradigm differ from earlier scientific accounts is in the fact that their success points the way towards even more general accounts. To develop this point: consider the successful emergence of a scientific account of colour vision (described in Chapter 5). The combination of evidence from psychology and neurophysiology led to an explanation of both the trichromatic and opponent-process aspects of colour perception. But this successful explanation does not of itself suggest how to tackle, for example, the problems of shape or movement perception. In contrast, the success of one application of Marr's approach strongly encourages the belief that the computational approach may be equally powerful when applied to other, very different phenomena.

There are two reasons why Marr attained a high level of rigour in his work. First is the clear distinction he drew between the appropriate levels at which a process may be understood: the computational theory, the algorithm and the implementation. Marr argued, convincingly, that many confusions over vision in the past arose because of misunderstandings about which level of explanation was appropriate in a particular context. There are those who believe that Marr's distinction between the three levels of explanation are not always appropriate. For example:

> While I do not disagree with Marr's basic argument, I would like to suggest that when dealing with *biological* systems the only sure way to progress is to deliberately get 'confused' between these different levels of analysis. . . . The reason for this is that the organization of biological systems is dictated just as much by constraints of hardware (and by the organism's evolutionary history) as by the 'computational problem'.
>
> (Ramachandran, 1990)

Ramachandran supports this assertion by reminding us that knowledge of the double-helix structure of DNA *preceded* understanding of its function. Modern researchers appear to have accepted the value of Marr's distinctions between levels of understanding; nevertheless, Ramachandran's argument carries weight.

Another reason why the computational approach has achieved such rigour arises from the ways in which theories advanced by Marr and other workers have been rendered explicit. To see whether an idea actually works when written into a computer program is a powerful check against vagueness and imprecision: it is no longer possible to define problems out of existence, nor is it acceptable to explain things by appealing to concepts which (a) remain undefined, such as Prägnanz, or (b) are descriptions rather than explanations, such as 'perceptual constancy'. Everything must be explicit.

One of the arguments against the computational approach has been that it represents a new mentalism; that the computer is an inappropriate model of the perceiver; and that by omitting the phenomenological aspects of perception the theory cannot ever do full justice to its subject matter.

To conclude this section it can be asserted that there is as yet no satisfactory general theory of visual perception. No theory adequately handles all possible transactions between the regions of the orienting model described in Chapter 1. For example, no theory has adequately united a full analysis of the environment *and* the cognitive aspects of seeing. No general theory has thoroughly incorporated and explained the motor aspects of seeing. The direction of the interactions between the regions is not yet clear: the extent to which perception is determined by stimulation (involving bottom-up processes) or knowledge (top-down processes) has not been agreed upon.

Since the first edition of this book was published, an important article has appeared which argues that in fact a general theory of perception may not be achievable. In what he describes as 'The utilitarian theory of perception', Ramachandran (1990) has developed a powerful case against the possibility of such a general theory.

In summary, Ramachandran's argument runs as follows. Through millions of years of evolution, trial and error solutions have led to the 'bag of tricks' which we call perception. Numerous rules-of-thumb and heuristics survived, not because of their elegance or beauty, but simply because they worked (the reason for the term 'utilitarian'). Ramachandran argues by analogy. Consider the vertebrate digestive system: mastication, peristalsis, and enzyme actions form a sequence in the breakdown of food. But they did not evolve as a single, coherent system: teeth evolved independently from enzymes. Similarly, the ossicles of the middle ear were once parts of the hinge mechanism in the lower jaw of our reptile antecedents. Evolution leads to solutions which work, but they are always the minimum solutions, not the most elegant.

If Ramachandran is correct, the perception of, say, colour and motion may have little in common. They comprise part of the 'ragbag' of tricks adopted during evolution. It follows that the search for general laws and general theories of perception may be doomed to failure. Ramachandran's article contains accounts of fascinating discoveries of the extent to which 'quick but dirty' solutions characterize the ways in which vision can be shown to respond when conditions allow. His article should now be read in full. The message is pessimistic, but it is also very thought-provoking.

There is a curiously interesting link between the work of Ramachandran, an active researcher, and a recent book by a philosopher, Dennett (1991). Dennett's book is a major work and cannot be summarized in a few sentences. For the present purpose, we can refer simply to one of Dennett's examples. Imagine entering a room plastered with small identical photographs of, say, Marilyn Monroe. We look at one and recognize it. Then we become aware of the fact that all the walls are covered by this same image. But much of this information is contained in peripheral vision. A question that used to be asked was, how do we fill in or complete our perception under such complicated conditions? Dennett's answer is that we don't: there is no need to. Why not *assume* (albeit unconsciously) that all the pictures are identical? There is no need to work at this—let it be.

SOME GENERAL REMARKS ON THEORIES OF VISUAL PERCEPTION

It has not been possible in an undergraduate text to describe all theories of visual perception, although many others have been mentioned in passing in earlier chapters. For reasons of space, we have omitted important theories from a number of areas in visual perception. These include: vision and attention, theories of reading, theories and systems of perspective, theories of motion perception, perception and aesthetics, ethology, the effects of brain damage on seeing, cross-cultural studies. The list is dismayingly long, but interested readers with access to good libraries should easly find enough material to enable them to begin their studies of areas of interest.

It must be remembered that some of the issues raised in this book are themselves worthy of book-length treatment. However, in each of the earlier chapters an attempt was made to provide enough references for the interested reader to pursue topics to greater depth.

At this point a few general remarks will be offered concerning the theoretical approaches described in previous sections. What, if anything, can be distilled from them?

The first obvious point is that there are too many irreconcilables between the various theorists to permit any general fusion of ideas. The differences, for example, between empiricist views of perception and those of the Gestalt theorists, or between Gibson and Marr, are such that they cannot all be right. Nor does it seem reasonable to suppose that the truth must lie between the rival views: they are too different for that.

It is, however, possible to hope that each of the approaches described has merit and that for this reason there may be implications for future theorists. Here are what seem to us to be the best aspects of each approach.

1. Laboratory studies of the highest quality are now possible. Psychophysics continues to provide psychologists and others with powerful means of obtaining precise data from perceptual experiments. The challenge will be to extend this work to perception under real-world conditions.

2. The power of neurophysiology will enable certain new models of the brain to be tested, particularly those of the type proposed in parallel distributed processing (PDP) models. Neurophysiology will provide knowledge useful for those who work at what Marr described as the stage of implementation of a theory.

3. Brunswik's emphasis on the probabilistic nature of cues should be remembered in future theorizing, together with his pleas for more representative designs in psychological experiments.

4. New theories will have to recognize and explain those dynamic aspects of perception discovered by Gestalt theorists, in particular the tendency towards Prägnanz and the fact that stimulus interactions produce new emergent properties.

5. Gibson's work has shown (a) that perceivers are active, not passive, and that sensory and motor systems should be viewed together as integral components of perception; (b) that light may be (usually is) rich in

information and that the study of any perceiver should therefore begin
with an exhaustive examination of the ecological niche occupied by the
perceiver; (c) that the dualism implicit in the animal/environment dicho-
tomy may actually impede our understanding of the nature of perception.
6. The role of central factors in perception has been most brilliantly demonstrated by workers in the empiricist tradition. The question now is to
   discover whether or not all perceiving is like this, or whether there are
   indeed situations where stimulation can specify objects and events without
   recourse to additional constructive processes.
7. To the extent that future theories of visual perception will be self-consciously
   scientific, they may be guided by the clarity and power of Marr's analysis of
   what it takes to understand any process. The standards Marr set for clarity
   and explicitness should serve as a model for theorists in the future.

Those seem to be the safest and best conclusions arising from any comparison
of the selection of theoretical approaches outlined in this book. We shall
return to some of these conclusions during the following sections which contain some further general remarks on theorizing.

The remainder of this chapter is in four sections. First, an attempt will be made
to show the challenge offered by visual perception; why it can be expected to
continue to fascinate researchers and theorists. Then a list will be given of some
of the achievements to date: the gains which have been made because some
theorists have attempted to develop general theories of the type described in
previous chapters. We shall then repeat the claim that there has not yet been a
satisfactory theory of vision, and, in the third section, shall attempt to explain this
by describing some of the problems facing theorists in this area. Finally, some
speculations will be offered concerning the next generation of theories of visual
perception.

THE CHALLENGE OF VISION

The theme of this book is seeing and attempts to explain it. But seeing is part
of the daily life of anyone who can read this book. We are as familiar with
seeing as with anything; so familiar that it is easy to overlook what an achievement seeing represents. Underlying this awareness of a solid, coherent world
are the activities of many neurons—saline-filled tubes—and that is all. How
do they do it? That is the ultimate question, but it is unlikely to be answered
for a very long time.

There are, of course, many other important problems facing contemporary
theorists and fortunately these are of a rather more tractable nature. They
are, however, so difficult that they will probably occupy the attentions of
researchers for many years to come. Four examples will prove this point.

What is meant by 'seeing'?

In December 1959, a 52-year-old man, described as the patient S.B., underwent a corneal graft operation to restore his vision. What is important about this event is that S.B. had been blind for more than 50 years. He had some sight as an infant (how much is not known with certainty) then, following a neglected eye infection at around the age of 10 months, he was admitted to an institution for the blind, where he received the whole of his academic and technical education. Shortly after the successful operation S.B. was examined by two psychologists (Gregory and Wallace, 1963), who later took him on a visit to the London Science Museum where he was shown a lathe:

> We led him to the glass case, which was closed, and asked him to tell us what was in it. He was quite unable to say anything about it, except that he thought the nearest part was a handle. (He pointed to the handle of the transverse feed.) He complained that he could not see the cutting edge or the metal being worked, or anything else about it, and appeared rather agitated. We then asked a Museum Attendant for the case to be opened, and S.B. was allowed to touch the lathe. The result was startling; he ran his hands deftly over the machine, touching first the transverse feed handle and confidently naming it as 'a handle', and then on to the saddle, the bed and the head-stock of the lathe. He rans his hands eagerly over the lathe, with his eyes shut. Then he stood back a little and opened his eyes and said: 'Now that I've felt it I can see.'
>
> (Gregory and Wallace, 1963)

What did S.B. mean by 'see'? The visual image of the lathe remained the same, but something must have changed in S.B.'s head. What was it? In what way could he *not* see before using his sense of touch? Was the change in S.B.'s visual perception akin to Fodor and Pylyshyn's (1981) distinction between *merely* seeing the Pole star and seeing it *as* the Pole star? Questions surely for a general theory of visual perception.

Different eyes

Reference has been made throughout this book to 'the eye' and 'the visual system'. In fact, apart from a few references to vision in monkeys and cats, all the main discussions have been about the human eye and the human visual system. But there are millions of different eyes. Vision in insects, for example, is based upon a different set of structures from those of any vertebrate, and visual information goes to a very different form of central nervous system. At present, we can only make a few educated guesses at what it must be like to see as a fish, a bird, or a flea. Even the lives of our pets remain deeply mysterious. It is a serious flaw in recent documentary broadcasts on animal vision that visual input is mistaken for visual perception. A familiar trick is to film the world through a segmented lens and then say that this is what the perception of an insect with a compound eye must be like. This is a major fallacy: we view the resulting picture and interpret it with highly developed brains; it is simply impossible to know how the output from a segmented eye looks to an insect.

Building seeing machines

There is one activity that makes visual research different from that in other sensory areas, and almost unique in science generally. One of the goals of a growing number of researchers is to understand vision and then build a seeing machine. To date, this has inspired some highly original and interesting work. And it has also provided a valuable check upon loose speculation and the imprecise analysis of problems.

> . . . The first great revelation was that the problems are difficult. Of course, these days this fact is a commonplace. But in the 1960s almost no one realized that machine vision was difficult. The field had to go through the same experience as the machine translation field did in its fiascos of the 1950s before it was at last realized that here were some problems that had to be taken seriously. The reason for this misperception is that we humans are ourselves so good at vision.
>
> (Marr, 1982)

In other words, building a seeing machine is going to be very difficult, not least because there are some formidable philosophical problems associated with this whole enterprise which raise doubts as to its feasibility. These will be mentioned later. For now, it is sufficient to say that here is a real goal for general theorists. But if it can be attained and a machine becomes able to do enough to make us say that it can see, then the builders may be in the unique position of knowing with certainty that some of their ideas on vision are correct. The reader will not be surprised to learn that this is a research area of vast commercial potential. Robots able to discriminate quickly and accurately between objects in the environment would have immense value. The implications of machine vision are so important that this is one area where researchers are unlikely ever to be short of funds.

Of course, no existing theory has come close to meeting any of these challenges. They were included at the start simply to show what fascinating challenges they are, fascinating enough, surely, to continue to attract ingenious and creative people into visual research.

SOME OF THE GAINS MADE DURING THE SEARCH FOR GENERAL THEORIES

General theories of visual perception have done two of the things expected of all scientific theories: they have often converted masses of data into manageable forms; and they have attempted to explain things. In Chapter 2 on psychophysics, for example, it was shown how early work on thresholds led to Weber's Law. Anyone who knows this law has an overall view of several hundred sensory threshold results, and this is invaluable. In the same area, the theory of signal detection explains the pattern of above-chance guessing which is commonly found in threshold tasks. These represent two real gains arising as a result of forming general theories, and numerous other examples are contained in earlier chapters of this book. Here now are some more specific achievements.

Many general properties of vision have been discovered

For example, it is one thing to know that observers tend to see objects as the same size irrespective of distance, and to be able to measure the magnitude of this effect. It became even more interesting when it was realized that shape perception also tends to veridicality. But when the same effect became apparent in colour perception it was clear that here was a general characteristic of visual perception. (The realization that a comparable effect can occur with loudness suggests that the effect is even more general.) However, to recognize the fact that perceptual constancy *is* a general characteristic of vision requires a theory, for data from different experiments are merely data: something more is required before their more general significance can be recognized, and that something is a theory (in this case it was the Gestalt theory).

All the theories described in this book have become broader with time. They have sought to embrace increasingly disparate sets of phenomena. For example, Gibson's demonstrations of the role of invariants in the perception of simple geometric shapes has been extended to include the match between the cardioidal strain transformation and the ageing of the human face. Even further from the original demonstration is the discovery of invariants in sound patterns which can specify the likelihood of collision. But would sound patterns have been examined for this property prior to Gibson's theory?

The range of application of theories has broadened

For example, the theory of signal detection arose as a way of thinking about the behaviour of an observer attempting to detect weak signals against a noisy background. It was a new theory in psychophysics. But within a few years of the announcement of the theory of signal detection, it had been used to explain the role of acupuncture in the treatment of pain: whether the technique changes the subjective intensity of pain, or only willingness to report it. This is more than a clever extension of an idea: TSD offered a different way of looking at pain behaviour, a new way of measuring pain responsiveness, and techniques for analysing the psychophysical data. It was a genuine extrapolation from a theory.

In a similar manner, the empiricist/constructivist approach convinced many that here was a theory which could account for many of the dynamic aspects of perception, for example the ability of perceivers to go beyond the sensory evidence—the closing of gaps, the correct identification of ambiguous stimuli through the use of context, and many other tendencies which have been described in Chapter 6. But then an extrapolation of the same theory to the geometric illusions allowed Gregory to suggest 'inappropriate constancy scaling' as a possible explanation of these strange phenomena.

Theories have led to improvements in technique

Here the influences may operate in two directions: techniques can influence theory—as was asserted in Chapter 1. Typically, however, when a new theory appears it will often popularize new techniques of experimentation and/or data analysis. Consider the history of psychophysical theories. Fechner and all psychophysicists since him knew that observers make errors when detecting faint signals. As was shown in Chapter 2, these errors can be simple misses, when the observer simply fails to report the signal, or they can be 'false positives' when the observer says that a signal is present when it is not. But how to allow for these false positives during threshold measurement? One answer is to encourage observers to maintain a low false positive rate and then adjust their scores whenever false positives appear in the data: the classical correction for guessing.

The theory of signal detection changed all that. By distinguishing between signal present/signal absent trials and between hits, misses and false positives, data could be collected in a much more revealing way. Add to this the observer's assessment of his or her confidence in any judgement and one achieves some very informative data. But the analysis of these data requires the use of tables of the ordinates of the normal curve, together with two new measures: d', a measure of sensitivity, and beta, a measure of the position of the observer's criterion stated in units based on ordinates of the normal curve. These measures were not available to Fechner. In fact, d' and beta were created as quantifying statistics within the new theory. Once available, however, they started to be widely used by psychologists in a variety of situations. The theory of signal detection came to exert a powerful influence upon research in the 1960s and 1970s, partly as a result of the new techniques conceived within this theoretical framework.

Theories have become more precise and scientific

Two of the hallmarks of any scientific theory are that its terms are precisely defined and that the theory is testable and therefore falsifiable. Of course not everyone agrees that the best solution to problems in psychology will always be scientific ones, a point which will be returned to later. For the moment we shall assume that it is in fact desirable for theories of perception to be as scientific as possible.

If this assumption is agreed upon then it can be claimed that there has been real progress in theorizing. Consider, for example, the Gestalt theory (Chapter 3). Certain key terms within the theory lacked precise operational definition. For example, the concept of Prägnanz was described in a manner which made it seem very interesting and important, with many convincing illustrations. But how did one measure it? How could one be sure that some novel stimulus array would show high or low Prägnanz? Was Prägnanz a descriptive shorthand for such factors as balance, simplicity and symmetry, or was it an explanatory concept: things being seen as coherent wholes *because* they had high Prägnanz?

In another part of Gestalt theory dynamic brain forces were stated to be the underlying causes of the Gestalt laws. but how could these forces ever be measured or assessed by *psychological* methods? Köhler had moved the central explanatory part of a psychological theory beyond the reach of experimental psychologists. (Tests were eventually made, and are described in Chapter 3, but these required techniques from another discipline.)

Brunswik wrote of the 'stupidity of the senses', by which he meant the inability to compensate for visual illusions once one knows the details of their construction. But to what extent did he claim this as a general principle? There are, after all, numerous examples (some of which would have been known to Brunswik) showing that perceivers can be very flexible in their behaviour: the recovery from mild sensory distortion, the ability to reinterpret ambiguous patterns, or to extract meaning from corrupted or noisy displays. Where does 'stupidity' begin and end?

In contrast, more modern theories of visual perception are much more precise. Gibson made important use of the term 'optic flow' in his theory. More recent work has shown possible constraints upon what optic flow can in fact specify (it doesn't indicate the point of collision if a surface is approached with the head slightly averted, for example). And Gibson seriously underestimated the difficulty of extracting the higher-order invariants from optic flow, as Marr was able to show. Nevertheless, there was never any doubt over what Gibson actually meant by the term 'optic flow', it was well defined.

By the time Marr's computational theory of vision was published, even higher standards of precision had been reached. One of Marr's enduring contributions will probably be the rigour which he introduced into the activity of theory construction. We have already described Marr's distinctions between the computational theory, the algorithm, and the implementation. But the whole of *Vision* is an object lesson in precision and clarity, attributes which owe much to the discipline required when converting ideas into working computer programs.

PROBLEMS REMAINING FOR THEORIES OF VISUAL PERCEPTION

The four examples given above serve to support the claim that real progress has been made. Nevertheless, formidable obstacles remain.

First, it must be accepted that vision must be very complicated indeed. Recognizing this fact will make the next section seem less negative and pessimistic. Think of the things which vision can do. Reflect on the last time you drove or were driven down a motorway on a wet night. That you are alive to tell the tale says a lot about vision: it provides the basis for judgements of speed and distance under difficult conditions, for moving in and out of lanes, steering half a ton of steel between and around hazards. All this while thinking about the depth induced by random-dot stereograms. Or think of being forced to sit at the end of a row in a crowded cinema: how distorted the screen seems at first, but how quickly it comes to appear normal. Then think about walking down the cinema steps without consciously looking at them.

All the phenomena described in this book reinforce the conclusion that vision is remarkable. It has defeated some of the best thinkers of their time. There have been few better scientists than Helmholtz, and he left many problems unsolved. The Gestaltists were clever and creative researchers, but their theory is flawed. Marr has been described as a genius, and yet some aspects of his work have been shown to be wrong.

Three of the formidable problems facing any who search for general theories of visual perception will now be described.

The definition of a stimulus

It is manifestly true that the job of vision is to inform us of things and events in the external world. The medium by which information is carried to the eye is, of course, light. Sometimes light is informative, sometimes not. When it is informative the term 'stimulus' tends to be applied. It is therefore clearly desirable, when constructing theories, to be able to define, measure, and, where necessary, control stimuli. But what *is* a stimulus?

This is one of those problems which gets more difficult the more one thinks about it. And there is a noticeable lack of agreement between theorists over this basic issue. It is also one which has exercised many philosophers.

A sensible aim would be to try to describe any stimulus in terms of its physical characteristics—this would seem to be a natural starting point for any scientific endeavour. After all, part of the success of chemistry and physics, at least in the early days of those subjects, lay in the ability to define and measure such basic entities as atoms and molecules. Is it likely that a comparable degree of objectivity and precision over stimuli will eventually be achieved? The answer is, probably not. Here are some reasons why.

Imagine that one is participating in a psychophysiological experiment. Electrodes have been attached to the back of the head in order to monitor some of the activity of the visual cortex. Every half second a flash of light is delivered to the eye. Then, without warning, the sequence is broken by omitting one of the flashes. What happens? Well, the gap would be noticeable—it would capture the attention as a novel *event*. And the subsequent renewal of vigour in the electrical responding of the visual cortex would confirm this introspection. Now, was the missing flash a stimulus? It surely possesses many of the characteristics we would wish to assign to stimuli on common-sense grounds. But can it be measured? No, of course not, for the missing light has no physical existence: it is something which might have occurred but did not—the dog that failed to bark in the night.

An equally important phenomenon has been described in the account of Gestalt theory (Chapter 2): sources of stimulation interact to yield novel perceptions. In the phi phenomenon, for example, the seen movement cannot be explained or predicted from a description of either of the pair of inducing lights—it depends upon their spatial and temporal *relationships*. At the heart of the Gestalt theory is the axiom that wholes are more than the sum of their parts, and Gestalt publications bristle with demonstrations of this effect, although the Gestaltists were never able to offer quantitative data on this point.

Thus it seems certain that any description of a stimulus in isolation will prove to be inadequate and it will usually be necessary to consider other stimuli which (a) might have been present or (b) are present and capable of interacting with the original stimulus.

Another difficulty arises from the fact that stimulus definition is theory-dependent. Psychophysicists would not describe patterns in terms of their Fourier transforms unless they believed that the visual system also performed such analyses. If it is assumed that perceptions are hypotheses, then a stimulus is something which can stand as evidence against which these can be tested: we have described the danger of infinite regress in this way of thinking. In the theory of signal detection, purely internal events can be responded to as if they arose from external causes, so that the final definition of a stimulus becomes some above-criterion subjective event. Gibson objected to any definition of a stimulus as a momentary happening, something frozen in time. Instead, he considered that that which endured or was invariant over change was the basis for a given percept. Gibson also emphasized that activity on the part of the perceiver was a source of stimulation, although it is not always easy to see how such stimulation could be measured. Marr's focus is upon spatial variations of intensity and so on in the visual image. Although he acknowledges that Gestalt-type interactions occur, his theory nevertheless concentrates upon the analysis and processing of separate parts of the image: none of his algorithms deals specifically with whole/part effects, nor is it easy to see how any could. The differences between these theoretical approaches go some way towards explaining why there is no single definition of a stimulus.

The appropriate level of explanation

At issue here is the level at which visual phenomena should be described and explained.

It was pointed out in Chapter 5 that there have always been those who prefer to explain perceptual phenomena in terms of neural mechanisms rather than psychological constructs. This form of reductionism has yielded important insights into the nature of perception; and the interaction between the disciplines of experimental psychology and neurophysiology has been a fruitful one. But, as was argued in Chapter 5, there is a fundamental flaw in the idea that the eventual explanation of perception will be physiological: namely, that neurophysiology remains 'inside' the organism, while perception involves the external world. Neural events may be isolated entities, but stimuli arise from within a context, a context which shapes our conscious experience. A general theory of vision will have to respect this fact, and this means that the language of such a theory is more likely to be psychological than physiological.

However, even if the emphasis in the future is away from physiological reductionism, there will still be a problem over the best level at which to write a theory. Assumptions of similarity between humans and computers led to computational theories. Recognition of certain dynamic properties of vision encouraged thinking in terms of vectors and fields. Those who claim that phenomenal experience must be accounted for by theories will write in the appropriate language. And anyone wishing to theorize only at the most formal and abstract level will adopt the language of mathematics. It is a sobering thought that, years from now, a general theory of vision may indeed be so abstract and complex that few workers now alive would be able to understand it. But it is as yet unclear what level of explanation will be adopted in such a theory.

The place of subjective experience in perceptual theory

Suppose that there was a respected general theory of visual perception, a theory which successfully handled the main phenomena of colour, shape, depth, motion and so on. Would the theory be limited to human perception? Many theorists have clearly believed that their work could embrace non-human species: the Gestalt theorists demonstrated some of their effects in apes and chickens; Brunswik studied probability matching in rats; direct perceptionists talk about different species in different ecological niches; Marr speculates about the landing behaviour of the house fly; cortical edge detectors were first demonstrated in cats. However, although much is known about vision in a few non-human species, we have no way of understanding the quality of their conscious experiences, if any. As was stated earlier, we cannot know what it is like to see as a fly.

We are, however, intimately aware of our own consciousness, of what seeing is like 'from the inside'. In actual research it is possible to adopt a tough-minded, behaviourist approach to perception, measuring human and animal performance in similar ways. There is then no place for introspection, only controlled, measurable responses. But where do the researchers' ideas come from, if not from their own subjective experiences? The Purkinje shift—changes in the relative brightness of blue objects with changing illumination—can be demonstrated via the objective operant behaviour of humans or animals. But why should anyone think to do so, unless they had *noticed* the effect (Purkinje was lying in bed when he noticed it—off colour perhaps?). Should perceptionists deliberately omit from their theories that which is part of their daily experience?

Discussions such as this may be dismissed as relevant only to the origins of scientific theories, not to the logic of the theories themselves. After all, it could be argued, much has been learned about the behaviour of honey bees without anyone knowing what it is like to use the sun's position in a signalling dance. And one of the most powerful binocular illusions—Pulfrich's Pendulum[1]—was discovered by a one-eyed man. But, for example, would a purely objective research into colour vision ever have discovered that certain colour combinations are very unpleasant, or that some colours appear warm, others cold, or that some people hear coloured sounds?

It is equally important that experience also tells us what does *not* happen during perception. For instance, our noses are constantly in view but not seen: no formal account of a visual experiment ever includes the nose in a description of the stimulus array—it doesn't need to, for noses are not important in seeing, *and it is subjective experience which tells us this.* We can learn to see that objects occupy less of the visual field when they recede from us (and artists must be able to do this), but phenomenally they remain the same size. Which of these ways of perceiving the objects should the theorist be concerned with?

---

[1] When a pendulum, swinging across one's visual field, is viewed with a dark filter in front of one eye, the swing changes into a 3D ellipse in which the pendulum appears to move towards and away from the viewer.

The strongest claims for the inclusion of subjective experience in accounts of perception have been made by modern phenomenologists. They insist that our perception of, say, a house, transcends any limited vantage point: we 'see' the volume of the house, its solidity, even when the only visible aspect is the front. Our phenomenal experience includes the knowledge that we are 'inside' our bodies. We know what things would look like from alternative vantage points.

The problem of conscious experience has now been alluded to several times in this book. It is, however, so important that one final example must be presented.

We have all had the experience of perceiving some thing or event with unusual clarity. At its most dramatic this happens when we witness a violent, sudden accident. But there are other times when one simply feels calm or quiet and yet strangely attentive. It is as if one has achieved a new sharpness of focus in which things are seen as if for the first time.

Developing a scientific account of seeing is very different from the creation of an original work of art; the two activities attract different personalities motivated by different goals. But when it comes to describing the more elusive aspects of experience, who is to say that the artist is not the better analyst? Here is a short sequence from a twentieth-century novel. After reading it do you not agree that it is reminding us of what it is like to perceive something intensely; that the description is as interesting in its way as anything to be found in more scientific accounts?

Two men are making a coffin:

> The lantern sits on a stump. Rusted, grease-fouled, its cracked chimney smeared on one side with a soaring smudge of soot, it sheds a feeble and sultry glare upon the trestles and the boards and the adjacent earth. Upon the dark ground the chips look like random smears of soft pale paint on a black canvas. The boards look like long smooth tatters torn from the flat darkness and turned backside out.
>
> Cash labours about the trestles, moving back and forth, lifting and placing the planks with long clattering reverberations in the dead air as though he were lifting and dropping them at the bottom of an invisible well, the sounds ceasing without departing, as if any movement might dislodge them from the immediate air in reverberant repetition. He saws again, his elbow flashing slowly, a thin thread of fire running along the edge of the saw, lost and recovered at the top and bottom of each stroke in unbroken elongation, so that the saw appears to be six feet long, into and out of pa's shabby and aimless silhouette. . . .
>
> The air smells like sulphur. Upon the impalpable plane of it their shadows fall as upon a wall, as though like sound they had not gone very far away in falling but had merely congealed for a moment, immediate and musing. . . .

> (William Faulkner, *As I Lay Dying*)

Faulkner has used his formidable powers of description to put into words something of the essence of perceiving. In a sense, we are there with him, watching this strange scene. And the ways in which he has noticed things—the muffled sounds, the subtle gradations of light and shade—remind us that there is a lot to the business of perceiving, and a long way to go before it is understood. Will computer simulations ever do justice to these aspects of awareness? Can they be captured in scientific accounts of perception? It will be fascinating to see how these formidable problems are approached in the future.

The evolutionary background to human vision

About six million years ago the earliest humanoids split from the apes. Within another million years our ancestors had become fully bipedal. Then, in the last two million years, the human brain developed more rapidly than any other organ in evolutionary history. It was during these last two million years that the human visual system attained its present form and, presumably, its remarkable range of functions.

But the environment which exerted the selective pressures that shaped the evolution of perception was very different from that which most of us inhabit today. Now our daily lives bring us into regular contact with signs and symbols. We live in a built environment—a place of sharp edges, flat surfaces and artificial lighting. Our bodies have a natural speed across two-dimensional surfaces of four or five miles per hour but are frequently moved passively through three dimensions at speeds one hundred times greater than this. There are many highly unnatural environments.

Although this question has been raised several times in this book, it is worth one last mention: Can we expect a single theory to explain perception of the natural *and* the artificial world? That is to say, there may be one set of mechanisms (describable by one set of laws) which will ensure that, for example, singleness of vision and stereoscopic fusion are achieved in the lit environment; but there can be no such inbuilt mechanism to allow us to fly in clouds. That is something which we can learn to do, provided we have access to the right instruments. Instrument flying undoubtedly involves perception as well as skill, but is it the same sort of perception as, say, normal stereopsis? If not, where is the dividing line to be drawn?

As has been shown in previous chapters, the extent to which a perceptual theorist remains aware of the evolutionary background to vision determines, in part, those things which are emphasized in his or her theory. R.L. Gregory is much more concerned to explain illusions than is J.J Gibson, who regards these as arising from essentially unnatural patterns of stimulation. It is almost a truism that the more cognitive a theorist is, the greater will be the emphasis upon those things over which we cognate: pictures, puzzles, words, lists. But is seeing a word the same as seeing a face? Do we 'read' these two types of pattern in the same manner? This leads naturally to a much larger question as to which sets of phenomena—the natural or the artificial and symbolic—should be researched. Which offers the greater chance of success?

THEORIES AND THE FUTURE

Futurology is not to everyone's taste. It is certainly not to the author's. And yet the reader who has come this far has a right to some sort of personal statement; after such a lengthy attempt to be dispassionate and fair, it seems only right to offer some views on theories of visual perception. This should not be read as a prediction concerning 'the' final theory of vision, as nobody can be expected to know what form such a theory will take; rather, it is a guess concerning the next important general accounts of visual perception, the future equivalents of something as important in their way as was the Gestalt theory. Here are eight assertions. They should be read with an appropriate degree of scepticism.

1. *Rivalry will continue between theories.* This claim is reinforced by many of the points listed below. It is going to be very difficult, if not impossible, to reconcile a scientific account of perception (possibly based on a computer model) with the claims of phenomenologists. The need to describe and explain human awareness can be expected to form the ground for much future debate among theorists.
2. *The phenomenological component in theories will grow.* This is predicted simply on the basis of a probable future swing away from the reductionist, mechanist approach that has dominated Western psychology this century.
3. *General theories will be mainly concerned with human perception.* It will be possible to explain some aspects of perception in other species, of course. Much is already known about, say, vision in insects. But most species are simply too different from us in structure and lifestyle for their perceptions ever to be predicted from a human theory. We know how bats navigate, but cannot imagine their phenomenal world.
4. *Future theories will include more thorough analyses of the environment.* It seems certain that the successes of direct perception and the computational approach, both of which owe much to precise analysis of the nature of the physical world, will inspire others to extend this type of work.
5. *Theories will have a functional bias.* To repeat Jung's phrase, 'We are of an immense age'. As an increasing effort is made to plot the evolutionary background from which humans emerged, rapid gains in knowledge seem almost inevitable. Recent advances in evolutionary theory have explained

such apparently baffling problems as the Panda's sixth finger (read Gould, 1980, in order to experience the excitement of this type of research). Can we not expect similar researches to uncover the functional significance of, for example, the human tendency to see vertical lines as longer than physically equal horizontal ones; why faces with large pupils strike us as more attractive; or why the human visual system is modifiable only during the first few months of life?

6. *Research and theory will continue to be influenced by technical developments.* Those who have not experienced the effects of some major new technique in perceptual research may find it difficult to imagine the impact these can have on ways of thinking. For example, it was customary until recently to describe the performance of the eye in terms of (a) its acuity and (b) its sensitivity. The advent of visual gratings and the associated idea of spatial frequency analysis, tuned spatial frequency channels and the contrast sensitivity function completely changed our ideas about these aspects of vision. This is a very familiar story in psychological research and could be illustrated by many more examples. The point is that psychologists and physiologists are not the only people who are thinking about problems of seeing: engineers, physicists, zoologists and mathematicians, can all claim a legitimate interest in the problem. As more and more of their techniques are adopted, the impact of these other disciplines on perceptual theory and research can be expected to become increasingly dramatic.

7. *Models will increase in importance.* This relates to the last point and is too obvious to need stressing. We have already shown how available models determine psychological thinking. As new and more powerful computer systems emerge, these will inevitably be used as models of the brain by many psychologists.

8. *Simulation will become increasingly common.* Thirty years ago very few perceptionists had access to computers; now they are to be found in every laboratory. It would be hard to exaggerate the impact of these remarkable machines in experimental psychology. That they have provided a very seductive model of the perceiver has been discussed at some length in earlier chapters. Computers have also changed the ways in which actual experiments are conducted. For example, it is no longer necessary always to specify the ordering of stimulus presentations at the start of an experiment. Because the computer can react much faster than any experimenter, the observer's performance can be assessed from trial to trial, and subsequent presentations can be modified accordingly. As an example of the possibilities afforded by this speed and power, consider the dynamic 'staircase' tracking procedures now used in the determination of sensory thresholds (Chapter 2). Such work would have been impossible prior to the advent of computer-controlled displays.

There is, however, another way in which computers are having an impact on perceptual research and theorizing, and this is their ability to simulate processes. In the past, a typical sequence would be along these lines: someone has an idea—a possible explanation of some perceptual phenomenon, a critical test of a controversial theory, or simply a hunch about how something comes about. An experiment is designed, equipment built, participants recruited. Some weeks or months later the data are ready for analysis. Interesting results may or may not be found and the experiment may be repeated with certain modifications, and so on. This is slow, inefficient, and often frustrating work—ask any experimenter. It is often realized, half way through an experiment, that something is wrong, that things could have been done in a different way. However, the rules of experimentation and the demands of statistical analysis mean that the experiment must be run to the end. These are the major problems: the minor ones are that people don't turn up, mothers of young infants change their minds, animal research is discouraged.

But some ideas about perception can be tested, at least in the first place, without using observers at all: a computer will suffice. What is required of course is complete clarity of thought. Each and every part of the hypothetical process which it is desired to simulate must be programmed. But this can be a valuable discipline: it is no longer possible to be vague, to employ undefined terms; everything must be made explicit for the computer. Once started, the simulation will be run at high speed, and the input variables can be modified at will. In this way, several thousand hours of possible experimentation can be compressed into a few days. We have described one famous use of simulation to test a perceptual hypothesis in Chapter 8, when the Marr–Poggio model of stereopsis was outlined. The success of this and other recent simulations is a clear pointer to the future.

That is the last speculation. One thing is certain, however, and that is that vision will always fascinate. The visual sense is, above all, the channel through which curiosity becomes manifest. Think, for example, of the crowds which gather to see the rare artefacts of other civilizations: Tutankhamen's mask, the horses of ancient China. Watch people at sporting events, in the cinema, in front of television sets. Ask why it is that every well-known beauty spot has a continual stream of visitors, gazing out across the view.

There has as yet been no satisfactory general theory to explain how we see the world, none that has been able to satisfy all demands of breadth, precision and falsifiability which are required of good theories. Perhaps this chapter has helped to explain why. But we should not be disheartened: visual perception utilizes not only the eye—which is a structure of formidable complexity—but the brain: ten thousand million cells interacting in ways as yet not understood. Underlying our experience of seeing is the most complicated system ever known. Explaining vision will not happen tomorrow, but there are many interesting things to attempt in the meantime.

NOTES ON CHAPTER 9

Some of the issues addressed in this chapter are clearly philosophical. Readers wishing to know more about theory, explanation, and the philosophical problems associated with reductionism and the computer metaphor of the mind should start by reading the following: Chalmers (1982), Dreyfus (1972), and Russell (1984). For somewhat more advanced discussions of artificial intelligence and the computer metaphor see Dreyfus and Dreyfus (1985) and Winograd and Flores (1986).

Contemporary editions of the journal, *The Behavioural and Brain Sciences* should be watched for interesting debates on some of the issues raised in this chapter.

References

Adrian, E.D. (1928). *The Basis of Sensation*. London: Christophers.

Ames, A. (1949). *The Nature and Origins of Perceptions* (Preliminary laboratory manual). Hanover, New Hampshire: The Hanover Institute.

Arnheim, R. (1949). The Gestalt theory of expression. *Psychological Review*, **56**, 156–171.

Arnheim, R. (1956). *Art and Visual Perception*. London: Faber.

Arnheim, R. (1969). *Visual Thinking*. Berkeley: University of California Press.

Arnheim, R. (1987). Prägnanz and its discontents. *Gestalt Theory*, **9**, 102–107.

Attneave, F. (1955). Symmetry, information, and memory for patterns. *American Journal of Psychology*, **68**, 209–222.

Bahnson, P. (1928). Eine Untersuchung über Symmetrie und Asymmetrie bei visuellen Wahrnehmungen. *Zeitschrift für Psychologie*, **108**, 129–154.

Barlow, H.B. (1953). Summation and inhibition in the frog's retina. *Journal of Physiology*, **119**, 69–88.

Bartlett, F.C. (1932). *Remembering*. Cambridge: Cambridge University Press.

Beck, J. (1966). Effect of orientation and of shape similarity on perceptual grouping. *Perception and Psychophysics*, **1**, 300–302.

Békèsy, G. von (1930). Über das Fechner'sche Gesetz und seine bedeutung für die Theorie der akustischen Beobachtungsfehler und die Theorie des Horens. *Annalen für Physik*, **7**, 329–350.

Blackwell, H.R. (1953). Psychophysical thresholds: experimental studies of methods of measurement. *Bulletin of the Engineering Research Institute of the University of Michigan*, No. 6.

Blakemore, C. (1974). Developmental factors in the formation of feature extracting neurons. In F.G. Worden and F.O. Smith (eds), *The Neurosciences, 3rd Study Program*. Cambridge, Mass.: MIT Press.

Blakemore, C. (1990) (ed.). *Vision: Coding and Efficiency*. Cambridge: Cambridge University Press.

Blakemore, C. and Campbell, F.W. (1969). On the existence of neurons in the human visual system sensitive to the orientation and size of retinal images. *Journal of Physiology*, **203**, 237–260.

Blakemore, C. and Cooper, G.F. (1970). Development of the brain depends on visual environment. *Science*, **228**, 477–478.

Blakemore, C. and Sutton, P. (1969). Size adaptation: a new aftereffect. *Science*, **166**, 245–247.

Boring, E.H. (1950). *A History of Experimental Psychology*. New York: Appleton-Century-Crofts.

Bornstein, M.H., Kessen, W. and Weiskopf, S. (1976). The categories of hue in infancy. *Science*, **191**, 201–202.

Bowmaker, J.K. and Dartnall, H.J.A. (1980). Visual pigments of rods and cones in a human retina. *Journal of Physiology*, **298**, 501–511.

Brehmer, B. (1984). Brunswikian psychology for the 1990s. In K.M.J. Lagerspetz and P. Niemi (eds), *Psychology in the 1990s*. North Holland: Elsevier.

Broadbent, D.E. (1958). *Perception and Communication*. London: Pergamon.

Broadbent, D.E. (1985). A question of levels: comments on McClelland and Rumelhart. *Journal of Experimental Psychology: General*, **114**, 189–192.

Brown, S.C. (ed.) (1974). *Philosophy of Psychology*. London: Macmillan.

Brown, R.W. and McNeill, D. (1966). The 'tip of the tongue' phenomenon. *Journal of Verbal Learning and Verbal Behaviour*, **5**, 325–337.

Bruce, V. and Green, P.R. (1990). *Visual Perception. Physiology, Psychology and Ecology* (2nd edition). Hove: Lawrence Erlbaum Associates Ltd.

Bruner, J.S. (1957). On perceptual readiness. *Psychological Review*, **64**, 123–152.

Bruner, J.S. and Goodman, C.C. (1947). Value and need as organizing factors in perception. *Journal of Abnormal and Social Psychology*, **42**, 33–44.

Bruner, J.S., Goodnow, J.J. and Austin, G.A. (1956). *A Study of Thinking*. New York: Wiley.

Brunswik, E. (1938). Psychology as a science of objective relations. *Philosophy of Science*, **4**, 227–260.

Brunswik, E. (1939). Probability as a determiner of rat behavior. *Journal of Experimental Psychology*, **25**, 175–197.

Brunswik, E. (1948). Statistical separation of perception, thinking and attitudes. *American Psychologist*, **3**, 342.

Brunswik, E. (1952). The conceptual framework of psychology. In *The International Encyclopedia of Unified Science*, **1**, 10. Chicago: University of Chicago Press.

Brunswik, E. (1955). Representative design and probabilistic theory in a functional psychology. *Psychological Review*, **62**, 193–217.

Brunswik, E. (1956). *Perception and the Representative Design of Psychological experiments*. Berkeley: University of California Press.

Brunswik, E. and Kamiya, J. (1953). Ecological cue-validity of 'proximity' and other Gestalt factors. *American Journal of Psychology*, **66**, 20–32.

Butterworth, G. (1983). Structure of the mind in human infancy. In L.P. Lipsitt and C.K. Rovee-Collier (eds), *Advances in Infancy Research*, Vol. 2. Norwood, New Jersey: Ablex.

Butterworth, G. (1988). Events and encounters in infancy. In A. Slater and G. Bremner (eds), *Infant Development*. London: Lawrence Erlbaum.

Campbell, F.W. and Robson, J.G. (1968). Application of Fourier analysis to the visibility of gratings. *Journal of Physiology,* **197**, 551–566.

Chalmers, A.F. (1982). *What is This Thing Called Science?* (2nd edition). London: Open University Press.

Chapman, C.R., Chen, A.C. and Bonica, J.J. (1977). Effects of intrasegmental electrical acupuncture on dental pain: an evaluation by threshold determination and sensory decision theory. *Pain,* **3**, 213–227.

Chasles, M. (1830). Note sur les propertiétés generales du système de deux corps semblables entr'eux et placés d'une manière quelconque dans l'espace; et sur le déplacement fini ou infiniment petit d'un corps solide libre. *Bulletin des Sciences Mathématiques,* Férussac, **14**, 321–326.

Cherry, E.C. (1953). Some experiments on the recognition of speech with one and with two ears. *Journal of the Acoustical Society of America,* **25**, 975–979.

Chomsky, N. (1965). *Aspects of the Theory of Syntax.* Cambridge, Mass.: MIT Press.

Churchland, P. (1984) *Matter and Consciousness.* Cambridge, Mass.: MIT Press.

Clarke, F.R. (1969). Confidence ratings, second choice responses and confusion matrices in intelligibility tests. *Journal of the Acoustical Society of America,* **32**, 35–46.

Clark, W.C. and Yang, J.C. (1974). Acupunctural analgesia? Evaluation by signal detection theory. *Science,* **184**, 1096–1098.

Coren, S. (1986). An efferent component in the visual perception of direction and extent. *Psychological Review,* **93**, 391–410.

Corso, J.F. (1970). *The Experimental Psychology of Sensory Behavior.* London: Holt, Rinehart & Winston.

Costall, A. (1981). On how so much information controls so much behaviour: James Gibson's theory of direct perception. In G. Butterworth (ed.), *Infancy and Epistemology.* Brighton: Harvester Press.

Creelman, C.D. (1962). Human discrimination of auditory duration. *Journal of the Acoustical Society of America,* **34**, 582–593.

Cutting, J.E., (1982). Blowing in the wind: perceiving structure in trees and bushes. *Cognition,* **2**, 25–44.

Cutting, J.E. (1986). *Perception with an Eye for Motion.* Cambridge, Mass.: MIT Press.

Cutting, J.E., Vishton, P.M. and Braren, P.A. (1995). How we avoid collisions with stationary and moving obstacles. *Psychological Review,* **102**, 627–651.

Dartnall, H.J.A., Bowmaker, J.K. and Mollon, J.D. (1983). Human visual pigments: results from microspectroscopic results from the eyes of seven persons. *Proceedings of the Royal Society of London, Series B,* **220**, 115–130.

Day, R.H. (1989). Natural and artificial cues, perceptual compromise and the basis of veridical and illusory perception. In D. Vickers and P.L. Smith (eds), *Human Information Processing: Measures and Mechanisms.* North-Holland: Elsevier Science Publishers, pp. 107–129.

Day, R.H. and Power, R.P. (1965). Apparent reversal (oscillation) of rotary motion in depth: an investigation and a general theory. *Psychological Review,* **72**, 117–127.

DeCasper, A.J. and Fifer, W.P. (1980). Of human bonding: newborns prefer their mother's voices. *Science,* **208**, 1174–1176.

DeCillis, O.E. (1944). Absolute thresholds for the perception of tactual movement. *Archives of Psychology,* **294**, 1–52.

Dennett, D.C. (1991) *Consciousness Explained.* London: Penguin Books.

DeValois, R.L. (1960). Colour vision mechanisms in monkey. *Journal of General Physiology,* **43**, 115–128.

Dienes, Z. and McCleod, P. (1993). How to catch a cricket ball. *Perception,* **22**, 1427–1439.

Dreyfus, H.L. and Dreyfus, S.E. (1985). *Mind Over Machine.* New York: Macmillan.

Dreyfus, H.L. (1972). *What Computers Can't Do: A Critique of Artificial Reason.* New York, Harper & Row.

Dziurawiec, S. and Ellis, H.D. (1986). Neonates' attention to face-like stimuli: Goren, Sarty and Wu (1975) revisited. Paper presented at the Annual Conference of the Developmental Section of the British Psychological Society, University of Exeter, September 1986.

Earle, D. (1985). Perception of Glass pattern structure with stereopsis. *Perception,* **14**, 545–552.

Ehrenfels, von C. (1890). Über Gestaltqualitäten. *Vierteljahresscher für Philosophie,* **14**.

Eijkman, E. and Vendrik, A.J.H. (1963). Detection theory applied to the absolute sensitivity of sensory systems. *Biophysics Journal,* **3**, 65–77.

Ellis, W.D. (ed.) (1938). *A Source Book of Gestalt Psychology.* London: Routledge & Kegan Paul.

Engen, T. (1971). Psychophysics 2. In J.W. Kling and L.A. Riggs (eds), *Woodworth and Schlosberg's Experimental Psychology,* London: Methuen.

Fechner, G.T. (1860). *Elemente der Psychophysik.* Leipzig: Breitkopf & Hartel. (English translation of Vol. 1 by H.E. Adler (1966). New York: Holt, Rinehart & Winston.)

Feynman, R.P. (1985). *QED: The Strange Theory of Light and Matter.* London: Penguin Books.

Fodor, J.A. (1983). *The Modularity of Mind.* Cambridge: Mass.: MIT Press.

Fodor, J.A. and Pylyshyn, Z.W. (1981). How direct is visual perception? Some reflections on Gibson's 'ecological approach'. *Cognition,* **9**, 139–196.

Fodor, J.A. and Pylyshyn, Z.W. (1988). Connectionism and cognitive architecture: a critical analysis. *Cognition* (to appear).

Frisby, J.P. (1979). *Seeing.* Oxford: Oxford University Press.

Galanter, E.H. (1962). Contemporary psychophysics. In *New Directions in Psychology*. New York: Holt, Rinehart & Winston.

Gibson, E.J. (1982). The concept of affordances in development: the renascence of functionalism. In W.A. Collins (ed.), *The Concept of Development. The Minnesota Symposia on Child Psychology*, **15**, 55–81.

Gibson, J.J. (1950). *The Perception of the Visual World*. Boston: Houghton Mifflin.

Gibson, J.J. (1961). Ecological optics. *Vision Research*, **1**, 253–262.

Gibson, J.J. (1966). *The Senses Considered as Perceptual Systems*. Boston: Houghton Mifflin.

Gibson, J.J. (1967a). New reasons for realism. *Syntheses*, **17**, 162–172.

Gibson, J.J. (1967b). Autobiography. In E.G. Boring and G. Lindzey (eds), *History of Psychology in Autobiography*. New York: Irvington.

Gibson, J.J. (1971a). A preliminary description and classification of affordances. Unpublished manuscript reproduced in E. Reed and R. Jones (eds) (1982). *Reasons for Realism*. Hillsdale, New Jersey: Lawrence Erlbaum Associates.

Gibson, J.J. (1971b). The information available in pictures. *Leonardo*, **4**, 27–35.

Gibson, J.J. (1976). The myth of passive perception: a reply to Richards. *Philosophy and Phenomenological Research*, **37**, 234–238.

Gibson, J.J. (1977). The theory of affordances. In R.E. Shaw and J. Bransford (eds), *Perceiving, Acting and Knowing*. Hillsdale, New Jersey: Lawrence Erlbaum Associates.

Gibson, J.J. (1979). *The Ecological Approach to Visual Perception*. Boston: Houghton Mifflin.

Gigerenzer, G. and Murray, D.J. (1987). *Cognition as Intuitive Statistics*. Hillsdale, New Jersey: Lawrence Erlbaum.

Gilchrist, A.L. and Jacobsen, A. (1983). Lightness constancy through a veiling luminance. *Journal of Experimental Psychology: Human Perception and Performance*, **9**, 936–944.

Glass, L. (1969). Moiré effect from random dots. *Nature*, **223**, 578–580.

Goren, C.C., Sarty, M. and Wu, P.Y.K. (1975). Visual following and pattern discrimination of face-like stimuli by newborn infants. *Pediatrics*, **59**, 544–549.

Gould, S.J. (1980). *The Panda's Thumb*. London: Penguin.

Gould, S.J. (1981). *The Mismeasure of Man*. Harmondsworth, Middlesex: Penguin Books Ltd.

Granrund, C.E., Yonas, A., Smith, I.M., Arterberry, M.E., Glicksman, M.L. and Sorkness, A.C. (1984). Infants' sensitivity to accretion and deletion of texture as information for depth at an edge. *Child Development*, **55**, 1630–1636.

Gregory, R.L. (1961). The brain as an engineering problem. In W.H. Thorpe and O.L. Zangwill (eds), *Current Problems in Animal Behaviour*. Cambridge: Cambridge University Press.

Gregory, R.L. (1963). Distortion of space as inappropriate constancy scaling. *Nature*, **199**, 678–680.

Gregory, R.L. (1970). *The Intelligent Eye*. New York: McGraw-Hill.

Gregory, R.L. (1974). Perceptions as hypotheses. Chapter 9 in S.C. Brown (ed.), *Philosophy of Psychology*, London: Macmillan.

Gregory, R.L. (1980a). Perceptions as hypotheses. *Philosophical Transactions of the Royal Society of London*, **B290**, 181–197.

Gregory, R.L. (1980b). Choosing a paradigm for perception. In E.C. Carterette and M.P. Friedman (eds), *Handbook of Perception*, Vol. 1. New York: Academic Press.

Gregory, R.L. (1995). Black boxes of artful vision. Chapter 1 in R.L. Gregory, J. Harris, P. Heard and D. Rose (eds), *The Artful Eye*. Oxford: Oxford University Press.

Gregory, R.L. and Wallace, J.G. (1963). Recovery from early blindness: a case study. *Experimental Psychology Society Monograph Number 2*. Cambridge: W. Heffer & Son.

Gross, C.G., Rocha-Miranda, C.E. and Bender, D.B. (1972). Visual properties of neurons in inferotemporal cortex of the macaque. *Journal of Neurophysiology*, **35**, 96–111.

Grossberg, G.M. and Grant, B.F. (1978). Classical psychophysics: applications of ratio scaling and signal detection methods to research on pain, fear, drugs, and medical decision making. *Psychological Bulletin*, **85**, 1154–1176.

Haber, R.N. and Hershenson, M. (1980). *The Psychology of Visual Perception*. New York: Holt, Rinehart & Winston.

Hammond, K.R. (ed.) (1966). *The Psychology of Egon Brunswik*. New York: Holt, Rinehart & Winston.

Hartline, H.K. (1938). The response of single optic nerve fibres of the vertebrate eye to illumination of the retina. *American Journal of Physiology*, **121**, 400–415.

Hartine, H.K. (1940). The receptive field of the optic nerve fibres. *American Journal of Physiology*, **130**, 690–699.

Hatfield, G. and Epstein, W. (1985). The status of the minimum principle in the theoretical analysis of visual perception. *Psychological Bulletin*, **97**(2), 155–186.

Hearnshaw, L.S. (1964). *A Short History of British Psychology, 1840–1940*. London: Methuen.

Hebb, D.O. (1949). *The Organization of Behaviour*. New York: Wiley.

Helmholtz, H. von (1924–1925). *Helmholtz's Physiological Optics*. Translated from the third edition (1909–1911) by J.P. Southwell (ed.). Rochester, New York: Optical Society of America.

Helson, H. (1947). Adaptation level as frame of reference for prediction of psychophysical data. *American Journal of Psychology*, **60**, 1–29.

Helson, H. and Kosaki, A. (1968). Anchor effects using numerical estimates of simple dot patterns. *Perception and Psychophysics*, **4**, 163–164.

Henle, M. (1984). Isomorphism: setting the record straight. *Psychological Research,* **46**, 317–327.

Hering, E. (1890). Beitrag zür Lehre vom Simultankontrast. *Zeitschrift für Psychologie und Physiologie der Sinnesorgane*, **1**, 18–28.

Hess, E.H. (1965). Attitude and pupil size. *Scientific American,* **212**, 46–54.

Hess, E.H. (1975). The role of pupil size in communication. *Scientific American,* **222**, 110–119.

Hildebrandt, S. and Tromba, A. (1985). *Mathematics and Optimum Form.* New York: W.H. Freeman.

Hine, T.J., Cook, M. and Rogers, G.T. (1995). An illusion of relative motion dependent upon spatial frequency and orientation. *Vision Research,* **35**, 3093–3102.

Hochberg, J.E. (1968). In the mind's eye. In R.N. Haber (ed.), *Contemporary Theory and Research in Visual Perception*. New York: Holt, Rinehart & Winston.

Hochberg, J.E. (1971). Perception. In L.A. Riggs and J.W. Kling (eds), *Woodworth and Schlosberg's Experimental Psychology* (3rd edition). New York: Holt, Rinehart & Winston.

Hochberg, J.E. (1973) Organization and the Gestalt tradition. In E. Carterette and M. Friedman (eds), *Handbook of Perception*, Vol. 1. New York: Academic Press.

Hofsten, C. von (1983). Foundations for perceptual development. In L.P. Lipsitt and C.K. Rovee-Collier (eds), *Advances in Infancy Research*, Vol. 2. Norwood, New Jersey: Ablex.

Horn, B.K.P. (1974). Determining lightness from an image. *Computer Graphics and Image Processing*, **3**, 277–299.

Hubel, D.H. and Wiesel, T.N. (1962). Receptive fields, binocular interaction and functional architecture in the cat's visual cortex. *Journal of Physiology,* **166**, 106–154.

Hubel, D.H. and Wiesel, T.N. (1968). Receptive fields and functional architecture of the monkey striate cortex. *Journal of Physiology,* **195**, 215–243.

Hubel, D.H. and Wiesel, T.W. (1977). Functional architecture of macaque monkey visual cortex. *Proceedings of the Royal Society of London,* **198**, 1–59.

James, W. (1890). *Principles of Psychology.* New York: Holt.

Jerome, E.A. (1942). Olfactory thresholds measured in terms of stimulus pressure and volume. *Archives of Psychology,* **274**, 1–44.

Johansson, G. (1950). *Configurations in Event Perception*. Stockholm: Almqvist & Wiksell.

Johansson, G. (1964). Perception of motion and changing form. *Scandinavian Journal of Psychology,* **5**, 181–208.

Johansson, G. (1977). Spatial constancy and motion in visual perception. In W. Epstein (ed.), *Stability and Constancy in Visual Perception*. New York: Wiley.

Judd, D.B. (1951). Basic correlates of the visual stimulus. Chapter 22 in S.S. Stevens, *Handbook of Experimental Psychology*. New York: Wiley.

Julesz, B. (1960). Binocular depth perception of computer generated patterns. *Bell System Technical Journal*, **39**, 1125–1162.

Julesz, B. (1971). *Foundations of Cyclopean Perception*. Chicago: University of Chicago Press.

Julesz, B. (1981). Textons, the elements of texture perception and their interactions. *Nature*, **290**, 91–97.

Kanizsa, G. (1979). *Organization in Vision: Essays on Gestalt Perception*. New York: Praeger.

Katz, D. (1951). *Gestalt Psychology*. London: Methuen.

Katz, S. (1987). Is Gibson a Realist? In A. Costall and A. Still (eds), *Cognitive Psychology in Question*. Brighton: Harvester Press.

Kaufman, L. (1974). *Sight and Mind: an Introduction to Visual Perception*. New York: Oxford University Press.

Kelley, G.A. (1955). *The Psychology of Personal Constructs*. New York: Norton.

Koffka, K. (1915). *Reply to Benussi*. Reprinted in W.D. Ellis (ed.) (1929) *A Source Book of Gestalt Psychology*. New York: Humanities Press.

Koffka, K. (1924). *The Growth of the Mind*. London: Routledge & Kegan Paul.

Koffka, K. (1935). *Principles of Gestalt Psychology*. New York: Harcourt Brace.

Kohler, I. (1955). Experiments with prolonged optical distortion. *Acta Psychologica*, **11**, 176–178.

Köhler, W. (1920). *Physical Gestalten*. Reprinted in W.D. Ellis (ed.) (1929), *A Source Book of Gestalt Psychology*. New York: Humanities Press.

Köhler, W. (1925). *Reply to G.E. Muller*. Reprinted in W.D. Ellis (ed.) (1929), *A Source Book of Gestalt Psychology*. New York: Humanities Press.

Köhler, W. (1940). *Dynamics in Psychology*. New York: Liveright.

Köhler, W. (1947). *Gestalt Psychology*. New York: Liveright.

Krueger, L.E. (1989). Reconciling Fechner and Stevens: toward a unified psychophysical law. *Behavioral and Brain Sciences*, **12**, 251–320.

Kubovy, M. and Pomerantz, J.T. (1981). *Perceptual Organization*. Hillsdale, New Jersey: Lawrence Erlbaum.

Kuffler, S.W. (1953). Discharge patterns and functional organization of mammalian retina. *Journal of Neurophysiology*, **16**, 37–68.

Kuhn, T.S. (1970). *The Nature of Scientific Revolutions* (2nd edition). Chicago: University of Chicago Press.

Külpe, O. (1904). Versuche über Abstraktion. *Berlin International Congress of Experimental Psychology*, 56–68.

Land, E.H. (1985). Recent advances in Retinex theory. *Vision Research*, **26**, 7–21.

Land, E.H. and McCann, J.J. (1971). Lightness and retinex theory. *Journal of the Optical Society of America*, **61**, 1–11.

Land, M.F. (1981). Optics and vision in invertebrates. In H. Autram (ed.), *Handbook of Sensory Physiology*, Vol. 7/6B. New York: Springer.

Lashley, K.S. (1950). In search of the engram. *Symposium of the Society of Experimental Biology*, **4**, 454–482.

Lazarus, R.S. and McCleary, R.A. (1951). Autonomic discrimination without awareness: a study in subception. *Psychological Review*, **58**, 113–122.

Lee, D.N. and Reddish, P.E. (1981). Plummeting gannets: a paradigm of ecological optics. *Nature*, **293**, 293–294.

Leeper, R.W. (1966). A critical consideration of Egon Brunswik's Probabilistic Functionalism. In K.R. Hammond, (ed.). *The Psychology of Egon Brunswik*. New York: Holt, Rinehart & Winston.

Lettvin, J.Y., Maturana, H.R., McCulloch, W.S. and Pitts, W.H. (1959). What the frog's eye tells the frog's brain. *Proceedings of the Institute of Radio Engineering*, **47**, 1940–1951.

Lipsitt, L.P. and Rovee-Collier, C.K. (eds) (1983). *Advances in Infancy Research*, Vol. 2. Norwood, New Jersey: Ablex.

Luce, R.D. (1960). Detection thresholds: a problem reconsidered. *Science*, **132**, 1495.

Ludel, J. (1978). *Introduction to Sensory Processes*. San Francisco: W.H. Freeman.

MacLeod, R.B. and Pick, H.L. (eds) (1974). *Perception: Essays in Honour of James J. Gibson*. Ithaca, New York: Cornell University Press.

MacNichol, E. (1964). Three-pigment color vision. *Scientific American*, **211**, 48–56.

Mandler, J.M. and Mandler, G. (1969). The diaspora of experimental psychologists: the Gestaltists and others. In D. Fleming and B. Bailin (eds), *The Intellectual Migration, Europe and America, 1930–1960*. Cambridge, Mass.: Harvard University Press.

Mark, L.S. (1987). Eye-height-scaled information about affordances: a study of sitting and stair-climbing. *Journal of Experimental Psychology: Human Perception and Performance*, **13**, 361–370.

Marr, D. (1982). *Vision: A Computational Investigation into the Human Representation and Processing of Visual Information*. San Francisco: W.H. Freeman.

Marr, D. and Hildreth, E. (1980). Theory of edge detection. *Proceedings of the Royal Society of London*, **B207**, 187–217.

Marr, D. and Poggio, T. (1976). Cooperative computation of stereo disparity. *Science*, **194**, 283–287.

Marr, D. and Poggio, T. (1979). A computational theory of human stereo vision. *Proceedings of the Royal Society of London*, **B204**, 301–328.

Maturana, H.R., Lettvin, J.Y., McCulloch, W.S. and Pitts, W.H. (1960). Anatomy and physiology of vision in the frog (*Rana pipens*). *Journal of General Physiology*, **43**, 129–176.

Mayhew, J.E.W. and Frisby, J.P. (1981). Psychophysical and computational studies towards a theory of human stereopsis. *Artificial Intelligence,* **17**, 349–385.

McClelland, J.L., Rumelhart, D.E. and Hinton, G.E. (1986). The appeal of parallel distributed processing. In D.E. Rumelhart and J.L. McClelland (eds), *Parallel Distributed Processing.* Cambridge, Mass.: MIT Press.

McGinnies, E. (1949). Emotionality and perceptual defense. *Psychological Review,* **56**, 244–251.

Michaels, C.F. and Carello, C. (1981). *Direct Perception.* Englewood Cliffs, New Jersey: Prentice Hall.

Michotte, A. (1946). *La perception de la causalité.* Louvain: Institut Superieur de Philosophie.

Miller, G.A. (1964). *Psychology, the Science of Mental Life,* London: Hutchinson.

Minsky, M. and Papert, S. (1969). *Perceptrons.* Cambridge, Mass.: MIT Press.

Møller, A. (1992). Females prefer large and symmetrical ornaments. *Nature,* **357**, 238–240.

Møller, A. (1994). Sexual selection in the Barn Swallow (*Hirundo rustica*). VI: Patterns of fluctuating asymmetry and selection against asymmetry. *Evolution,* **48**, 658–670.

Møller, A. (1995). Bumblebee preference for symmetrical flowers. *Proceedings of the National Academy of Science, U.S.A.,* **92**, 2288–2292.

Møller, A., Soler, M. and Thornhill, R. (1995). Breast asymmetry, sexual selection, and human reproductive success. *Ethology and Sociobiology,* **16**, 207–209.

Moray, N. (1994). *Ergonomics and the Global Problems of the 21st Century.* Keynote address at the International Ergonomics Association Meeting. Toronto, August 1994.

Morgan, M.J. (1977). *Molyneux's Question: Vision, Touch and the Philosophy of Perception.* Cambridge: Cambridge University Press.

Morgan, M.J. (1984). Computational theories of vision (Review of Marr). *Quarterly Journal of Experimental Psychology,* **36A**, 157–165.

Neisser, U. (1967). *Cognitive Psychology.* New York: Appleton-Century-Crofts.

Neisser, U. (1976). *Cognition and Reality.* San Francisco: W.H. Freeman.

Noble, W.G. (1981). Gibsonian theory and the pragmatist perspective. *Journal for the Theory of Social Behaviour,* **11**, 65–85.

Norman, D.A. (1988). *The Psychology of Everyday Things.* New York: Basic Books.

Norman, D.A. (1992). *Turn Signals are the Facial Expressions of Automobiles.* Reading, Mass.: Addison-Wesley.

Norman, D.A. (1993). *Things That Make Us Smart.* Reading, Mass.: Addison-Wesley.

Norman, D.A. and Draper, S.W. (eds) (1986). *User-Centred System Design.* Hillsdale, New Jersey: Erlbaum.

Orchard, G.A. and Phillips, W.A. (1991). *Neural Computation. A Beginner's Guide.* London: Lawrence Erlbaum Associates.

Pantle, A. and Sekuler, R.W. (1968). Contrast response of human visual mechanisms to orientation and detection of velocity. *Vision Research,* **9**, 397–406.

Petermann, B. (1932). *The Gestalt Theory and the Problem of Configuration.* London: Kegan Paul, Trench & Trubner.

Petrinovich, L. (1979). Probabilistic functionalism: a conception of research method. *American Psychologist,* **34**, 373–390.

Petter, G. (1956). Nuove ricerche sperimentali sulla totalizzazione percettiva. *Rivista di Psicologia,* **50**, 213–227.

Pittenger, J.B. and Shaw, R.E. (1975). Perception of relative and absolute age in facial photographs. *Perception and Psychophysics,* **18**, 137–143.

Pittenger, J.B., Shaw, R.E. and Mark, L.S. (1979). Perceptual information for the age level of faces as a higher-order invariance of growth. *Journal of Experimental Psychology: Human Perception and Performance,* **5**, 137–143.

Pomerleau, D.A. (1989). ALVINN: An Autonomous Land Vehicle In a Neural Network. In D.S. Touretzky (ed.), *Advances in Neural Information Processing Systems.* New York: Morgan Kaufmann.

Popper, K.R. (1960). *Conjectures and Refutations: the Growth of Scentific Knowledge.* London: Routledge & Kegan Paul.

Porter, P.B. (1954). Find the hidden man. *American Journal of Psychology,* **67**, 550–551.

Poulton, E.C. (1968). The new psychophysics: six models for magnitude estimation. *Psychological Bulletin,* **69**, 1–19.

Pylyshyn, Z.W. (1979). The rate of mental rotation of images: a test of holistic and analogue hypotheses. *Memory and Cognition,* **7**, 19–28.

Quine, W.V. and Ullian, J.S. (1970). *The Web of Belief.* New York: Random House.

Ramachandran, V.S. (1990). Interactions between motion, depth, color and form: the utilitarian theory of perception. In C. Blakemore (ed.), *Vision: Coding and Efficiency.* Cambridge: Cambridge University Press.

Reed, E. (1982). Descartes' corporeal ideas hypothesis and the origin of scientific psychology. *Review of Metaphysics,* **35**, 731–752.

Reed, E.S. (1987). James Gibson's ecological approach to cognition. In A. Costall and A. Still (eds), *Cognitive Psychology in Question.* Brighton: Harvester Press.

Restle, F. (1979). Coding theory of the perception of motion configuration. *Psychological Review,* **86**, 1–24.

Rock, I. (1983). *The Logic of Perception.* Cambridge, Mass.: MIT Press.

Rock, I. (1995). *Perception* (2nd edition). New York: Scientific American Books.

Rogers, S. and Costall, A. (1983). On the horizon: picture perception and Gibson's concept of information. *Leonardo,* **16**, 180–182.

Rosenblatt, F. (1959). Two theorems of statistical separability. In *The Mechanisation of Thought Processes* (Proceedings of a Symposium held at the National Physical Laboratory, November) Vol. 1. London: HMSO.

Rubin, E. (1915). *Synsoplevede Figurer*. Copenhagen: Glyndendalska.

Rumelhart, D.E. and McClelland, J.L. (1986). *Parallel Distributed Processing*. Cambridge, Mass.: MIT Press.

Rushton, W.A. (1964). Colour blindness and cone pigments. *American Journal of Optometry and Archives of the American Academy of Optometry,* **41**, 265–282.

Russell, J. (1984). *Explaining Mental Life*. London: Macmillan.

Sanford, R.H. (1936). The effects of abstinence from food upon imaginal processes: a preliminary experiment. *Journal of Psychology,* **2**, 129–136.

Sedgwick, H.A. (1980). The geometry of spatial layout in pictorial representation. Chapter 2 in M. Hagen (ed.), *The Perception of Pictures*, Vol. 1. New York: Academic Press.

Sekuler, R. and Blake, R. (1985). *Perception*. New York: A.A. Knopf.

Selfridge, O.G. (1959). Pandemonium: a paradigm for learning. In *The Mechanisation of Thought Processes*. London: HMSO.

Selfridge, O.G. and Neisser, U. (1960). Pattern recognition by machine. *Scientific American,* **203**, 60–68.

Senden, M. von (1960). *Space and Sight*. London: Methuen.

Shannon, C.E. (1948). A mathematical theory of communication. *Bell Systems Technical Journal,* **27**, 379–425.

Shaw, R.E., McIntyre, M. and Mace, W. (1974). The role of symmetry in event perception. In MacLeod, R. and Pick, H. (eds), *Perception: Essays in honour of James J. Gibson*. Ithaca, New York: Cornell University Press.

Shepard, R.N. (1984). Ecological constraints on internal representation: resonant kinematics of perceiving, imagining, thinking, and dreaming. *Psychological Review,* **91**, 417–447.

Shepard, R.N. (1990). *Mind Sights*. New York: W.H. Freeman.

Shepard, R.N. and Metzler, J. (1971). Mental rotation of three-dimensional objects. *Science,* **171**, 701–703.

Simon, H.A. and Newell, A. (1958). Heuristic problem solving: the advance in operations research. *Operations Research,* **6**, 6.

Slater, A. and Morison, V. (1985). Shape constancy and slant perception at birth. *Perception,* **14**, 337–344.

Sommer, R. (1959). The new look on the witness stand. *The Canadian Psychologist,* **8**, 94–99.

Spence, K.W. (1956). *Behavior Theory and Conditioning*. New Haven: Yale University Press.

Sperry, R.W. (1951). Mechanisms of neural maturation. In S.S. Stevens (ed.), *Handbook of Experimental Psychology*. New York: Wiley.

Sperry, R.W. and Miner, W. (1955). Pattern perception following insertion of mica plates into visual cortex. *Journal of Comparative Physiological Psychology*, **48**, 463–469.

Sperry, R.W., Miner, W. and Meyers, R.E. (1955). Visual pattern perception following subpial string and tantalum wire implantations in the visual cortex. *Journal of Comparative and Physiological Psychology*, **48**, 50–58.

Staniland, A. (1966). *Patterns of Redundancy*. Cambridge: The University Press.

Stevens, K.A. (1978). Computation of locally parallel structure. *Biological Cybernetics*, **29**, 19–28.

Stevens, S.S. (1957). On the psychophysical law. *Psychological Review*, **64**, 153–181.

Stevens, S.S. (1959). Cross-modal validation of subjective scales for loudness, vibration, and electric shock. *Journal of Experimental Psychology*, **57**, 201–209.

Stevens, S.S. (1961). The psychophysics of sensory function. In W.A. Rosenblith (ed.), *Sensory Communication*. New York: Wiley.

Stevens, S. S. (1962). The surprising simplicity of sensory metrics. *American Psychologist*, **17**, 29–39.

Stevens, S.S. and Galanter, E.H. (1957). Ratio scales and category scales for a dozen perceptual continua. *Journal of Experimental Psychology*, **54**, 377–411.

Stevens, S.S., Morgan, C.T. and Volkmann, J. (1941). Theory of the neural quantum in the discrimination of loudness and pitch. *American Journal of Psychology*, **54**, 315–335.

Sutherland, N.S (1957). Visual discrimination of shape by octopus. *British Journal of Psychology*, **48**, 55–70.

Svaetichin, G. (1956). Spectral response curves from single cones. *Acta Physiologica Scandinavica Supplementum*, **134**, 17–46.

Svaetichin, G. and MacNichol, E.F. (1958). Retinal mechanisms for achromatic vision. *Annals of the New York Academy of Sciences*, **74**, 385–404.

Swets, J.A. (ed.) (1964). *Signal Detection and Recognition by Human Observers*. New York: Wiley.

Swets, J.A. (1973). The receiver operating characteristic in psychology. *Science*, **182**, 990–1000.

Tanner, W.P. and Swets, J.A. (1954). A decision-making theory of visual detection. *Psychological Review*, **61**, 401–409.

Tanner, W.P., Swets, J.A. and Green, D.M. (1956). Some general properties of the hearing mechanism. *University of Michigan Electronic Defence Group Technical Report No. 30.*

Thompson, R.F. (1967). *Foundations of Physiological Psychology*. New York: Harper & Row.

Thorpe, W.H. and Zangwill, O.L. (eds) (1961). *Current Problems in Animal Behaviour*. Cambridge: Cambridge University Press.

Tinbergen, N. (1951). *The Study of Instinct.* London: Oxford University Press.

Titchener, E.B. (1901). *Experimental Psychology: A Manual of Laboratory Practice.* New York: Macmillan.

Todd, J.T., Mark, L.S., Shaw, R.E. and Pittenger, J.B. (1980). The perception of human growth. *Scientific American,* **242**(2), 132–144.

Uhr, L. (1963). Pattern recognition computers as models for form perception. *Psychological Bulletin,* **60**, 40–73.

Ullman, S. (1979). *The Interpretation of Visual Motion.* Cambridge, Mass.: MIT Press.

Ullman, S. (1980). Against direct perception. *The Behavioural and Brain Sciences,* **3** (whole issue).

Valvo, A. (1971). *Sight Restoration after Long-Term Blindness: The Problems and Behavior Patterns of Visual Rehabilitation.* New York: American Foundation for the Blind.

Wald, A. (1950). *Statistical Decision Functions.* New York: Wiley.

Walls, G.L. (1942). *The Vertebrate Eye and its Adaptive Radiation.* Birmingham, Michigan: Cranbrook Institute of Science.

Warren, W.H. (1984). Perceiving affordances: visual guidance of stair climbing. *Journal of Experimental Psychology: Human Perception and Performance,* **10**, 683–703.

Watt, R.J. (1988). *Visual Processing: Computational, Psychophysical and Cognitive Research.* London: Lawrence Erlbaum.

Watt, R.J. and Morgan, M.J. (1985). A theory of the primitive spatial code in human vision. *Vision Research,* **25**, 1661–1674.

Weber, E. (1846). Der Tatsin und das Gemeingefühl. In E. Wagner (ed.), *Handwörterbuch der Physiologie,* **3**, 481–588.

Wells, G.L., Lindsay, R.C.L. and Ferguson, T.J. (1979). Accuracy, confidence and juror perceptions in eyewitness identification. *Journal of Applied Psychology,* **64**, 440–448.

Wertheimer, M. (1912). *Experimental Studies on the Seeing of Motion.* (Reprinted in T. Shipley (1961). *Classics in Psychology.* New York: Philosophical Library.)

Wertheimer, M. (1923). Untersuchungen zur Lehre von der Gestalt, 2. *Psychologie Forshung,* **4**, 301–350. (Republished in Ellis, W.D. (ed.) (1938) *A Source Book of Gestalt Psychology.* London: Routledge & Kegan Paul.)

Winograd, T. and Flores, F. (1986). *Understanding Computers and Cognition.* Norwood, New Jersey: Ablex.

Woodworth, R.S. and Schlosberg, H. (1955). *Experimental Psychology* (3rd edition). London: Methuen.

Author index

Subject index